Promotional Marketing

SIXTH EDITION

Promotional Marketing

How to create, implement and integrate campaigns that really work

Roddy Mullin

KoganPage

LONDON PHILADELPHIA NEW DELHI

First published as *Sales Promotion* in 1989 by Kogan Page Limited
Sixth edition published as *Promotional Marketing* in 2014

2nd Floor, 45 Gee Street
London EC1V 3RS
United Kingdom
www.koganpage.com

1518 Walnut Street, Suite 1100
Philadelphia PA 19102
USA

4737/23 Ansari Road
Daryaganj
New Delhi 110002
India

© Roddy Mullin, 2014

The right of Roddy Mullin to be identified as the author of this work has been asserted by him in accordance with the Copyright, Designs and Patents Act 1988.

ISBN   978 0 7494 7246 7
E-ISBN   978 0 7494 7247 4

British Library Cataloguing-in-Publication Data

A CIP record for this book is available from the British Library.

Library of Congress Cataloging-in-Publication Data

Mullin, Roddy.
  [Sales promotion]
  Promotional marketing : how to create, implement & integrate campaigns that really work / Roddy Mullin.
    pages cm
  Revised edition of the author's Sales promotion.
  ISBN 978-0-7494-7246-7 (paperback) – ISBN 978-0-7494-7247-4 (ebook)   1. Sales promotion.
2. Marketing.   I. Title.
  HF5438.5.M85 2014
  658.8'2–dc23
                                                                    2014025419

Typeset by Graphicraft Limited, Hong Kong
Print production managed by Jellyfish
Printed and bound by CPI Group (UK) Ltd, Croydon, CR0 4YY

CONTENTS

LIST OF FIGURES, TABLES, CASE STUDIES AND BRIEFS

Figures

Tables

Case studies

Briefs

PREFACE

Promotional marketing is any marketing initiative, the purpose of which is to create a call to action that has a direct and positive impact on the behaviour of a targeted audience by offering a demonstrable, though not necessarily tangible, benefit.

(IPM DEFINITION)

This book replaces the fifth edition of *Sales Promotion*. It turns out that its Preface (written in 2009) was remarkably prescient in predicting the increase in internet purchases (obvious, but the extent now is near unbelievable), the use of the mobile and the rise of experiential marketing. These topics are covered in this new book. The definition here is broader than that just for sales promotion and consequently this book covers more than just what used to be called 'sales promotions' (the latter now defined as promotions within the retail space, historically controlled by sales teams).

Opportunity knocks

For those involved with promotions (10 per cent of UK jobs are in retail, so there is a certain career in it) there is a golden opportunity now, especially for any 'millenials' (people under 30 years old) who are up to speed with the latest communications, social media and technical developments such as the 3D printer, QR codes, NFCs (near field communications), augmented reality and apps. Research (highlighted in Colin Harper's book *Beyond Shopper Marketing*) shows the amazing divergence between what marketers believe and the reality of what customers actually think. Marketers are really out of touch. Existing marketers need to apply self-recognition criteria and use facts from insight to up their game. Academics should cease teaching the 4Ps, killed off by Ogilvy over a decade ago, and accept that sales and marketing, above and below-the-line, have merged and that short- and long-term relationships with the customer need to be considered at the same time when drawing up a marketing plan. Millenials unencumbered with these hang-ups should be truly creative and use all the new technical advances available, including inventing new uses for them, grasping the power of promotions described in this book to make money for their employers and at the same time advance themselves. Call them 'entrepreneurial marketers' if you like, who are focused and only satisfied when the shopper makes a purchase as a direct result of the targeted communication and persuasive messages that they – these millenials – have constructed.

A promotional marketer has to have a broader understanding of marketing and how people communicate and how to communicate to them messages via their preferred media, format and language. Communication is a skill that is essential in life and mastering it is the way to the top. It is the key skill for leadership. Some of the millenials should harness the power of pure promotional marketing for other purposes, for example making 21st century diplomacy work, assisting learning by people at all levels (using learning apps) especially for difficult topics such as leadership and marketing and even instilling moral values that used to be learnt at home, in school and from faiths. The hope is that one or two millennial readers will take up these challenges and apply in full the promotional marketing definition above, using the discoveries and techniques described in these pages. Those who employ millenials need to find ways to lead and manage them to let them blossom.

How the customer views promotional marketing

In a way it is easier to describe what is not promotional marketing; it is marketing that only serves to inform – there is no call to action whatsoever. Gatwick Airport has an advertisement on the London Underground that states that a second runway is required – no action or response needed. An advertisement urging to give up smoking or hand in guns during an amnesty offers demonstrable benefits. Where to draw the line? Few are going to communicate any product or service without some benefit, tangible or otherwise. No client (even a government) is likely to pay for a non-beneficial marketing communication. This conundrum really makes the point that the blurring of the various media suggests that all marketing initiatives are promotional; advertising, publicity, direct mail, the internet – the lot. Fortunately, for customers – the shoppers/buyers – all marketing communications are indeed promotional; they see no difference. Someone is urging them to buy or do something. This matches the discovery that it is the subconscious mind that makes most decisions for us on purchasing, or ignores or accepts dictats from the state.

The marketing industry needs to rethink itself and consolidate to match the shoppers' perception of marketing communication. That suggests that integrated communication as one is the answer – for both the long and the short term – with the single purpose of persuading shopper/buyers to buy a product or service, whether it's your brand, your client's brand or your suppliers' goods and services. That point of view – promotional marketing is all marketing communication – means the marketing industry needs to organize itself to seamlessly deliver this unified purpose, for any and all marketing messages.

IBM now advocates the simple strategy of putting the customer at the centre of its business through IBM's vision, described in its document 'Portraits of a smarter planet': in essence the future chief marketing officer is seen by IBM as achieving three things: harnessing data about the shopper to paint a predictive picture of each shopper as an individual (from social media, transaction data, etc), creating systems of engagement so that the business protects and shapes desire (upgraded CRM), and designing the culture and brand so that they are seamless (reputation, trust building and delighting customers). This mammoth task is made possible through technology

– 'listening' to social media and 'engaging' with customers for life, while predicting the future needs of shopper/buyers from observation of their purchasing habits.

The previous paragraphs envisage the future; but here and now, the reality is that marketing communications is carried out in silos – advertising in all its forms, publicity, direct mail, etc. Older marketers are generally only competent in one aspect. To avoid a heavy volume covering all marketing silos, this book will focus on the global picture as far as deciding on promotional objectives and examine in detail the promotional offers (called promotions hereafter) that result and how to implement them. Messaging that is purely to build on the engram, creating the brandgram, insight to ascertain the customer view, CRM and how to influence social media and the technology that supports it all, are not covered in detail in this book. The chapter on how promotional marketing fits into marketing and business, in the previous edition of this book, has been removed.

What's new?

The need for brand managers, retailers and suppliers to appreciate that the shopper is discerning and builds up a 'mind file' of brands and won't buy if he or she does not love the brand. Philip Clarke, CEO of Tesco, has come to realize this (reported in the *Daily Telegraph* in February 2014). His solution (and now Morrisons) is to reduce Tesco's profit margin and costs (known as deep-cut price promotions) is wrong and generates negative brand engrams. A 2014 In-Store survey shows that 64 per cent of shoppers look for added value; 55 per cent of respondents say they now shop at Aldi and Lidl. Shareholders and investors note that price discounts also hit the bottom line. Shoppers do look for value for money but also a shopping experience that is fun and has a positive impact, with a brand of which they approve. The best way to create fun and impact is to go for promotions. That is where Tesco's CEO should put Tesco's money; not more miserable cheeseparing. The book hopes to persuade you that using promotions to create a call to action is a large part of the answer to getting people to buy.

Chapter 1 introduces what is really new; matters that are expanded on in subsequent chapters. For the shopper, according to research, it is the amazing part that their subconscious plays in purchasing; the solution is to place and build, through multimedia, sufficient messages to reach the shoppers' tipping point which persuades them to buy. This book examines the role of promotions and how to use them in that persuasion process. The mobile, with the internet, has transformed the way we communicate and access information, which means the brand manager, retailer and supplier need to match the much enlarged shopper's expectation. The way to exploit these new technologies is covered in this book.

How consumers feel and how they behave is complex – know thy customer is the message. That's why Chapter 2 is about the customer and understanding the engram and how the shopper's 'mind file' on any product or service is built on by a discerning marketer to produce the desired brandgram.

NFC allows the mobile phone to become both an Oyster card (in London) for purchases under £10 and a credit card. Combined with other existing mobile capabilities, such as GPS and mobile internet, it means that where a retailer is prepared for mobile credit card purchases and the customer has indicated a preference for SMS receiving, new opportunities occur. Many stores in the United States are so enabled! For example, as customers enter the store sales promotions can be texted to them, steering them to particular parts of the store. At a political or charity meeting the audience, if so persuaded, could gift money on the spot (chuggers do this in the street). If a consumer has forgotten a birthday and/or wishes to send a surprise gift, he or she texts the outlet as the person arrives for lunch and a pre-paid bottle of champagne awaits him or her, possibly with an additional promotion gift from the restaurant as an incentive to both buyer and recipient. You can now use an app to tell a waiter you are ready to order or to bring the bill (**www.getwaiter.com**). Warm feelings all round!

The speed of communications and 'word of mouth' through web blogs, tweeting and e-mails continues and means that false or misleading claims about products or bad service are rapidly disseminated, as are significant good news and there are specialist web sites too which exist for universal voucher dissemination.

What's not new?

Research shows a majority of retailers still do not understand marketing, they often do not employ anyone trained in marketing (and as directors or partners they are not trained in marketing themselves) and they have not carried out customer research to obtain insight nor considered any strategic marketing. Unbelievable! They are unaware that a promotion is anything other than discounting. Where retail customers are considered and their needs met through marketing and attention at the point of sale, they return and shop again and again.

The Preface to the previous edition reported disastrous results over the Christmas period for some retailers; John Lewis was an exception. In 2014 it is déjà vu: John Lewis achieving an increase in sales over the Christmas 2013 period. Well done! It must be doing a lot right and should be studied closely! It has now overtaken M&S in trading revenues as has Next (convenience seems to be a reason for their success – they deliver).

The importance of the customer

Shopper marketing was originally jargon from across the Atlantic, but it has been successfully practised in the UK for some years. The key to winning at shopper marketing is an intimate knowledge of the journey to purchase for each customer for each product or service. Once this is known you can clearly chart the points at which marketing communications should be made and deliver them in a form that matches the customer communications canvas (see *Shoppernomics* by Roddy Mullin and Colin Harper for a full description). While on jargon, I note 'brand activation' and 'retail activation' are expressions creeping in as alternatives to parts of promotional marketing and are unhelpful to the practitioner who is just trying to sell to the shopper/buyer. You, as a practitioner, need to give the shoppers/buyers an engram on which to build your brandgram and achieve excess share of voice (locally or for your niche) to help them reach the tipping point at which the promotion persuades them and they buy.

For firms that outsource sales (known as 'field marketing') the efforts now being made by field marketing companies to add value for their clients by defining the journey to purchase and recommending when and how to promote should produce even greater rewards. Experiential marketing is becoming 'brand experience'. If selling is not a firm's core business, then it makes sense to adopt field marketing (see *The Handbook of Field Marketing*, by Alison Williams and Roddy Mullin). In the UK, retailer, supplier, bank and financial service, mobile phone and utilities companies often do not seem to be on the same wavelength as the customer. Know and research your customer's journey to purchase. Among the IPM (old ISP) award winners were two awards, excellent examples still (in Chapter 2 as case studies) that were for groups of targeted customers who were carefully researched. The importance of knowing the customer was clearly understood here. The winners of the awards extended the understanding of customers to achieving clear marketing effectiveness: Kellogg's 'Win a day as a Zookeeper' increased sales by 76 per cent as well as adding £3.8 million of value to participating customers, demonstrating novelty and solid sales achievement promotion work.

Over many years customers build a perception in their minds, a view of your brand (their version of your brandgram), and they compare it with your competitors' brandgrams. At the decision point, the point of purchase (POP) or point of sale (POS), where 70 per cent of retail buying decisions are made according to Mintel, something persuades them to buy from one supplier rather than another. This is their choice and they need to make it in your favour. Consider examples such as shampoo or toothpaste – theoretically there are some 1,300 toothpastes to choose from – which one will the customer select? The strength of the brand may be the decider, but as statistics tell us, and as you will see in this book, it is likely to be a promotion that does the job of persuading. So there is a need to make sure the promotion is there, that it is creative and 'brand complementary' and that it is in a message that matches the customer's communication canvas. Customers are returning from their interaction with the internet and now want a retail experience from shops, so promotions continue to be the answer for the future there as well.

What is the difference between POP and POS? A Point of Purchase Advertising Institute (POPAI) representative describes the difference as being one of greater consideration with POP (where the whole rationale of the customer is taken into account) rather than a simple POS (for example, a 20 per cent off on-packet flash). POSAI rather than POPAI of course does not read as well, according to their representative.

The 'hammered' retail side in April 2014

It has been a real roller-coaster ride for retail for the last seven years. Starting in the United Kingdom over the Christmas period 2006, trading was the worst since records began in 1986. Figures shortly after that indicated both a small volume decrease of 1.8 per cent in January and a discounting of 33.7 per cent on goods sold in January over December; in other words, straight discounting – even at that amazing level – did not persuade consumers to buy. Seventy per cent discounting is not uncommon now. The poor retail situation has continued, with newspapers reporting 'grim news' and 'high street shock'. The move to eco-friendly living, 'repair and reuse' rather than 'throw away and buy (new)', was having an effect. Commentators unsurprisingly reported that customers were 'changing their buying habits', saying customer service with a human face was becoming really important. The ups and downs continued with many high street names going into administration.

The rise and rise of the internet continued having an impact. For retailers the question must be: 'If 70 per cent of buying decisions are made at the point of sale, what do I have to do to turn that to my advantage?' Though that percentage may be true we now know that in fact shoppers' subconscious and 'mind file' systems have already prepared them for the decision. However, shoppers may deviate and override their subconscious if something catches their interest. What might that be? Promotional marketing is the answer, whether in an advertisement on the way to shop or as a promotion on the internet and certainly at the point of sale – a sure-fire decider everywhere, especially if it is creative, fun, exciting the shopper – a sales promotion in the retail space!

Promotion: better than just discounting

So what can the marketer do for the retailer? First it is even more important to be in tune with the customer, so find out, through research, the customer's needs and communication preferences: gain Insight. Clearly, next up, an excellent website is important. Examples such as Amazon, eBay and Argos spring to mind, as they are the most used websites in the United Kingdom. Remember you have to drive customers to your website and that can be with a promotion. Thirdly, 'self-service' in stores without a human face no longer seems to work, so if you do not go for outsourcing the sales function through field marketing, investment in real sales staff, not shop assistants (order taking only!), is an alternative. This must match the brand and the customer need, with proper training, incentives and motivation (vouchers?) for staff. Finally, because straight discounting does not work and it may kill the brand perception too, some other marketing mechanism is needed. This is where the range of techniques of promotions comes in, though not all are relevant all the time and they depend on market conditions. Figures show that UK companies favour promotions over all other forms of marketing. They can't all be wrong – so join them.

The value of marketing

Think figures for a moment and the perceived difficulty in measuring marketing – for example, how much is spent to change attitudes or awareness and is that valuable? Take the investor who clearly sees a value in the intangible, the brand. Brand finance research of the top 25 stock markets found that 61 per cent of equity value is intangible, of which a brand typically accounts for 25 per cent. The concept of intangible value is widely recognized and accepted by investors and, as they pay the money and reap returns, it is measurable.

Marketing spend can also seem pretty intangible, but it is possible to measure and manage that too. How should the spend on marketing within a company be measured and controlled? Let's look at the business and marketing within that context. The accountants' view is threefold: keep costs tight, reduce the item cost and leverage sales. What does that mean for a company? By way of example: if the item is sold at £100 and the production cost is £70, then with the overhead (administration, management, marketing) at say £27 per item you make £3 profit at the end of the day (or £3,000 for 1,000 items sold). To an accountant, a company makes more money by attacking each of the three. Reduce the product cost (for example, by sourcing from countries that have low labour and manufacturing cost). Reduce the overhead (always difficult and unpopular, and the benefit of a larger size comes in here – it's easier to cut bits from a large organization than from a small one where any cut is significant). Marketing is often attacked under this category – it is the first to lose out unless a clear value benefit of each pound spent is available (or persuade the accountant to consider marketing as revenue expenditure). Finally, leveraging sales: for example, if you increase sales of 1,000 items by 10 per cent, ie sell 1,100 items, bringing in £110,000 at a cost of £77,000, and your overhead remains at the same level per item (ie £27,000), then your profit is doubled to £6,000. So a 10 per cent sales increase gives double the profit. Leveraging sales in this way is a persuasive argument, but it does not take the cost of generating that extra revenue into account (often mistakenly through price discounting which eats into the £6,000) nor does it demonstrate the effectiveness of the marketing spend included in the normal overhead cost. So a marketer in a company needs to know just how beneficial the spend of every pound on marketing is, both in the overhead budget and in the spend required to kick the leverage into action; otherwise expect the marketing budget to be cut. The message is simple: measure your marketing spend. We could call this marketing spend 'revenue expenditure' rather than overhead (see above); it is what you spend to generate revenue. So how much do you spend, need to spend, and on what, as both overhead marketing and extra marketing, to increase revenue by raising the level of sales by 10 per cent?

Spending on marketing is something you can plan to do as both a contingency and a routine activity. The contingency part is important in marketing, as customers are swayed by messages and events and a business needs to capitalize on this when it happens. This book will show that promotions are excellent for doing this. If you plan to measure in advance too, then promotions can demonstrate their value to accountants by way of the return generated for the revenue expenditure made. Some of the IPM awards given as case studies in this book describe planned examples of measurement and the returns that are possible, in one case for just a few thousand pounds of 'revenue expenditure'! For a client selling inflatable swimming pools, a contingency of on-call advertising was prepared for use with the local radio station for when a hot spell happened, along with some premium sales promotions as the icing on the cake. The cost of the radio advertising – the revenue expenditure – was set against the extra sales made, discovered by asking all the purchasers how they heard about the sales offer. Interestingly, POPAI considered that measurement should mimic advertising in trying to evaluate impact, awareness and reach, rather than ROI. The IPA suggests measuring penetration.

Overview of the book

This book's purpose is primarily to help you decide on the most suitable promotions to use and when, in the building of the shopper's 'mind file' leading to a 'buy' decision. With all the research pointing to an actual shift to the new media – internet or mobile in particular – any marketer has to communicate through both. Mobile is estimated to be just four years behind the internet. More households have a mobile than a landline – so mobile internet will take over from PCs. Research shows the 18–35 age group recognizes mobile advertising and view it twice as much as TV. Research also indicates that people use mobiles morning and evening but use a PC in the middle of the day, if at all.

Research for this book shows that readers and agencies want case studies: a few new and many from years gone by are included here. Thousands are now given online: search the trade bodies (MAA, DMA and IPM) members websites for these. I am really grateful to the agencies and their clients who generously gave permission to use case studies here this time – they would of course welcome enquiries from any potential clients or jobseekers (including marketing communications apprentices seeking jobs); see Chapter 15. A new form of information is included in this book – the Brief, which is an extract from somewhere: a newspaper, journal or magazine, either in print or online or heard at a seminar to illustrate a point in the text.

For some time I have been writing and lecturing that a 'promotion' can and should be added to all forms of advertising/marketing communication whatever channel or media is used. A promotion is a separate marketing tool from just communicating a message and in this book I have tried to illustrate the benefits (see Chapter 5). I continue to see a loose use of the words 'marketing mix' for 'promotional mix': the former is the offer (see Chapter 2); the latter is how it is promoted, ie the channels and media you use and with a promotion added to communicate awareness, brand values, desire, fun and support for the shopper's decision to purchase.

The readership of this book has broadened over the years. The text here is tuned to make it easier to take in what is needed to gain the international IPM Diploma. Some self-study questions are now placed at the end of each chapter. For past readers, though, the overall purpose of the book remains the same. It is a 'how to do it' volume for practitioners who are looking, in 2014, for a way to sell more to existing customers and to attract new customers. As before, the book considers using promotions when things go wrong. The competition for customers is fierce: finding new ones, persuading others to switch and then retaining them are ongoing tasks. Promotion is primarily about retail but, as everyone in business, charities and the professions is a consumer too, they all recognize promotions, and promotions can be used in these non-retail sectors to great effect. The difference is that the promotion benefit may go to the buyer or charity rather than the business or organization in B2B. A case study of a public sector award winner is included here – the Metropolitan Police trying to reach and communicate with black gun-carrying youths.

The web allows you, as the reader, to keep right up to date. Check out as a high priority the website at **www.theipm.org.uk**. It has the latest information.

The first part of the book looks at all the issues that promotion practitioners should consider. Promotion is seen as a part of the whole marketing effort, making its contribution in a consistent manner to build the brandgram in the shopper's subconscious 'mind file' or to drive profit through sales. Promotion has a role to play in overall marketing, and operates within legal constraints and codes of practice. What promotions can achieve, how they can be implemented and the importance of creativity are covered here. The second and third parts of the book deal with techniques and implementation. International promotions, whether in one or many countries, appear in Chapter 12.

For those new to this book: welcome! Promotions are a wonderful way to attract the customer. Just think back to the last time you remembered an advertisement from the press or TV. To attract you sufficiently for you to remember it, the advertisement was probably close to offensive, was humorous, or made a promotion offer. If this rings a bell, you have discovered the truth behind promotions: they attract and make advertising memorable. If your brand is not suited to humour or prepared to offend, then only a promotion remains. The same applies to direct mail or door-to-door literature. You usually recall direct marketing later, only if it includes a promotion. Clearly, promotions are a key factor in awareness raising and generating interest across all marketing communications.

Understanding how customers react to marketing – and particularly to promotions – is key to success. The rationale, the reasons and the thinking behind using promotions, the promotion mechanics (how the customer can respond) and the production of a promotion are all in the book. Individual techniques, the promotion itself, how the promotion works, what to look out for (tips) and how to measure the success are there too.

In Chapter 15, reference is made to websites where up-to-date codes of practice, the law relating to promotion, and examples can be found. Reference is also made to other magazines (including online) and books dealing with topics that impact on promotion, such as creativity, controlling agencies, direct marketing (which covers some of the production of promotions), marketing accountability/revenue expenditure (justifying marketing spend) and the strategic use of promotions.

Do participate in promotions as a customer – it is an easy way to learn. Analyse them. Why did you participate? Did it persuade you to do what they wanted? Did you feel better about the brand? Find a brand that is communicating and not offering a promotional offer and consider how you feel about that.

Register and look at the IPM website for the latest batch of awards and use them as case studies. This book includes a selection from the 2013 awards as there are some old ones that still have lessons for us all. I am particularly happy to see B2B and charity award categories in the IPM awards. This demonstrates the universal appeal of promotions to the customer. The DMA also has awards at **http://dma.org.uk/get-inspired**.

I hope I have communicated my passion and enthusiasm for marketing and here, promotions in particular. I can but commend the reader to the book.

PART ONE
The context

Introduction

Promotional marketing in action

A promotion – adds fun and spontaneity, rewards, stimulates and excites – to a message and persuades the mind of shoppers, (buyers and even retail therapists!) to reach a tipping point – and buy!

In 2014, relying on a promotion at the point of sale (a sales promotion!) to work wonders is not enough. Seventy per cent of buying decisions may be made there, but shopper insight now shows that unsurprisingly, on the journey to purchase, the shopper builds up a 'mind file' on a brand, product, retailer or supplier and adds every relevant message to that mind file whether from advertising, direct messages, online or through the post, social media and word of mouth or indeed personal experience. This mind file builds to a tipping point for the shopper or buyer as to whether to purchase or not; the final spur to purchase, a promotion, will tip the balance and get the shopper to buy. The promotion may be a 'sales promotion' only offered at the point of sale, but may well be a promotion offered along the journey to purchase. 'Buyers' for B2B are given a mention here as they too are human beings and the same logic operates for them as for shoppers, though they are more constrained by process and their work culture (see Chapter 2).

A key to future success for each marketer is to really understand the mind file construction of shoppers and buyers from insight gleaned from big data and market research, then to build, through a range of channels tuned to the shopper, the messages that persuade and convince, until the shopper's tipping point is reached. Technology in 2014 allows a marketer to analyse data for better insight and to be more precise in targeting messages, which means there is less waste and sending of inappropriate messages to the wrong shoppers, which can irritate and put off a purchase by the shopper.

The Christmas/Winter 2013/14 retail experience should at last confirm to retailers that it is neither the 'online versus bricks-and-mortar' debate nor price discounting that works. Yes, shoppers are buying more online (non-food grew by 19.2 per cent in December according to BRC and KPMG) and online sales now account for 18.6–21 per cent of all retail sales, depending on which survey you view. But those well-established in-store and online businesses such as Next and John Lewis did well, as did smaller supermarkets such as Aldi and Lidl, independents and other small chains.

Fat Face refused to follow the rest and did not discount at all, reporting a 5 per cent increase in sales in the five weeks prior to 4 January 2014. By resisting pre-Christmas discounting, Asda has seen the biggest ever Boxing Day trading day sales in its history. Primark did well (12.4 per cent increase in sales) without an online presence at all. ASOS online-only fashion sales were up 38 per cent overall including a 69 per cent increase in Europe. But the Giants such as Tesco (with the largest online sales at 45 per cent of the grocery market), Debenhams (both advanced online, an app and in-store), Morrisons (which has only just started online) and M&S (large and early discounting) did poorly. Why? Something other than internet presence or price discounting affected sales. Graham Ruddick, the retail correspondent of the *Daily Telegraph* reports that Clive Black, an analyst for Shore Capital warns the data (here he includes Sainsbury's as well) shows it is anti-corporatism that is to blame. Research into shopper's engrams suggests it is something else. It is the failure to understand the new insight that the subconscious mind rules the shopper more than brand managers, retailers and suppliers realize, requiring a sequence of promotional messages that inspire, reward, excite and are just simply fun, perhaps with a sales promotion at the point of sale as the icing on the cake (and not necessarily a price discount!) that achieves the shopper's tipping point – which is when they buy. If the shopper's subconscious mind picks up adverse comments or reports, these can persuade against buying a particular brand. The horse meat debacle, a failure to stock a preferred brand, poor shopper/staff interaction, poor handling of a customer issue, running out of promotional goods, all can affect the subconscious. Tesco in February 2014 is at last recognizing that this is true of its brand and that it needs to 'make Tesco loved again', according to Philip Clarke, its Chief Executive. The loving bit has to rebuild on the Tesco engram – its brandgram.

More on the downside: though customer service is expected to be extremely shopper-friendly, some retailers still have account-driven processes that can put off customers for good. Typical are the mobile phone companies which, when banks make errors with direct debits, do not inform customers of impending doom, but just cut off broadband or mobile access at a whim. This may in future be taken as affecting customers' human rights, as so many government services require online response and if a mobile phone company cuts off the line and the broadband, customers are totally bereft. The same applies to utilities and banks: a mindless pursuit of process that helps no one, especially customers. Such experiences lose customers and all the potential customers that they tell. It is as bad as a shopper discovering that the stock for a sales promotion has run out: retailers are expected to stock what has been offered; similarly, cinema chains offering screenings that are 'no shows' when customers arrive can expect little sympathy. Eurotunnel's 20th anniversary promotion with a £20 return journey attracted plenty of new customers on 20 February 2014. How sad that they were subjected to long delays and put on later trains; being packed into departure lounges too small to accommodate the extra numbers, where the restaurants had closed (they were not aware of the promotion) and the cafés ran out of food – all because they ran the normal two trains per hour instead of doubling it to four, when implementing the promotion. The staff did apologize (for the lack of trains), but it could have been so different with lots of new impressed Shuttle customers, instead of the reality of tired and hungry (angry) families. An excellent promotional idea that failed in its execution.

Remember to think retail therapy as well as shoppers' commodity buying. People go shopping for a rewarding experience. No one buys chocolate to be miserable, so make your promotions add to the fun of buying any product or service. If the fun goes out of it, so does the spirit that makes buying and selling part of our lives, whether as customers or as business clients. Indeed, of all the marketing tools available to the marketer, a promotion can most readily be used to give that sense of fun to the customer. To excite, make the shopping experience stimulating and rewarding. A shopper should leave a website or store, a cinema, a restaurant or a café; finish a journey; end a call centre 'chat' with a feeling that the experience was worthwhile and with a raised perception of the brand. A promotion is the icing on the cake that makes it memorable.

The marketer has other 'customers' to consider: the shareholder, the employee and the management team, which raises some serious points. Parts of this book 'talk' about detailed mechanics – how the customer or buyer responds – and the codes of practice that apply. It's also impossible to look at price promotions without some reference to economics. There is an important need for accountability and measuring the success of marketing activities; awards now consider the return too. There's hard graft and detail in promotions. At its heart is the serious business of building long-term, profitable customer relationships. Good promotions are not a substitute for serious thinking or for building deep staff and customer relationships; they are a part of the same process.

To what promotions do shoppers/customers respond? For door drops, research for the DMA shows 96 per cent of consumers are aware of them and 72 per cent take action on money-off coupons, with 80 per cent following up supermarket offers. Research in the United States shows 84 per cent believe a sales promotion enhances the brand, with 69 per cent agreeing that a sales promotion does this on its own and 44 per cent saying it generates a favourable attitude to a TV advertisement. Research shows that over 70 per cent of the population has taken part in competitions or games on products and services, with almost 60 per cent of the population actively participating in some form of promotion in any given month, whether entering a competition, sending in for a free gift or using a money-off coupon. This makes participating in promotions one of Britain's biggest active leisure activities. Compare that with, for example, the 11 per cent of the UK population participating in golf in any way over a year.

The best basis for understanding promotions is from the inside. Get involved in promotions: collect coupons, send in for offers and seek out special offers. Have a look at how others do it. Study the rolls of honour and the winners of the latest IPM competition. Read why the judges awarded the prize. Did those awarded exceed the target set for the response? How many participated? Did it prove the marketing activity was successful, ie the promotion worked and exceeded its objective?

The extent of promotions

A promotion can be anything from an invitation to test drive a new car, sampling a perfume as you pass a cosmetics counter, watching a stallholder demonstrate a new gadget or a sales promotion to stimulate a purchase at the point of sale (a BOGOF, extra fill, products with a chance to win a prize, purchase something else for a reduced price or a branded item, an offer of a cheap holiday or a bar code on your mobile to redeem a free drink when in range of a particular bar). A cursory check in your supermarket, your local paper or pub and the direct mail sent to both your home and your business address will give an immediate feel of the extent of promotions.

A 'sales promotion' is defined as a promotion within the retail space, normally short term and tactical, for a product; historically sales promotions were controlled by a sales team. Promotions are planned as part of a campaign, but they can be brilliant when planned as a contingency promotion. Offering a free umbrella with a product purchased when it's raining; adding a local discount to clear near date-expired or end-of-line stock; or match pricing a local rival's promotion to upset their sales; there is no limit.

A promotion is found whenever a supermarket offers 'three for the price of two', a pub offers a happy hour, an insurance or charity mailer offers a free pen for reply-ing or a product offers a free draw, competition or mail-in. On the mobile phone too, if permission has been given, offers will appear for drinks happy hours and estate agents' latest houses and flats coming onto the market, to allow the favoured to see them early. Whatever the consumer gives permission for, will appear on a mobile. The mobile phone can also be used to respond to advertisements, texting a number with a code word. 'Mobile vouchers' allow a message to be sent back that includes access to a promotion, including at the point of purchase, through a bar code reader. Apps facilitate reading QR codes. As a marketer, if you are not doing so, you should 'go mobile'. Sir Philip Green goes further and warns in an article in the *Sunday Telegraph* that retailers that don't invest in new technology will be left behind. Top Shop is spending £50 million on digital feedback and moving stock some 8 million miles a year around his stores to keep the right stock in front of the right customers. Lidl now seems to be expert at this as a quick check of stores in Clapham Junction and Cirencester will reveal: the stock is quite different in each, presumably matched to the local shoppers.

What does a promotion achieve? In this world of choice, a good promotion will stop customers for a moment, make them think about a brand and product and, if it has the right impact, move them to make a decision to follow up the promotion. There are hidden benefits – if customers take up your 'three for the price of two' offer they will not be purchasing a competitor product while using yours, and their experi-ence of enjoying a product or service is a great influencer on future purchases. Indeed, a second promotion delivered with the product or service when customers take up the first promotion can entice them to make their next purchase of that product or service. In mobile marketing parlance: use a bounce back or two.

For the customer as consumer at the point of sale, there are now too many choices. Careful placement (merchandising; see Chapter 7) can ensure your customer finds your product. You can pay for specific positioning and check it with field marketing. But there are, for example, around 1,200 brands of hair shampoo to choose from. What do consumers do? They are busy people who make their buying decisions and choice of brand from the offers available. This is not new. People have always looked for what is 'in season', what is a bargain, what is familiar and has met their need before. Shopkeepers and stallholders in previous centuries would make an 'on-the-spot offer' to help persuade people to make a purchase; a sales promotion is the modern equivalent when no salesperson (field marketer) is there.

More is now spent in all companies on promotion than on all other advertising, including direct marketing. You should note that price promotions – a very large part of promotions – may not always be counted as expenditure, but as lost income. Expenditure on altering packs and products for a promotion may also not be counted as promotional expenditure. Also check the basis for comparisons; it used just to be media spend for advertising. According to a University of Westminster Business School study for the Institute of Promotional Marketing (IPM), the 2014 spend on promotions in the United Kingdom will be £55 billion. This includes £14 billion on FMCG price discounting and £27 billion on other price discounting, leaving £14 billion on the sort of promotional offers covered in this book. On a like-for-like basis, some £8 billion is spent on advertising in UK.

If you are not undertaking promotions in your organization, you should be wondering why everyone else is. The figures given above demonstrate that promotions are no longer an also-ran in the business of marketing products and services, but one of the most important tools available to companies and a major part of our day-to-day lives. To find out why they are likely to become even more important in the future, read on.

Why promotions have grown

There are eight main reasons for the extensive growth of promotions and for managers finding that promotions are essential to building customer relationships:

1 Firms are getting better at what they do. Promotions offer a tie-breaker in markets in which most products are excellent. It's no longer enough to have an excellent product at an excellent price. Companies everywhere are facing declining real differences between products and services, increased distributor power and faster communication of alternatives. They have to fight harder and faster for every sale.

2 Customers look for more from the brands they buy. An experiential or sales promotion offers novelty, excitement and humour at the point of purchase, which customers respond to. Firms are having to rethink the relationship between attitude and behaviour (see Chapter 2). Trying to create awareness of and a positive attitude to a brand by means of advertising is seen as less effective than building on the engram over a succession of messages that achieves excess share of voice, finally encouraging a sale through a promotion, which all leads to a long-term relationship and further purchases of the brand.

3 The pressure to achieve short-term results is growing but should be resisted (see Chapter 2). This demand for short-term profit performance continues to grow, despite people urging a long-term view. The fortunes of brands and companies are increasingly volatile. Promotions can be devised in quieter

times as a contingency and implemented as necessary, taking effect far more quickly than other forms of marketing. This is the way ahead, but only if the engram exists and has been built on to produce a favourable brandgram!

4 TV audiences are fragmenting as the number of channels grows, making it more expensive to reach certain audiences even though TV advertising has probably never been cheaper. The decline in community identity at a local level is making it more difficult to reach particular groups (such as the young) via local media: the young tend to switch off from TV advertising and Twitter, although they do register cinema advertising.

5 The growth in the sheer number of competing brands and products is leading people generally to switch off from many of the advertising messages beamed at them (including using TIVO).

6 Advertising research has shown that the sales effects of TV advertising over a four-week period are between two and seven times greater when the advertising coincides with promotions. This important finding came from a survey of 21 different brands in eight different consumer goods markets that integrated the shopping behaviour of 9,000 households with TV viewing data. In the case of two out of 11 established brands where the effect of TV advertising with and without promotional activity could be measured, TV advertising was only effective when promotions were also taking place. The same result is now coming from surveys into internet and mobile buying. It might be said that the only advertising that works and registers with audiences is that which amuses, offends or offers a promotion.

7 A promotion can be applied anywhere in the cycle to retain a favourable customer relationship, for example if a sale is lost or a computer automatically penalized a customer when there was, in fact, a justification for his or her action. A promotion, particularly a sales promotion, is an excellent way to restore or retain goodwill.

8 In mobile marketing a second lesser promotion in a bounce-back can make all the difference to retaining customer interest and future responses. The same applies to the offer of samples – give one for immediate use and provide a second to allow the customer to recall the sample's effect (and brand name!) later, or to hand on to a friend or colleague.

How to use this book

There are three parts to this book.

Part One, the context, has two chapters: this one, which sets the current scene, and Chapter 2 which starts with the customer and describes the component parts of the offer a business makes to the shopper or buyer. It sets out from recent insights how they behave, the importance of the engram and building the 'mind file' and the six message opportunities, including achieving excess share of voice, that drive a shopper to the tipping point, when they decide to buy. There are barriers that should be removed. B2B buyers have additional hurdles to overcome.

Part Two comprises seven chapters:

Chapter 3 describes the importance of creativity in promotions.

Chapter 4 discusses the suppliers that are there to help.

Chapter 5 covers non-participative, passive promotions without offers and the media that deliver them.

Chapter 6 looks at how shoppers can actively pursue and take up promotions offered through mobiles, websites and other associated technologies and what retailers, brand managers and suppliers can do to support this activity.

Chapter 7 describes participative promotions (brand experiences) where a business can foster and encourage shoppers to buy.

Chapter 8 describes what promotions can do in all the other media and channels.

Chapter 9 covers the five standard promotional offers.

The nine chapters in Parts One and Two are crucial for understanding what promotions can and cannot do. If you are tempted to dive straight into the implementation and skip these chapters, resist. You can use the techniques of implementation to best effect only if you are clear about the why, when and how of promotions.

Part Three is the implementation of promotions – the techniques to apply:

Chapter 10 is about in-house activity – shopper marketing – to gain insight into the shopper, and how to structure and organize a business to undertake promotions, and how to avoid disaster and ensure that all the elements work together.

Chapter 11 covers how to implement a promotion.

Chapter 12 looks at the important area of international promotions. The rise of Central Europe as a new market is reflected in this chapter, along with the Far East. Even if your concerns are local, the chapter is full of ideas.

Chapter 13 covers the legal aspects of a promotion, sets out the principles behind the UK Code of Sales Promotion Practice and discusses recent case studies of promotions from the Advertising Standards Authority (ASA). The CAP code describes the rules that apply in UK and in other countries. It is a must, as a reference, for any promotion you run.

Chapter 14, on marketing effectiveness and accountability, is essential for ensuring that your promotions meet the marketing objectives you set.

You will find Part Three useful for years to come. You may not want to read it all at once. You will probably want to dip into it and refer to it for the nuts and bolts of techniques you may want to use now or in the future. If you are studying for a marketing course, you will find the data you need on the range of techniques available to you.

The final chapter of the book contains further information, listing useful addresses, books, magazines and courses. The organizations listed have a short descriptive entry to explain how they can best help you, most compiled their entries themselves.

There are case studies and briefs throughout the book, illustrating the text and giving examples (and in one historic case, the worst) in promotional practice. Use these for ideas for your business sector and your business challenge. They have been placed generally at the end of the chapter to which they mainly refer, but they illustrate the many types of promotions and their use in different business sectors. Be aware that although, for completeness, the range of case studies and techniques is extensive, some are probably less relevant today for certain target audiences; for example, the advent of low-cost airline fares made flight tickets less 'rewarding' as a promotion than in previous years, though this could change. I won tickets to Paris on Eurostar and was delighted to do so. The problem with including case studies and briefs is that they inevitably seem out of date; however, a creative marketer will be able to use an old case study or take the point made in a brief as the basis of an idea and update the promotion. Take a look at the Institute of Promotional Marketing website at **www.theipm.org.uk** and the Marketing Agencies Association website at **www.marketingagencies.org.uk** which, in addition to including examples of promotions in their awards sections, have links to IPM and MAA members' websites with even more case studies.

The
shopper/buyer

02

The increased power of the customer

The shopper/buyer has become more powerful because of near-universal communication (and the technology that has enabled it) and the access a shopper/buyer has to an amazing amount of information. The supplier, retailer and brand managers have to live with this, but if they use big data and social media research and the insight they provide, they can discover a lot about shoppers/buyers, who they are, who buys what, what triggers the purchase and how to communicate with them. The shoppers/buyers' expectations have changed as well: quality, value, relationships, competent service and delivery with consistency rank high in their evaluation of the brand, supplier and retailer. This matters as the shopper/buyer builds a 'mind file' that stores all the information, even over many years, which is brought forward from their subconscious as their version of a brandgram, when a proposition to buy arises.

Segmenting

Customers display many different shopping personalities according to the time, place or context of the purchase. The business executive may be buying top travel packages one moment and the next organizing an economy family break. Within a few hours an office manager may be purchasing office materials, spending on entertainment at lunchtime with colleagues and then, after leaving work, go food and retail shopping with the children before returning home to shop online. The shopper is still one individual with a singular and distinct social, educational and cultural background, but represents multiple customer personalities. The supplier or retailer that fails to recognize this chameleon-like aspect is likely to fail the customer relationship test.

The customer applies a different buying process to different purchases. Obviously acquiring a pair of socks may require no thought and allow an instant purchase – where the product subsequently can be rejected if the purchase is mistaken. There are not many parameters when considering sock (or commodity) purchase. When buying a car, a rigorous examination of alternatives, consultations and research is undertaken: the cost of insurance, tax, fuel consumption, in addition to performance, reliability and resale value. In fact car sales staff report that some shoppers know more about the car than they do – all the shopper is then looking for from the salesperson is a better deal than a competitor car showroom. Factors affecting the shopper perception may be the cost of purchase in relation to shopper income or available cash or credit, but here the salesperson can invoke feelings that the shopper is worth it and overcome price resistance. (The salesperson must not assume anything about the shopper or whether they can afford to buy. Pity the Swiss sales girl who reckoned Oprah Winfrey was unable to pay for a handbag, in 2013.)

The shopper's emotional state at the time of purchase can encourage impulsiveness. Heightened emotion associated with a promotion, work, professional recognition, being on holiday, being in love, can encourage us to bypass our normal caution and restraint. The status of products and services may also influence a purchase: some customers are heavily influenced by the impression a branded item portrays and their own perception of how people view others who own such branded goods. A customer attitude to purchase can be altered by the perception of an economic recession, the influence of green issues, medical disclosures, press speculation and whether they can be seen to shop in certain premises. The recent extended recession made economy brand shopping quite chic for otherwise high net worth individuals; shopping at Lidl or Aldi with an Audi, BMW or Range Rover is no longer socially unacceptable, nor is shopping at pound shops.

To target by gender, demographic or socioeconomic station is no longer adequate: brand marketers must reach, engage, convert and amplify the offer (see below) to the specific shopper – the one who will buy, share, post, tweet and participate in branded programmes and events. The shortest path to this shopper is through a well-targeted, measured and well-messaged existing user base. The importance of well-planned and holistic CRM practices has never been greater.

Myer (Australia) advised by Sarah Richardson of Global Loyalty Pty Ltd (see Chapter 15), segment its customers into five categories, according to the way they shop as much as on the basis of what they buy. These are:

1 Busy Belinda: always in a hurry and often with kids.
2 Premium Polly: loves designer and high-end trends.
3 Trendy TJ: a wannabe Premium Polly.
4 Low Involvement Lou: would rather not shop if she can help it.
5 Discount Dora: loves to grab a bargain.

This has helped its marketers and staff in assessing how to treat shoppers.

Target shoppers and insights

Research from eBay published in 2014 shows some 75 per cent of UK shopping spend is by 'super shoppers' who make up 18 per cent of the population (see Brief 2.3). For top-end products and services these wealthy people must be sought out; the same principle applies to other types of shopper who have an interest in any specific product range. For many years it has been possible to construct a profile of a preferred customer and then find potential customers with similar profiles and the channels to reach them. Those with a sport, hobby or specific need will generally search out their niche suppliers and retailers. A retail outlet such as a supermarket which is tied to a location and offers a standard range of brands, or a niche product supplier, need to establish what the local shoppers' profiles are (or the niche segment shoppers' characteristics are) and what they buy and then stock that range and similar brand lines. Centralized purchasing does not work for such retail outlets and the local manager must have the power to acquire shopper insight and then decide what to stock, the promotions to run and the messages to communicate (Lidl seems to be good at this).

Those who lead the pack, the 'future shapers', must also be identified from among customers and be engaged with. Future shapers are identified as:

- valuing authenticity and originality in all they buy and experience;
- being well informed and hugely involved in the products, services and thus brands they buy;
- individualistic, doing things their way and trying to persuade suppliers to convert to that way;
- time-poor and valuing anything that saves them time;
- socially responsible, exercising ethical awareness via product and brand choices;
- curious, open-minded and receptive to new ideas;
- advocates of new ideas – and they spread the word.

Before you go any further, for every customer segment that you decide to select as a target (you do not need to target every one), you should apply the following method. Erase from your mind your own thinking and prejudices. Learn to listen, observe and grasp how your target thinks, communicates and comes to conclusions. You need to understand them and how they react. This method has been described as 'self-recognition criteria' – accepting that the way you think and react is wrong for any target you are analysing. You should not make any assumptions about the target customer (research into marketers finds their assumptions about customers are grossly out of kilter with reality). Find out from analysis of big data and the insight from research. Now you have an open mind about the customer, let's examine how to respond to the customer, how customers express their needs and what makes them tick.

Reacting to the shopper

1 Anchor your proposition as the supplier, brand manager or retailer for each product or service, using the customer view of the Six Cs component parts of the offer (see below) to produce the customer value proposition (CVP).

2 Ensure that you locate and understand who your target shoppers are and from insight know that the offer you propose matches the Six Cs components for your target shoppers. You may have to change the offer to achieve alignment or find a way to realign your shoppers to your offer.

3 Take account of the recent research finding on the part shoppers'
subconscious plays when they are choosing what to buy, which requires
a sequence of messages delivered by different media to achieve an 'excess
share of voice' and to build the 'mind file' of the shopper; you need to reach
the shopper's tipping point that persuades them to buy (adding a promotion!).
The insight should also be used to confirm that the shoppers' engram and
'mind file' for your product or service is near what you would wish for your
brand – compare their version with your brandgram. If it is not as you would
wish you will need to act to remedy this by additional messaging.

4 Make sure you have the logistics in place to deliver your product or service
and any promotion – customers are really put off if a brand they seek isn't in
stock. (Remember the shortage of Easter eggs in the shops in 2013 and 2014!)

These four steps provide a clear way ahead for the marketer to define marketing
objectives and so make a plan for message communication through each medium.
From that analysis readily arises the promotional objectives – Who do you want
to do what? – along the route to purchase that converts the shopper's arrival at the
tipping point into a sale, which is what this book is about.

The Six Cs – the offer

The six components are:

1 *Cost* (of lifetime purchase) within a value perception. That value perception
is personal and includes a quality-of-life assessment, social, cultural, or status
reasons and the cost of time and travel to make a purchase, in addition to
longer-term servicing and maintenance costs.

2 *Concept:* the product and service, incorporated with brand values, benefits
and advantages over competitors; a warranty, fitness for purpose and a
returns policy are assumed and of course there is the distinctive shopper
marker – its engram (and the subconscious 'mind file' built on it).

3 *Convenience:* of payment method, location, availability of item and ideally
24/7 purchase and delivery.

4 *Communication:* the seamless arrival of appropriate and timely messages
through preferred media and channels. The communication must not be
complex or dull and put the concept across in terms the consumer commonly
uses. The mobile internet is the consumer technology of the future; shoppers
communicate with each other (social media) and expect the brand to operate
two-way communication too.

5 *Customer relationship:* the customer expects to have a relationship, be treated
with respect and be recognized at any interface (the involvement criterion)
with the supplier or retailer, with all reasonable questions answered and
problems arising resolved speedily and fairly.

6 *Consistency:* the same values of the brand and messages at all customer
interfaces – brand surety if you like; research shows that inconsistency can
lead to a loss of 30 per cent of sales.

Matching the offer to the shopper/buyer

Once the offer is determined, it needs to be matched to what the shopper/buyer expects. This is an iterative process. See if the shopper buys from the offer – the CVP you have created. If it is right, you will make sales!

The shopper's engram and 'mind file'

The shopper's subconscious plays a key part in buying. Something in the brain, which shoppers do not articulate when questioned, is prompting their behaviour. The shopper appears to build a 'mind file' about brands, products and services around a core 'hook', identified as the engram, and only when a tipping point of sufficient marketing communications is reached with messages that build the 'mind file' will the shopper buy that brand, product or service. This 'mind file' may be subconscious but it can be built on and encouraged by the discerning marketer on the shopper's journey to purchase. An expansion of the reasoning for the engram concept is given in *Shoppernomics*, by Roddy Mullin and Colin Harper, which also describes the 'communication canvas' of a shopper and how to match marketing messages to it.

In essence the shopper's subconscious takes a logo, a smell, a jingle – but usually a visual indicator called a core visual mnemonic or CVM – that triggers a brand or product as an engram, and all experiences and messages, good or bad, as interpreted by the shopper, are added to that to build a 'mind file'. Each individual will store different experiences and take on the marketing messages in their 'mind file' and may build up, as a consequence, something quite different from the image intended by the brand manager, retailer or supplier. Insight from social media analysis will reveal what the shopper thinks, which can be accommodated or corrected to the preferred profile of the brand, known as a brandgram. Early research shows a brand manager's brandgram frequently differs from that held by shopper/buyers.

The shopper is unlikely to buy anything without having absorbed marketing communications and messages from many other sources (relatives, colleagues, friends and social media, advertising) into the adaptive subconscious, before entering the store or website. The shopper may be smart, sophisticated, cynical of marketing and advertising, time-poor and highly selective, but his or her subconscious will be working the whole time. The in-store environment is immensely complex, with many, sometimes thousands of products on display and lots of promotions, other shoppers and staff; how does the shopper set about the task of making purchases? Shoppers are pack-focused and interacting with packs is the primary task.

For a product, the packaging needs to stand out and do so in a very brief glance by the shopper, seeing a CVM which then triggers the engram with its mind file. Shoppers look for unique visual clues in prioritizing shape and colour over any words. The packaging is the most important form of communication for the shopper in store. The shopper subconsciously pays attention only to packs that are relevant to their store visit. Packaging design minimizes the effort and time involved in decision making. The CVM often has high recall; where it does not, conscious processing is required to make the decision to select a product.

Unfortunately market researchers are often unaware that the research they undertake exposes conscious attitudes and opinions to research stimulus material but rarely identifies the subconscious. Eye-tracking studies, for example, reveal where people look on a pack but, with honourable exceptions, studies do not reveal whether a dwell in one area is a result of trying to understand, or high levels of interest.

Twitter research can indicate how shoppers rate supermarkets and predict the need to change the customer relationship. Categorizing tweets in eight ways from Happiness to Disgust and examining each is revealing much about the 'herd' view of a brand – their depiction of the brandgram. It allows analysts to predict early on the eventual outcome of the common view of shoppers on brands, on retailers, on individual stores service and on anything else on which there are comments.

To build the engram 'mind file' some six communications are needed to deliver your messages. Initial messages provide information and come from the brand manager, retailer or supplier. They describe the product and associated services and the benefits and features. They must match the communication canvas in their delivery. The shopper/buyer will also search other sources, online forums, social media, etc for comments – clever marketers can encourage this. Some brands have used social media as the starting point – only then do they introduce the commerce element. Contacts with colleagues, friends and relatives need to be stimulated as they provide an important input to the mind file – sharing their views. The way into and in the shopping environment (online or in store) itself needs to send messages to the shopper. Excess share of voice plays an important part and can be achieved locally quite easily (excess share of voice is when the marketing communications exceed the market share). Point of sale material plays a further part. A promotion though, is the icing on the cake, adding fun, exciting the shopper/buyer and reaching the tipping point that persuades the shopper to buy.

Stock availability, logistics

Shoppers expect to see their preferred brands on the shelf. Shops and retail outlets are often centrally limited in the inventory they may stock even though outlets may do so: M&S will supply only 10 stores with some fashion items, and Homebase limits boards for cutting at some of its stores – meaning customers have to go elsewhere. Meanwhile other chains are prepared to move stock around (TopShop spends millions doing so); they rate customer satisfaction highly. Next also seems to have cracked the problem. One fashion chain went out of business some years ago through failing to research its customers – jackets with sleeves were stocked in the North of the UK and sleeveless jackets were sent South. Customers in each case preferred the opposite and a fortune, more than their profit, was spent correcting the error.

Technology's effect on shoppers

In the United States and Britain, around 50 per cent of the population own smartphones. In Britain the growth trend is also for mobile TV interaction and social interaction. The shopper is using web pages, on mobile, tablet and PC, both as a showroom and for actual purchase. The shopper seeks engagement with the brand, supplier and retailer. Personal recommendations, commentary and participation offer a great signal to those in one's sphere of influence: if delighted, shoppers are given the opportunity to share their passions. Shoppers are accustomed to moving from one technology to another – they expect the brand or retailer to do the same.

Games are another way to support brand advertising – principally through in-app purchases or free-to-play ('freemiums'). Cross-channel campaigns should exploit the differences between mobile and tablet, making the message a holistic experience, ie one message complements the other. Strategies that could be used include augmented reality, for example where a shopper clicks on a view and computer-generated pop-ups add information or descriptions to the scene; geo-location, where the mobile or tablet using GPS produces messages related to the shopper's location (usually near the retail store or a brand outlet); or a second screen when something seen on TV can be accessed by the shopper on mobile or tablet or through an app (even downloading the app while watching the ad on TV). 'Attract', 'engage' and 'delight' will be the marketers' watchwords. Make sure that any platforms you use work successfully in all of the regions and countries from which you draw your customers.

Measuring the effectiveness of all the above is a challenge and is covered in Part Three. Real-time intelligence where the brand and retailer pick up shopper reaction almost as it happens is needed to turn the quantities of data into relevant, actionable insight, transforming the end-user experience positively into purchases. The Kellogg's delivery overnight of on-pack gold medal winner naming, is an example of near real-time action. (Yes, Kellogg's had the packs printed with winners' names, filled and delivered overnight to the shops!)

How shoppers shop

What catches their eye? What messages persuade? How do shoppers gather and use information? The fact is that most decisions in-store are not purely rational: you have to accept there is a degree of randomness about the way a person shops. The shopping experience is basically a creative process. It is complicated by the 20 per cent of shoppers who are also un-persuaded and not concerned about price.

At the point of sale there is an involvement in purchase, dialogue, developing the customer relationship and 'nudging' the customer to purchase. MARI research (POPAI's Marketing at Retail Initiative) has discovered that what actually can and does make the difference to the purchase decision is the use of key words ('Free', 'New' or a £1 flash) or a promotion. Research indicates that 70 per cent of brand purchase decisions are made in store/on the web page. A number of models describe how people buy, one of which is the involvement model. The involvement model for buying is increasingly seen as a realistic description of the way in which consumers buy products and services. This ties in with the need for six messages that build the 'mind file' while instilling involvement. The model extends well beyond marketing: for example, religious bodies used to think that people started belonging to a church because they believed, often after a conversion experience. However, it is now understood that people belong before they believe. Studies in the United States have shown that people become involved in a church because of friends or family. It is often quite casual at first: only after a period of years do they come to realize that they believe. The process of 'belonging before believing' is about 'behaviour before attitude'. The involvement model suggests that if you involve shoppers in your product or service sufficiently they will believe in it and buy. The Ehrenburg model (Awareness-Trial-Reinforcement, or ATR) is based on the same 'early experience convinces' approach in the commercial world. This suggests that marketing campaigns that directly impact on the behaviour of customers succeed and the desired attitude to the product or service will follow. A creative promotion can do this; following the London 2012 Olympics, the distinctive symbols of success used by Mo Farah and Usain Bolt have been adopted by some brands. Advertising campaigns aimed primarily at creating awareness and attempting to change attitudes are less likely to succeed.

A promotion, offering a sample, or the deployment of experiential marketing can assist in a change in behaviour. Persuading someone to 'try' offers the chance to experience a product and the brand values that come with it. Once you have seen that the product or service matches or could match your preferred behaviour then, if the process continues, it is only a matter of time before the attitude follows the behaviour and the shopper buys the product or purchases the service. It follows that one should make use of this insight that behaviour precedes attitude; for example, the importance of bounce-backs in mobile marketing, which stimulates further involvement. A bounce-back is a second promotional offer when a shopper accepts a first promotional offer or responds to a requested action. It is a kind of thank you. Encouraging someone to try a product or service is often the best way to begin the process by which they become a long-term customer. Never give just one sample – always more – so that they can try one on the spot and the second when they will have more time to absorb the engram and get another opinion. Giving away more also looks generous and that is a plus to build into the 'mind file'.

Behaviour and attitude have a complicated relationship with each other. Surveys show that far more people think that regular exercise is a good thing (attitude) than actually practise it (behaviour). Surveys also show that people drink more alcohol (behaviour) than they are prepared to admit (attitude). For years, the government urged people to use seat belts (attitude), with only limited effect. It then passed a law making it illegal not to wear seat belts (behaviour). People grumbled at first, but buckled up. Over time, people's attitude changed to accord with the behaviour they had become accustomed to. This suggests that marketing campaigns that directly impact on the behaviour of customers succeed, and the desired attitude to the product or service will follow. A creative sales promotion can do this. Advertising campaigns aimed primarily at creating awareness and changing attitudes through adverts are less likely to succeed.

Loyalty, attitude and behaviour

Loyalty is supposed to be based on attitude; it is not necessarily a predictor of behaviour. Compromises do occur: behaviour beats attitude and loyalty when a customer is lured into buying a competitor product on price drop. Loyalty is also undermined by bulk-buy discounts, though the Office of Fair Trading intervention in November 2012 requiring the price of bulk purchases to be a genuine discount on the list price, suggests that customers are not all as streetwise as they are supposed to be. *The Grocer* has pointed out that in Asda supermarkets 44 per cent of all goods are now sold on promotion with 60 per cent of health and beauty products on a price promotion at any one time. There is a need to constantly promote products to maintain customer loyalty (and of course re-invigorate the engram). Errors in measuring loyalty can occur – DunnHumby tracking volume purchasing for Tesco recorded a particular product as 'low loyalty' and it was de-listed, whilst Morrisons' customers loved the same product. Brands are designed and built to secure loyalty and encourage purchase, generally at a higher or even premium price. Ehrenburg demonstrated that loyalty can be mapped as a statistical effect, resulting from the higher penetration that brands achieve with their higher marketing spend.

The strong trend to discounting is developing two types of consumer: the ones that are not driven by price alongside brand, and those that are. This suggests three different measures of loyalty: customers who are loyal under all normal circumstances, those who are loyal under discount (in particular when a shopper can 'larder fill') and those with no brand preference. IPM research with *Retail Bulletin* indicates a broad trend that loyalty cards have moved the two major users in the UK (Tesco and Boots; for the latter, 68 per cent of sales are from 70,000 Advantage card holders) above their expected market position. Loyalty cards also provide valuable data on shoppers.

Coupons or vouchers have the greatest effect (55 per cent buy a product they would not have otherwise), followed by in-store tasting, then a money-saving discount. Samples in any form work well, whether given away in store with other products or through door drops – even cover-mounted on magazines. Moneysupermarket.com estimated some 2.4 million vouchers are redeemed every day, representing £30 billion in a year. The positive impact of a coupon on customer buying behaviour even works when the value of the coupon is small – research indicating that there is no difference in response between a 15p off or a 75p off coupon or voucher.

The effective use of data

In 2013 Bronto surveyed retailers under three categories: store focused (only 20 per cent revenue from online), online focused (>50 per cent) and e-mail driven (40 per cent of business) and found that retailers took differing actions pre-purchase, in purchase and after purchase.

A retailer's pre-purchase communications are based on activities that signal that a consumer is shopping, but has not necessarily made a selection or is ready to purchase. This is a critical part of the purchase process because, when done well, retailers have the maximum opportunity to influence consumer shopping behaviour. The 53 per cent of retailers who collect product-level browsing data, however, are already way ahead of their competitors: they collect a large number of data points. Of those who collect product-level data (product category and specific product, price, product details, ratings or reviews, quantity, image, URL), more than 80 per cent of respondents leverage product category and SKU (stock keeping unit) information when using browsing data to target e-mail communications. What is interesting is how few retailers are leveraging product images: only 59 per cent. This is a great missed opportunity, as market research has continually shown that images have far greater suggestive impact on consumers than text.

In-purchase activities move shopping behaviour from browsing to the transaction itself. For retailers looking to build repeat business, an important point of continuity is using the transaction as a bridge to drive the next sale. Of those retailers who send transactional messages, most only send order and shipping confirmations. Fewer than one in four retailers are taking advantage of the revenue-driving potential and customer service engagement opportunities of a multi-e-mail post-purchase series. Even though 75 per cent of respondents automate data exchange between their e-commerce platform and their e-mail service provider, 34 per cent of respondents are not able to use that information to market to shoppers in the purchase cycle. For those who can leverage the data, they are nearly evenly split between the ability to use only e-mail-related purchase data (32 per cent) and data attributed to both e-mail and non-e-mail-related purchases (34 per cent). While possessing the data is a first step, using it can be a challenge. Of those who collect purchase-related data, nearly half (42 per cent) have not actually used the data in e-mail communications.

Once the purchase is completed, retailers should begin enticing that consumer to make his or her next purchase and become a loyal customer. What we see instead is that while retailers are interested in continuing the dialogue with a hopefully happy customer, those communications tend to not be very imaginative, focusing primarily on inactive purchasers (rather than recent purchasers) and doing basic segmentation of past purchasers. Only 24 per cent will customize campaigns to active purchasers beyond their transactional communications on order and/or shipping confirmations. The percentage is slightly higher, 31 per cent, among online-focused retailers, showing again that retailers who conduct the majority of their business online are more willing to experiment with communications that go beyond 'standard operating procedure'. It would seem that the scope for retailers to make shed-loads more sales is enormous.

The customer trigger, purchase stages and category interest

Triggers that kick start the shopper along the route to purchase can be almost anything – a comment by someone, reading a newspaper or magazine article, seeing something on TV or at the cinema or hearing something on the radio. A trigger may be one of the key words described earlier ('New', 'Free', a £1 flash) or time/date-related: a launch date for iPads or when tickets for a major event go on sale may be the start point. A particular interest of the shopper in a category – clothing, technology, music – may mean some shoppers are easier to trigger and start on the journey to purchase. Furthermore, since they have been along the path before, they travel the route faster, particularly if the brand, supplier or retailer communicates appropriate messages along the way. Once on the route to purchase, there are four generally acknowledged stages:

1 Taking in (absorbing) information, this is often subliminal.
2 Researching the proposed purchase by comparing alternatives (planning).
3 Setting out and completing the buying mission (obtaining).

4 Assessing the merits and value of the purchase (sharing: passing information to other shoppers).

Encounters with advertising

Brands used to rely on killer messages in their advertising (such as 'last day of sale' or 'final reduction'). Shoppers are generally immune to messages that are unrelated to a category in which they are interested. Brands have tried to use killer messages with social media, but the shopper no longer swallows the bait there either. Just 6 per cent of a brand's fans engage through Facebook via likes, comments and polls. The Facebook Edgerank algorithm decides which news feed items to put in front of a subscribing shopper. The algorithm considers the affinity (relevance to the shopper), weight (pictures and video carry more weight) and time decay of the news item. This means only a few will see a news feed. Until brands understand that social media are a network of influencers rather than a target, such advertising will be ineffective; the brand needs to embrace the empowered shopper, encouraging the influencers to comment favourably on the brand. For the shopper, advertising has to be useful, building positive relevant experiences. In the future, those who are marketing brands need to engage, respecting the shopper while allowing him or her to participate in the brand experience. The key concept here is experience – something such as the opportunity to compete in an online game or contribute to a sport, activity or hobby. The impact of this activity depends on the stage the customer is at on the journey to purchase, the particular media and how the customer is connected to it (the device they are using and its functionality), which is a key element of a customer's profile nowadays.

The role of influencers

It's not just advertising: customers are influenced by others when making purchases, and this influence must be understood. Viral marketing depends on this. You need to know how those around the customers, the people they follow and their perceived status, can influence their attitude and their buying behaviour. Social media, celebrities, a panel of experts, consumer programmes on the TV, are all influencers to different customers.

BRIEF 2.1 Future of retail is in 'bricks and clicks', says John Lewis

'Contrary to some headlines, we don't think that online shopping is replacing the high street, our shoppers tell us they still enjoy shopping as a leisure activity. John Lewis continues to draw customers with shop sales up.'

BRIEF 2.2   What will stores of the future be like?

Thomson's new-look shop in Bluewater features a video wall shop window, an 84 inch touch screen interactive map, and high-definition screens and projections throughout the store offer changing images and videos, with content that includes live weather information, reviews and destination videos.

BRIEF 2.3   The super shopper

Eighteen per cent of people who shop frequently compare prices by browsing online and account for 70 per cent of total UK retail sales (equivalent to over £200 billion in 2013) according to a study by eBay and Deloitte. Retailers need to target these people to boost their sales in all channels, the marketplace reveals.

B2B buyers are shoppers too

Oracle (September 2012) reports B2B customers now expect their provider to be accessible online with a user-friendly, B2C-like experience, for example accepting text messages as purchase orders.

Screwfix takes orders from builders directly and deliver to site. This is copying the just-in-time work practices of manufacturing, a proven cost-saving measure for the builder which enhances the direct sales for Screwfix.

Forrester Research reports that 'many B2B companies project that e-commerce will soon comprise 50 per cent of total sales', so B2B should follow B2C practice. With more competition and tighter budgets than ever before, a business needs to:

1 Identify your ideal customer – produce a profile.
2 Define a sales-qualified lead and the marketing processes to nurture it.
3 Develop the most appropriate messaging and execute a highly targeted multi-channel marketing strategy.
4 Create engaging content to attract and nurture.
5 Connect with prospects where they spend their precious time.
6 Utilize tele-nurturing and telemarketing for lead follow-up and qualification.
7 Pass the lead to sales.
8 Close the loop, measure, refine and report to the senior management team.

(Source: ReallyB2B, **http://cdn2.hubspot.net/hub/196544/file-222720429-pdf/docs/ B2B_Sales_and_Marketing_ebook_final.pdf**)

BRIEF 2.4   Build a business community

Social media marketing is the activity of the moment – if it's done right it can deliver enduring benefits for your business, which translates into better, more sustainable returns for your shareholders:

- Engagement. Interacting with your community members turns them into advocates.

- Loyalty. Customers appreciate the opportunity to provide their ideas and suggestions.

- ROI. A community with a defined strategy and clear goals can help your business reduce costs and increase sales opportunities, through FAQs, how-to videos, technical publications and by listening and responding to members' conversations.

CASE STUDY 2.1   Listerine's whiter-than-white mailing to dentists

The importance of researching the customer is illustrated here:

Pfizer Consumer Healthcare (Agency RMG Connect) sent out a Listerine mailing directed at the highly sceptical dental profession that is regularly bombarded with 'fact heavy' literature. Listerine prevents tartar build-up and helps keep teeth white. The visually striking letter spelling out these benefits was pure white and appeared to have no copy. Under a bright dentist's light it could be seen that the letter was printed in an embossed font. The letter had a fold-down reply-paid card enabling dentists to request samples and try the product for themselves. They would also be sent the offer of a subscription to a free trade magazine from which they could apply for further samples.

The mailing achieved a 14 per cent response rate against a target of 8 per cent. As many as 3,487 dentists ordered samples and subscribed to the quarterly magazine, exceeding the target by 172 per cent. This success was attributed to the intriguing nature of the mailing piece, which won over a tough audience.

CASE STUDY 2.2   Unilever Pot Noodle spinning fork

The Unilever promotion demonstrated a deep understanding of its target audience – the bloke's snacking audience. The objective was to drive sales growth and it achieved year-on-year value growth over the promotional period of 11 per cent with a sales uplift of 20 per cent. The focus was on the funny side of man's relationship with food and the need for a quick and easy taste hit. The promotion offered an on-pack instant win of a spinning fork together with a self-liquidating promotion for non-winners.

CASE STUDY 2.3   Mazda's Operation Renesis – Can you handle it?

Mazda's insight into its target audience of professional 30–45-year-old males was paramount in the success of its Operation Renesis campaign. Potential customers were challenged to participate in a unique experiential event in which they would be trained to drive like a special agent. Applicants completed an online profiling questionnaire to establish their suitability. Taking cues from 'Spooks' and 'The Bourne Supremacy', the three interactive driving zones included J-turns, avoidance driving and a proving ground complete with explosions and fog screens. The six most talented trainees won a training mission to Moscow.

The campaign delivered exceptional results, massively increasing the perception and awareness of the brand. It also generated significant PR through owners' clubs websites, YouTube and 'Top Gear' as well as creating an innovative property that can be leveraged in the future.

CASE STUDY 2.4   Metropolitan Police target gun crime

Gun crime is a major issue in London's black communities, with both offenders and victims becoming younger. In 2006, the Metropolitan Police, through Trident, a gun crime initiative, commissioned Roll Deep, a top Grime act, to produce an anti-gun music track, 'Badman'. It was distributed without Trident branding to selected club DJs and music shops, as well as being e-mailed to Roll Deep fans. Six weeks later the Trident involvement was revealed with the release of a branded video on its microsite, YouTube and RWD.com. It was also aired on

Kiss TV and MTV (without payment). Further support came from a hard-hitting poster campaign and visits to London schools by Roll Deep.

Specific results are confidential, but the exposure and reach outperformed all expectations. This proved that the young, streetwise black audience is not unreachable given the right approach.

Summary

Place the customer at the centre of your business. Start with the customer as shopper, identify your customer through insight, and think from the customer's viewpoint. Make sure your offer matches the customer need then build your preferred brand-gram in their minds, using the six message media to achieve excess share of voice and assist the tipping point with a promotion at the point of sale to persuade and get the shopper to buy.

Call it 'bonding with a brand', ie the customer has your brandgram in mind which is entirely positive and exceeds any loyalty. It is a CEO deliverable – to have a brand that is wholly loved. It gives a value far in excess of the bricks-and-mortar worth of a company. The Worshipful Company of Marketors showed in a booklet how, by discovering bonding with a brand as a measurement, it can be used to predict future share value (see **www.marketors.org**).

The most difficult element of a brand for any firm to manage is the 'psychological' part, that is, achieving and retaining ownership of a piece of the customer's mind. Companies often talk about 'creating an image'. They may do so in the minds of the staff who work long and hard to devise it. They only do so in customers' minds when customers adapt, develop and absorb that image as their own, built as a 'mind file' on the engram. Companies can offer an image, but they cannot make an image stick. If it is attractive and powerful and accords with customers' own experiences, it will form part of their image of the product or service. Thoughts and images in our own minds are, thankfully, beyond anyone else's total control.

Customers retain brandgrams; seeing an engram triggers a brand if the retention has been successful. The engram is a 'shorthand' memory device, a mix of logo, slogan or a feeling that the customer relates to 'advantage' with regard to a need. If you have such recall in a customer, you are made. But beware: if the concept you are selling does not match the perception, image and experience of the customer: you are far less likely to make a sale. You also need to nurture that retention constantly and favourably reinforce it. Reducing brand support marketing in a recession is fraught with long-term risk. Guard against operational measures that destroy the brand's value (think of banks, and horse meat!)

It is quite possible to have different perceptions of your brand in different parts of the globe or even in different parts of one country. Guinness for a time advertised in Africa unwittingly using a symbol that implied that Guinness improved fertility. Brylcreem was thought to be a food delicacy in an African country. A failure of branding, you might think – unless of course you are happy to sell with that branding mismatch.

It is also quite possible to reposition a brand. Sometimes this is essential to save a brand that has become dusty and is failing. Failures are often the seed corn of success if the lesson is understood. Lucozade was rebranded as a sports drink from its previous life as an expensive drink for when you were ill. It used to be said by the older generation that you knew you were really ill when the Lucozade appeared. How different it is now.

Self-study questions

2.1 To ensure you have understood, write a short sentence on each of the Six Cs – the offer – describing what needs of the customer each C covers. Then, as an exercise, write down the Six Cs of your own business or organization's offer. From that prepare a brand values statement (a brandgram): what you would want your customers to hold in their minds.

2.2 Describe the difference between attitude and behaviour. Which is more important to the marketer in the long term and which in the short term?

2.3 Why is understanding the customer first so important in business?

(Remember, the answers are in the text.)

PART TWO

What you can do to promote your brand, your products and your business

Why creativity is key

03

This chapter covers creativity – an essential ingredient to any promotion because, if it is to be noted by the shopper, your promotion must be different, fun, exciting, etc. Promotions die if they are not creative. What makes an ordinary promotion outstanding? How do you go about the process of translating promotional objectives into an idea that will achieve behavioural change? You have to be creative. Catch the imagination. This is the art of creativity.

Types of creativity

Creativity is a much misunderstood word. For some people, it is the opposite of order and structure. It is thought of as the free expression of feeling, of your deepest self. Some talk about creativity as if it were only found in the visual or dramatic arts, such as painting or dance. They have difficulty thinking of the creativity of the engineer or physicist, let alone of the business person. In business, 'creativity' can be understood to mean bending the rules; for example, the 'creative accountant' is a dodgy accountant, not an imaginative and effective one.

Advertising people have added to this confusion. 'Creatives' in many agencies are distinguished from the business people, the 'suits'. The background of creatives is normally in visual design, and their hearts may still be there. Awards for creativity given by the Design and Art Direction Association often put a premium on the clever, off-the-wall and fashionable. The Institute of Practitioners in Advertising (IPA) runs advertising effectiveness awards, which reward campaigns that achieve the greatest results for sales and profits. Some – but far from all – also win 'creative' awards.

In promotions, creativity does not mean free expression, exciting pictures, clever copy or off-the-wall concepts. It certainly does not mean dodgy practices. It means generating the most effective concept possible. In this, it goes back to the original meaning of creation or creativity. Chaucer writes, in *The Canterbury Tales*, of 'All things as God created, all things in right order.' Bringing into being the wonders of the world out of nothing was what Chaucer had in mind. On a smaller scale, generating something new where nothing was before is at the heart of creativity. It applies as much to the engineer as to the musician. Order, structure and fitness for purpose are not enemies of creativity, but part of it.

All promotions, sales promotions and indeed advertising and PR communicate with one person at a time, usually the reader of a leaflet, poster, mailshot or press or TV advertisement. But they are not atomized individuals: they are people who build their understanding by means of their interactions with friends, colleagues, families and communities. The more specifically you can define your target audience in both individual and group terms, the more precise will be your creative approach and the more effective your promotion.

If you are going to be responsible for creating a truly effective promotion, you must be really clear about what it is you need to achieve and be capable of imaginative, lateral thinking. If others are to create the promotion for you, then this chapter will help you provide them with the best brief possible.

It is a sad fact of life that, as people grow up, fewer and fewer show signs of creative ability. Research has shown that 95 per cent of children show strong creative tendencies, while only 5 per cent of adults show the same traits. We simply become less good at inventing and developing new and original ideas. This is partly because creativity is the one life skill that has seldom been taught at school or university and partly because our elders and peers stamp it out of us. Remember when you were caught jumping on the settee and told off for doing so? Your mother just saw you damaging the furniture. You were riding a horse, escaping from the enemy – exercising your creativity.

To create promotions, you do not need to jump up and down on your office chair, however much you might feel like doing so sometimes. You do need to suspend belief and really and truly imagine. Experience shows that latent creative ability can be liberated in most people. There are many exercises and procedures that can help you become more creative, and later in this chapter we will look at some techniques that can be helpful in a business context. They will help you structure your creative planning to enable you to create a truly great promotion rather than an imitation of someone else's idea. First, here a few case studies to stimulate and enlarge on the essence of creativity.

CASE STUDY 3.1   Osram

Truly great ideas stand the test of time. Osram had produced a new light bulb that lasted four times as long as a normal one but cost only twice as much. It was ideal for use in industry where bulbs are often changed all at once, towards the end of their life. Not only would the bulbs be cheaper over a period of time, but there would also be considerable savings in labour costs. However, industry was not buying them. Research indicated that this was because the maintenance department purchased bulbs and were usually instructed by finance departments as to the maximum amount they could pay. Maintenance staff were not allowed to suddenly spend twice as much as normal.

The 'Who do I want to do what?' question led to the answer. Maintenance and financial staff could only agree to buy Osram if they did so together. The solution was to send the chief accountant a cash box and explain that there was information inside the box on how to save more than 50 per cent on bulb replacement. The key was sent to the head of maintenance and this fact was also communicated to the financial officer. To read the information inside the box, both the financial and maintenance representative had to meet, and they were then in a position to have a short discussion.

Was it successful? Yes. A neat, elegant solution far more likely to succeed than a simple brochure mailing or trade press campaign. This promotion deservedly won an ISP Grand Prix award.

CASE STUDY 3.2   Sheraton Securities

Another elegant solution involved, of all unlikely things, a wellington boot. Sheraton Securities wanted to attract commercial property agents to visit its greenfield development site. These agents are inundated with similar requests and are regularly sent brochures and inducements. Sheraton chose to deliver personally one left wellington boot to 50 selected agents. It then advertised in the trade press: 'What possible use is one welly?', stating that the other boot was to be found on its development site. This humorous and off-beat approach succeeded in bringing the agents along.

CASE STUDY 3.3   Ramada

There are established hotels in Manchester and the new Ramada was just not reaching its targets. Of the many ways of promoting hotels, one of the best is to encourage positive recommendations from existing guests. How, though, can you do that? The bizarre solution was to put a plastic duck in each bathroom and tell the guests, by means of a card, that they could keep the duck. Alternatively, if they wished, they could have it sent anywhere in the world in its own special crate for only £2.50 plus postage.

This promotion not only succeeded, but made a profit. The cost of the duck and crate was far less than £2.50, and hundreds were sold to intrigued guests. This promotion won a European sales promotion gold award. It has also been used extensively since. I found a plastic duck in a Saigon hotel in 2009!

CASE STUDY 3.4   Cherry Blossom

How would you go about sampling thousands of consumers with a new shoe-cleaning pad? Cherry Blossom must have considered door-to-door sample drops, banded offers and all the other techniques. The one it used, however, was to link with the Boy Scouts, who at that time cleaned people's shoes outside supermarkets during Bob-a-Job week. Simple, cheap and a winner of several awards.

CASE STUDY 3.5   Shell's 'Make Money'

Many people still remember Shell's 'Make Money' promotion in the 1960s in which customers collected halves of banknotes. They could redeem them for their face value if they collected both matching halves. Obtaining that elusive matching £10,000 banknote half became compulsive, driving out any thought of visiting a competing petrol station. This promotion has been run several times in the United Kingdom and throughout the world. It works, again and again, and it has been copied over and over. It must be a great promotion.

All these promotions have a number of things in common. They are engaging. It is not immediately obvious what they are trying to achieve (the objectives are not showing). They were original when they were first implemented. They are very carefully targeted. The promotions' creators all clearly identified 'who it was that they wanted to do what'.

The Osram promotion clearly identified that the company wanted the accountants and the maintenance people to meet and discuss the benefits of the new bulb. The property developer wanted agents to come to its site. Ramada wanted people to tell their friends and business acquaintances about the new hotel. Cherry Blossom wanted people to try the new product and feel warmly about the company. Shell wanted people to come back to its petrol stations rather than visit those of its competitors. It is this clarity of the promotional objective and definition of the target audience that they all have in common. Once that is in place, humour, excitement, style, graphics and copy can be introduced in an appropriate way to enhance the overall offering to the customer.

What has clarity of promotional objectives got to do with creativity? Essentially, it is the key to success! Briefs often state that the objective is to increase sales by X or to increase distribution by Y. These are marketing objectives, not promotional objectives. A promotional objective is the answer to 'Who do I want to do what?' Remember that promotions are about changing behaviour. Setting the right objectives is often truly creative.

Thinking creatively

Very often a marketing objective will turn into a number of different promotional objectives as you ask the question: 'Who do I want to do what?' This is not a problem unless you try to achieve them all by the same promotion. Note that we are talking here about a promotion and not a promotional theme. You may decide on a theme that has several different promotions targeted at different audiences. Different people in the distribution chain will be motivated in different ways: the wholesaler, the retailer and the consumer all need to be attended to. Also, the same theme can be worked through different promotions over a period of time.

Let's take a typical brief, one that is often proposed by brand managers of lager beer: 'We want to generate sales of X cans during Y period. Our target market is C1/C2 men and women between the ages of 18 and 25.' Have you ever met a C1/C2, or indeed anyone aged 18 to 25? The group contains postgraduate students, marketing managers, soldiers, lathe operators, nurses, car mechanics, musicians performing classical and heavy metal music, teachers, truck drivers, jockeys, farm workers, photographic models and so on. How can you possibly attract all members of such a diverse group? The only thing they have in common is that they visit pubs and off-licences and like to drink lager. Think of them as a sociological category and you will end up with a bland promotion. Although not a bad promotion by any means, you will focus on the single thing they have in common and give away lager as an incentive – 10 per cent extra free, and buy five get one free, are standard promotions in this market. But is that the best that you can do?

Before you go any further, have you spotted the flaw in the description given? An assumption was made and this is always a mistake. 'Who' was assumed as existing lager drinkers. Perhaps the promotion could target wine drinkers. Never assume anything. In the case of Ramada, the normal action would have been to advertise to people who book hotels. The problem in that case is that these people are all over the world and do not see the same media. It would have been an impossibly expensive strategy.

The first task is to answer the 'who' part of the question. In our lager example we can list:

- existing drinkers of the brand;
- lager drinkers who buy other brands;
- ale drinkers;
- wine drinkers;
- people who vary what they drink;
- home drinkers;
- pub drinkers.

However, this only describes them in relation to their drinking; they have many other characteristics. They may be further categorized as:

- amateur pop singers;
- fashion followers;
- tennis players;
- golfers;
- classical music devotees; and so on.

Once we have decided the 'who', we must define 'what we want them to do'. The list could be:

- existing drinkers of the brand: suggest it to friends;
- lager drinkers who buy other brands: switch brands;
- ale drinkers: switch to lager, our brand;
- wine drinkers: try lager when it's hot weather;
- people who vary what they drink: be consistent, drink our brand;
- home drinkers: go to the pub;
- pub drinkers: take some home.

It is possible that some groups will have exactly or nearly the same 'what' as others, so it may be possible to use the same promotion. For example, the same approach may well work with ale drinkers and drinkers of other brands. Already we can see the opportunity for creatively engaging these different sorts of people in different ways. Now we have the 'who' and the 'what', it's time for the real creativity.

Let's study the second list of amateur pop singers, fashion followers, tennis players and the like. Remember that any one of the people in these categories may also be in one of the other categories, and the lists are by no means exhaustive. We have, therefore, the grounds for 35 possible promotional objectives. Let us take just one example: tennis players who vary their drinks. We can now start to build a picture of real people and work out how to motivate them. We know they are under 25. We know they drink a variety of things. We know they play tennis and are likely to visit the club bar. The answer to the question, 'Who do we want to do what?' is therefore: 'We want tennis players who are not consistent in their choice of drinks to try our lager once a week in their club after their game.'

Now we can begin to devise a worthwhile promotion for these people. We can imagine them as flesh and blood, coming in from the game, looking for a drink. We can imagine the place and the time of day. We can picture their friends and the things they will be talking about. It is far more real, far more focused, than trying to attract that sociological category, the C1/C2 person aged between 18 and 25.

A number of ideas immediately present themselves for encouraging tennis players who are not consistent in their choice of drinks to take a lager once a week after their game. A chance to play tennis with a celebrity? A discount on tennis kit? The chance to collect something for the club? However, tennis players are just one of our groups. A similar process will lead to similar thoughts about the classical music devotee who never drinks at home and the amateur pop singer who normally drinks beer.

Having categorized the consumers, it is worth looking at the intermediaries – at the publicans, managers of off-licences and supermarkets, cash-and-carry buyers and the rest. Like the consumers, they are immensely varied.

Let's assume that the tennis club idea proved a basis for a promotion themed on sport and leisure and designed to offer a range of celebrity sports opportunities. Now go back to our tennis club and develop the trade dimension of the promotion. Consider the bar steward. He will now become the 'who'. The 'what' might be: 'To suggest a cooling lager is best after a game.' It being a club, there may also be another 'who', the committee, which might have to give permission to allow the promotion to run. Should the club be given the opportunity to host the celebrity events or another incentive?

If you follow this method of identifying 'who' and 'what', you will quickly devise hundreds of different promotional objectives. This is delightful but you are unlikely to have the time to work them all up into full promotions – and you could not afford to run them all anyway. You need only work through those promotional objectives that are most likely to achieve the marketing objective. To do this requires careful assessment of the extent to which your promotional objectives will grip the underlying marketing objective.

There are a number of questions to ask about each of your promotional objectives and the initial promotional ideas that go with them:

- Is the particular audience a reasonable proportion of the total or can the idea at least be attractive to a wider group of people?
- Is it likely to be achievable within the budgetary, legal, timing and other constraints that you face?
- Does it lend itself to simple, clear expression to the trade and to consumers?

In this case, we may conclude that these tennis players form too small a group to be significant, but that there is an opportunity if we add them to a range of other active club sports.

The process of devising a promotion is far from over when you have a flipchart or whiteboard covered with possible promotions. However, to try to be creative without attempting to answer the 'who' and 'what' will usually result in promotions that are less effective than they could be.

In the case of the Ramada promotion, long before ducks or anything else was considered, it was realized that, mainly owing to budget limitations, the 'who' would be the guests and the 'what' would be telling their contacts about the hotel. It was as simple as that. The statement of the promotional objective in that case and in many others is creative in itself. In this case, the creative process then had to find a way of getting guests to talk about the hotel. Business hotels are not something one normally talks about (other than in negative terms) as they are fundamentally similar across the globe. A true creative leap was required. It was realized that one thing all guests do when they are in a business hotel room is to grab some relaxation time, often by taking a bath or a shower. We should catch them while they are relaxed and are likely to be receptive.

Brainstorming (or 'thought showering') is useful. Could we put a waterproof joke book by the bath? A bathroom karaoke kit? Something useful? Humour seemed appropriate and, eventually, along with boats came that deeply loved creature of children's baths, the duck. Brainstorming is not the only technique you can use: to devise good promotions, you need to use a range of creative techniques.

Creative techniques

Here are five creative techniques that are particularly useful in moving from 'Who do I want to do what?' to an effective promotion:

1 *Listing.* As we have already seen, making lists is a very useful technique. It was a straightforward process to list all the different types of young lager drinkers, for example. Lists help you order your thoughts and show up any gaps. They do have one disadvantage, which is that it is often difficult to see the connections between items on a list and particularly on several different lists. One way round this is to use the largest sheet of paper you can find and draw lines to show these connections. For example, you could link rugby players and golfers as people who would be members of a club and therefore involved with bar stewards.

2 *Mind maps.* Another way of showing connections is not to write a list but to draw a 'mind map', which is a formalized way of connecting ideas. Take a sheet of paper and start with one idea. It could be anything related to the subject, for example 'wine drinker'. Then draw a line from it. Along that line write connected ideas, for example 'sophisticated', 'educated' and 'travelled'. From each of these words draw other lines, and write the words that occur to you. For example, from 'travelled' you might write 'airline tickets', 'currency', 'passport' and 'duty-free'. Keep on doing this and the interconnected ideas stay together. Connections also appear that will not at first have struck you. For example, 'duty-free' brings you back to 'wine drinker'. Is there a promotional idea in that? Mind map software programs can help here.

3 *Thought showering (the old brainstorming).* Once you have really defined your chosen, practical promotional objectives, you may then decide to brainstorm. Brainstorming is not meant to be a woolly general discussion: set the objective for the session very clearly and ensure everyone understands it. For the Ramada promotion, it was: 'What can we put in a bathroom, in a business hotel, that will amuse the guests and encourage them to mention how good the hotel is to the person who booked it and to colleagues?' and the related one: 'Is it also possible to provide something that would act as a constant reminder to the guest?' It is useful to spend just a few moments on a warm-up exercise to get people into the right frame of mind. Perhaps you could examine where else the session could have been held that would increase the creativity level. The best hotel in the world? The most beautiful? Then imagine you are there. There are no right or wrong answers in a brainstorming exercise. It is important that people are not allowed to feel foolish or they will cease to contribute. They may have that brilliant idea lurking in their mind just waiting to pop out. Use affirmative expressions such as 'Yes, and...' rather than 'Yes, but...', let alone 'No, because...'.

4 *The village.* A very useful technique is to define all the types of 'who' and, in your imagination, people a village with them. Imagine the houses they would

live in, the places they would meet, the resources they would need, where they would go for fun and where they would shop. Then aim your promotion to appeal to the villagers. Think how they would react to it and how it would come up in their conversation. If it does not appeal to most of the villagers, you probably need to redefine your objectives or run more than one promotion.

5 *Being someone else.* If you feel you are not capable of solving the problem creatively, imagine someone you think could. Imagine a great artist – say, Picasso – or think about the most imaginative person you have met in your life. Then in your mind ask this person what he or she would come up with. A variation of this is mentally to take six people out to dinner and ask them what suggestions they have. Imagine a series of different people, the different perspectives they would have on the question and how they would discuss it among themselves. Why not even imagine one of the 'villagers' and ask him or her?

Practice makes perfect

Thinking about promotions can be turned into a party game, perhaps for use on long car journeys. Think of a product category you know and list all the brands in it. Then assume an objective and a set of mechanics and match the two together. Examine the following list of confectionery brands and promotional offers:

After Eight	Free Levi's jeans to be won
Yorkie	Win a racehorse
Jelly Tots	Free Mother's Day lunch to be won
Dairy Box	Win a holiday in LA
Toffee Crisp	Win a visit to Legoland
Drifter	Win a mountain bike
Lion Bar	Win a day out in a tank

Are they well matched? No. Why not give them a better matching, and then see if you can think of even better promotions to encourage repeat purchase for each of these brands?

Making the most of your idea

Deciding on your mechanic and theme as the answer to the 'Who is it we want to do what?' question is an important step. Now you must make it work well.

There may be some pitfalls you need to identify. In the case of Sheraton Securities' wellies, the different sizes of feet had to be taken into consideration. In the case of the Ramada duck it was recognized that, if it were left in the bathroom with no explanation, it might look as though the room had not been cleaned properly. People who took the duck, something the Ramada wanted them to do as a reminder of the hotel, might feel guilty. If they did so, they would be unlikely to carry the message about the benefits of the Ramada hotel in Manchester.

The problem was solved by printing a small card that introduced the duck and explained that it could be taken home or posted anywhere. The duck was also given a distinctive personality and distinctive packaging. Named 'Reggie', he was supplied with a specially constructed cardboard 'crate'.

It is essential to identify problems and practical difficulties, such as ensuring that a sales representative's car can carry sufficient quantities of your latest creative brainwave. More positively, you also have the ability to polish and extend the creative idea. However, beware of so extending the idea that it becomes impossibly complicated.

Mazda ran a competition that offered the chance to win a holiday. The stages involved required some imagination. Consumers were enticed by teaser ads in a newspaper, and directed to another and bigger ad; there they were asked to identify an island; then they had to go to their local Mazda dealer and identify three other photographs, identify another 'special photograph', complete an entry form and, should they so wish, phone a London telephone number for a clue. The persistent motorist would, however, have noticed that nowhere did a Mazda car appear, and at no stage did the Mazda dealer play a part in the promotion. Creativity? Not of a promotional kind.

The golden rule is to keep it simple and keep it relevant. The duck crate is an example of a simple extension that enhanced the promotion, yet the promotion would still have worked without it. That promotion was later extended further by putting the duck on Christmas cards and providing star staff with duck merit badges.

When you devise a promotion, be aware of what is current. You can often create far more interest about the activity at little extra cost. Linking in with a current fad can work. Golden Wonder crisps once offered embroidered jeans patches showing the Wombles. This was just as the characters became famous and as jeans patches became fashionable. It seemed that everyone was eating crisps all day, judging by the response. Be especially careful if you promote overseas: it is vital to know the traditions and expectations of your foreign consumers.

When you find a promotion that can be extended in many different ways, you know you have a winner. It is always worth polishing and extending an idea until you have bled it dry.

Once you have your promotional concept, there is a lot of work to be done to turn it into an effective operational plan. For this you need suppliers and an effective implementation strategy (see Part Three). In doing so, though, never forget the importance of the original idea: one that can extend and extend, one that is elegant and simple, one that you are really proud of. You will hear a voice in your head asking why no one has done it before. You will begin to fret that there must be something wrong. Don't worry. If you have followed the steps above you will have created a memorable promotion that will succeed. Congratulate yourself.

Innovation as an extension of creativity

'Innovation' literally means doing something new. It can also be inventing a totally new use for an existing product. Lucozade was originally an expensive drink for invalids. It was said that when a Mother bought Lucozade for a child you knew they were really ill. In a Dublin bar the marketing manager found Lucozade was being used as a mixer. Realizing there was no limit to what he could sell Lucozade as, he then had the idea of rebranding Lucozade as an energy drink for athletes – sales took off. Innovation usually occurs from 'thinking out of the box'. Clearly anything innovative must have a potential market.

This chapter has been full of examples of creative promotions. Many are from high-profile consumer fields. The two case studies that follow demonstrate that promotional creativity can be found on fairly sticky wickets – in promoting intellectual property law and in promoting an ageing car.

CASE STUDY 3.6   Eversheds

Intellectual property is a dry, complicated but increasingly important branch of the law. Most companies, not least promotion agencies, need to think very carefully about who owns the ideas, trademarks, designs and copy that their staff and subcontractors create. The trouble is, drawing up the necessary contracts is something that can always be put off until tomorrow.

The leading legal firm Eversheds wanted to promote its 'Intellectual Property Health Check'. An ordinary brochure would not have broken through the apathy. Instead, it sent a simple letter accompanied by a piece of wood with a hole drilled through it, marked with the Eversheds logo. It offered a prize for the best answer to two questions: 'What is it?' and, 'What intellectual property rights apply?'

The engagement of leading businesspeople in the questions was enormous. So too was the response. The object (which turned out to be a wine bottle holder) was genuinely intriguing. The follow-up letter contained winning solutions, an analysis of no fewer than five intellectual property rights that could apply to it and an invitation to arrange a 'Health Check'.

Eversheds deserved to succeed with this promotion. Simple and to the point, it showed that even lawyers could be creative! How exactly did Eversheds answer the 'Who do I want to do what?' question?

CASE STUDY 3.7   Rover Group

Rover was faced with the question of what to do to stimulate sales of the ageing and much-loved Mini (it has happened again since then!). Sales were to long-established customers who were declining in number. Could the Mini appeal to a younger generation who might not know it is even available? Potential customers needed to be made aware that they could still buy one, and that Rover's enormous range of options meant that they could virtually design their own.

The solution was found in an interactive internet site with a monthly competition to design your own Mini with real and fantasy features. Designs were entered on a gallery, where visitors to the site voted for the best design. The winner was rewarded with Mini merchandise, and winning designs were posted on a special page. Everyone won the chance to turn his or her design into a game and download it as a screensaver. Like any good website, it constantly changed. Developments included a walk-round film and a concept car section. These helped it to be one of the top 10 UK sites and to be voted Microsoft's site of the month as well as winning an ISP award. It was voted commercial website of the year in the UK Yell awards and best automotive site by New Media Age.

In its first four months, the site received 3 million hits, 5 per cent of them turning into brochure requests. The promotional mechanic of a design competition proved effective in engaging people with the Mini and with the differential advantage it had over newer cars: the capacity to design your own.

Think about the 'village' of visitors to this website. What other products and services featured on the internet would they like? What promotions could you devise to encourage them to visit your own company's website?

Summary

Creativity is about finding effective solutions. It requires the ability to think laterally and imaginatively, which can be developed with practice. There are several techniques that can be used, including mind maps and brainstorming.

Creative promotions arise out of close attention to the question: 'Who do I want to do what?' Once the process of answering this question is begun, hundreds of possible promotional objectives emerge. A really good idea can be versioned and developed in many ways.

Self-study questions

3.1 What are some of the leading techniques for developing creative ideas?

3.2 How would you go about answering the question, 'Who do I want to do what?' for a day at a theme park (maybe Legoland or Alton Towers)?

Essential support: suppliers

04

All promotions need suppliers, and complicated national promotions require an army of them: promotional and design agencies, premium sourcing specialists, printers, point-of-purchase manufacturers, handling houses and telephone response companies. Many of these will, in turn, have suppliers that are critical to the success of the promotion. This chapter describes them and deals with how to select and use them.

A promotion can present a particular difficulty in this respect if a company is not within the media or marketing industry. A company will normally have a wealth of experience of component suppliers and subcontractors for its core products and services. There will often be long-term supply agreements and careful supplier assessment in accordance with established quality criteria. In promotion, the picture is different: discontinuity is the rule. Promotions are different from one to the other so each promotion often needs different suppliers. One of the reasons there are so many case studies in this book, and not all new ones, is to provide a creative wealth of ideas that can be used as a basis for new promotions. Yet, in all this, the same requirements of quality assessment and value for money apply. For this reason, many firms try, where possible, to build long-term partnerships.

There are two models of supplier relationship: the 'quotation model', which assumes that you know what you want and can obtain the lowest price and best terms from a range of suppliers by setting out your specification as an invitation to quote; and the 'partnership model', which assumes that you will obtain the best solution by working with a chosen supplier from the earliest stage, incorporating the supplier's skills into the specification. This second model is often called 'partnership sourcing'.

Some organizations, particularly in the public sector, have rules that require them to obtain three quotations for every piece of work. Others believe that the constant use of tenders and quotations keeps suppliers on their toes. The risk in promotions is that you never use exactly the same product or service often enough to be able to specify what you want without the help of a supplier. That supplier is most likely to help if you build up a long-term relationship and bring the supplier into the planning of a promotion from the earliest stage.

Promotion agencies

Who they are

Most promotions are conducted by people who are not promotions specialists – marketing managers, sales managers, managers of small businesses and executives in general advertising agencies. In a number of large consumer goods companies, promotions are under the aegis of a (sales) promotion manager, but even then implementation is often the responsibility of non-specialist sales and marketing executives.

Many of the biggest and most high-profile promotions are developed and implemented by specialist promotion agencies. They are often called 'consultancies' because, unlike insurance or advertising agencies, they derive much of their income from fees rather than commission. However, promotion firms also derive a proportion of their income from selling artwork, merchandise, print and other services, which is not normal practice among consultancies. The word 'agency' is used here as the description commonly applied to firms engaged in providing marketing advice, consultancy and implementation.

Visit websites to find agencies. The DMA, IPM and MAA websites contain listings or contacts to obtain lists. The MAA offers a confidential Agency Selector service along with guides on writing a brief, creative critiquing, agency remuneration and the pitch process, all of which have been developed with the client trade body the Incorporated Society of British Advertisers (ISBA). Outside these lists, there is a wide variety of agencies that include the words 'promotion' in their list of services. Some are advertising agencies, which may or may not employ dedicated promotion specialists. Some are purveyors of particular promotional vehicles, such as travel or merchandise, and may be very competent, but they are not necessarily impartial about the types of promotion they recommend. Some are newer agencies, which may be extremely good, but have yet to qualify for MAA membership.

How they work

There are many different ways in which promotion agencies are set up, and this is reflected in their continuing diversity of structure. Some began as spin-offs of (sales) promotion specialists working in advertising agencies, others as the breakaways of advertising agency (sales) promotion departments, others from a base in supplying print, merchandise or incentives, and yet others (and this is increasingly the case) as greenfield start-ups that are meeting the growing demand for specialist promotion services. Nowadays the use of descriptions such as 'shopper marketing', 'brand delivery' is added to the agency title or they use way-out titles such as 'broccoli', 'juice', etc.

Despite the variety in their size and structure, promotion agencies have a number of features in common:

- They charge for creative and conceptual work on a fee basis that reflects their time input. This method of working, which is comparable to that of solicitors and accountants, means that it can be possible to use them simply for creative thinking and to do the organization and implementation of a promotion yourself.

- They are normally equipped to supply design, artwork, premium sourcing and a host of other services that are needed to make promotions happen. Sometimes these services are supplied in-house, sometimes they are supplied by subsidiary or associated companies and sometimes they are subcontracted. Agencies will always make a margin on these services, but their prices benefit from economies of scale and can be highly competitive.

- They work on an ad hoc or continuing basis. It is conventional for advertising and PR agencies to work with clients on a continuing, contractual basis. Promotion agencies like to do this, and increasingly do so, being paid a retainer rather than one-off fees. However, many clients still use them on an ad hoc basis, briefing them for particular promotions as and when required.

- They are increasingly involved in a broad range of marketing services. We discussed earlier the reasons for the growth of promotions. Most of these apply also to the use of an integrated mix of promotion, direct mail, PR and other tools assembled to meet particular needs. The disciplines of promotion agencies provide a good basis for providing these integrated marketing services, and many have taken up the challenge.

- Account handlers are heavily involved in the creative process. There is a tradition in advertising agencies for account handlers – the people who meet the clients – to be largely excluded from the creative process. In promotion agencies this is not the case. The creation of effective promotions is an interdisciplinary, brainstorming affair, simultaneously conceptual and practical, and the person you meet will play a central role in that process.

- They tend to be of moderate size. This reflects partly the relative newness of the industry and partly their low start-up costs. New agencies tend to be tightly run, enthusiastic and entrepreneurial and almost always run by the people who set them up.

- They are able to give impartial advice on the type of promotion that will most meet your particular needs. This is perhaps the greatest benefit of their fee basis of payment. They have no particular axe to grind over whether or not the promotion is a competition, an on-pack or a mail-in or uses travel, clothing or cash. In a world where there are many axes ground, that is a bonus in itself.

Promotion agencies earn their living from a combination of fees for time spent and mark-ups on goods supplied. The balance between the two will vary, but most commonly includes a fee for time spent, normally calculated at £60 to £372 per hour, depending on the seniority of the staff involved, and a mark-up on goods supplied (print, artwork, premiums and so on) of 15 to 20 per cent. These two combine to give an overall margin of 25 to 30 per cent (lower for bigger jobs and higher for smaller ones).

What to look out for

Choosing the right agency is a difficult process. The MAA offers a full intermediary service. Its consultants will search the MAA membership for the right-fit agency, deliver its credentials to you, organize chemistry meetings and if needed manage the entire pitch process, all within best practice guidelines through its Agency Selector service. Both the IPM and the MAA publish annual awards on websites and in brochures, detailing the best promotions of the previous year.

A relationship with a promotion agency normally starts with a pitch. The MAA and the ISBA have devised a set of guidance notes for pitches. They provide a good basis for the often vexed process of competitive pitches, and are obtainable from either the ISBA or the MAA (see Chapter 15 for details). The principles are to treat each other with fairness:

- Prepare the background information properly.
- Don't ask more than three agencies to pitch.
- Write a proper brief (see Chapter 11) and allow time for it to be responded to.
- Decide quickly and objectively.
- Give the losers the chance to learn how they could have done better.

Fees for pitches are a subject of regular dispute. The MAA's Code of Conduct discourages its members from making speculative pitches. The reason is that promotions are devised for a particular brief and so have no salvage value. Some companies pay agencies a briefing fee, sometimes known as a pitch or rejection fee. Nevertheless, if an agency produces acceptable work but the promotion is not run for reasons outside its control (for example, you have changed your own plans), it is only right that it should be paid for its work. It is an open question as to whether or not agencies should be paid briefing fees for competitive pitches. Agreeing to pay them intimates that it is recognized that each concept is tailor-made for each brief and has no salvage value. Equally, it is always possible to find smaller, hungrier agencies that will pitch for nothing.

In practice, most agencies are happy to compete against a reasonable number of others for a real piece of business, and all of them are happy to compete for ongoing business. The distinction is one of common sense. If you repeatedly brief half a dozen agencies for single promotions that may not even materialize, they are unlikely to find it profitable to respond. Conversely, if you brief a limited number for promotions that do materialize – and particularly with a view to establishing a long-term relationship – most agencies will respond professionally and effectively.

There are five key attributes that companies normally look for in their promotion agencies, which form a handy checklist for selection:

1 *Creativity.* The capability to produce promotions that are more imaginative, more effective and more eye-catching than you could do yourself is the fundamental reason for using an agency. Creativity should stand out in an agency's presentation of its work.

2 *Communication skills.* Promotions are produced to meet specific marketing objectives. In the way it presents its work, an agency should be able to demonstrate an understanding of a range of different marketing situations and of the techniques appropriate to communicating effective solutions.

3 *Budget control.* Implementing promotions requires a range of design, artwork, premium handling and other resources. It is not important that these

should all be in-house, but an agency should be able to demonstrate that they are to hand and that it can control them within your budget.

4 *Good service.* A successful promotional relationship requires client and agency to be on the same wavelength. It is important to meet the people you will actually work with, who are not necessarily those who make the new business presentation, and get on well with them. Just ask your team if they get on with the prospect agency; is the chemistry ok? If not, don't use them.

5 *Good track record.* The evidence from awards brochures and from the trade press is critical here, and a call to existing clients can also tell you about qualities of service and budget control that might not be obvious from published work. This is probably the best tip.

Having applied these criteria, you may end up with three agencies you feel you could work with. It is then common practice to put a brief to all three and to make a judgement on the basis of their response.

Once you have run a promotion with a particular agency, you will be able to judge its performance in practice. There are broadly three ways you can work in the longer term:

1 *Occasional supplier.* This is an arm's length approach – the agency is given the minimum information necessary for the job, is always in competition with others and is briefed only when the need arises.

2 *Rota member.* This is a compromise approach, where two or three agencies are put on a rota of agencies used by the client. Rather more information is given and some or all briefs will only be given to one of the agencies on the rota.

3 *Business partner.* Here, a single agency is appointed to work as an extension of the client's marketing department. Marketing plans are discussed jointly from an early stage, and a renewable contract establishes an ongoing partnership.

Agencies understandably dislike the first approach. It makes planning their own business difficult and results in a high percentage of wasted and unprofitable work. Clients that insist on 'occasional supplier' relationships can find that they are presented with off-the-shelf promotions, dusted down and rejigged without too much thought and effort, generally from second-rate agencies.

Clients are understandably wary of the third approach. It involves putting all their eggs in one basket and can lead to complacency and staleness on the part of the agency. Retainer fees, paid on a regular monthly basis, are liked by agencies as they provide a regular income. However, they only make sense when there is a steady, predictable flow of work.

For these reasons the second approach is often where client and agency find themselves in mutual agreement. It gives the client flexibility and it gives the agency a reasonable basis for predicting the amount of business it will get. Variants on this approach include using one core agency most of the time, but trying out others for particular briefs or in particular areas where the core agency may lack specialist expertise.

Is it worth letting between a quarter and a third of your budget go to the sales promotion agency? If the agency is any good, the answer is 'yes', and for three good reasons:

1 Part of the agency's margin will be covered by buying promotion items efficiently and by its ability to produce promotions cost-effectively.

2 Part will be covered by saving your time in devising, planning and executing the promotion.

3 Most important, a good agency will produce a promotion that is measurably more effective.

Handling houses

Who they are

Handling houses originated in the need for premium items to be warehoused, customer applications to be received and processed, and goods to be dispatched. From this basis, handling houses have grown into sophisticated businesses that offer data capture, database building, in-bound and out-bound telephone call centres, bar code scanning, downloading of e-mail sites and a range of customer interface operations.

How they work

Poor handling can destroy consumer confidence in a promotion and the brand behind it, as well as create considerable work for you as you try to limit the damage. Conversely, good handling can create added value in the information collected about participants in promotions, and build consumer confidence through the promptness and accuracy of your response to them. The following checklist identifies the details to be included in briefing a handling house:

- the promotion: incentive offered, instructions to applicant, any restrictions on entry;
- handling requirement: how it should be done, turnaround time;
- duration: start date, close date;
- response forecast: anticipated volume, variation over time;
- promotion media: on-pack, press, TV, direct mail;
- application format: coupons, leaflets, plain paper, telephone;
- point-of-purchase requirements: number, type, tolerances, count procedure;
- payment requirements: amount, coins, cheques, postal orders, credit cards, charge cards, tolerances, need to await cheque clearance;
- bank account: client's, handling house's, responsibility for charges;
- postage and dispatch: first-class, second-class, discounts for bulk mailings, recorded delivery, registered, carrier, cash floats for postage;

- packing: pre-packed, envelope, padded bag, carton;
- goods storage: quantities, period, special security;
- insurance: client's, handling house's;
- application details: captured manually, computerized, fields required, de-duplication, selections, sort criteria;
- reports: type, frequency, period covered, analysis headings;
- consumer relations: incorrect applications, correspondence, complaints, returns, exchanges, refunds;
- audit: retention of applications, record of dispatch dates;
- stock control: reorder levels, returns, final disposal;
- goods inwards: delivery dates, counting in, quality checks, receipts;
- security/confidentiality: expectations, special requirements.

Thinking through what you need under these headings will ensure that both you and your handling house know what is expected. You can also obtain an accurate quotation for the job. Clearly, this will vary depending on the amount of work involved. You should ask what a typical cost might be for receiving and checking three proofs of purchase and dispatching your item, or for setting up an in-bound telephone call number, receiving calls for a brochure, data capturing and posting the brochure.

What to look out for

If you brief your needs early enough, handling houses are an ally. The main decision you face is one of cost and sophistication. If all you need is the receipt of applications and the mailing of items, there are local facilities in most parts of the country that will do the job at low cost. However, this is probably missing an opportunity, in terms of both data capture and customer relations. More sophisticated operations cost more.

Points to look for include the audit trails a handling house offers for goods and cash, the scale of its computer operations, the training it gives to telephone staff, the efficiency and security of its warehousing and the nature and timeliness of its reports. All these mark out the sophisticated from the low-cost operation. Whatever type of handling house you use, make sure you have a good contract.

If you are running promotions regularly, it makes sense to build a long-term relationship with a handling house that becomes an extension of the company for both you and your customers.

Point-of-purchase manufacturers

Who they are

Drawn from a background in shop fitting or design, the leading firms are members of the Point of Purchase Advertising Institute (POPAI), set up in the United States in

1936, in Paris in 1989 and in the United Kingdom in 1992. Point-of-purchase manufacturers enable promoters to attract attention, communicate offers and brand image, and increase impulse sales at the point at which the great majority of purchase decisions are made. The activity used to be referred to as point of sale (POS), but the initials created confusion with electronic point of sale (EPOS). POP is clearer, but watch for the fact that POP is also the acronym for proof of purchase.

How they work

The incorporation of sound, light, movement and promotional offers in a single unit has moved POP well beyond its origin in cardboard dump bins or PVC shelf-barkers. There are wonderfully creative people called 'cardboard engineers' who make incredible designs. Some examples demonstrate the inventiveness and scope of POP:

- Cadbury's Crème Eggs enjoy a short but intense season between January and Easter. Advertising is wasted unless there is adequate display. A dumpbin with some new gimmick is the annual offering.

- Spillers Petfoods developed a 'shelf purrer' to launch its cat food brand Purrfect Selection. The battery-operated device sensed customers within a 12-foot radius and set off a voice message: 'Indulge your loved one with a can of new Spillers Purrfect.'

- A video display directs the audio to a particular spot at ear level, as if a person is standing next to you. This could be outside a shop window with the video inside and audio outside. Customers using a mobile could place an order when the store is closed, with payment collected and the item delivered the next day.

The primary applications of POP are in sectors that sell via retailers. Leisure outlets such as hotels, pubs and sports clubs are also important. However, POP is increasingly used to communicate brands well away from their normal sales outlets. Interactive displays in shopping centres, airports or anywhere else people gather can sell almost anything. Increasingly, the use of smart-card technology and interactive video and text messaging enables promoters to target particular offers to particular people, capture data about them and communicate product benefits and promotional offers wherever people have the time and propensity to respond. As people arrive at an airport in a new country, information on where they can buy their favourite brands can be made available to them instantly (along with the messages from the new mobile service provider and their charges!).

What to look out for

Promotion is about influencing behaviour. Consumer behaviour at the point of purchase is the behaviour that matters most. The enormous point-of-purchase operation to introduce the UK National Lottery was implemented in less than four months, long after other elements of the mix had been put together.

Critical points to look out for in using point of purchase are:

- Think early about POP needs and integrate them into your advertising and promotional planning.
- Use it to gain exposure in non-standard outlets; there are often great opportunities for joint promotions based on a POP unit.
- Make the best use of increasing opportunities for light, sound and movement; there are real benefits to being an innovator in POP.
- Think hard about the operational issues, especially who will distribute, site and install the units and (if high-tech) keep them running.

The leading manufacturers in the field are increasingly able to offer an all-in design-to-upkeep service. For details of them, contact POPAI (see Chapter 15).

Promotional risk management companies

Who they are

When it comes to setting up a promotion, there is an element of financial risk involved which can, if ignored, prove damaging to the promoter and the brand. If a promotion is a runaway success, with more people responding to it than you anticipated and, more important, budgeted for, huge financial costs may be incurred. Promoters therefore need to be aware of the risks and how they can protect themselves and their balance sheets.

Specialist promotional risk management companies, such as PIMS-SCA, exist to provide services that protect balance sheets against the risk of over-redemption. PIMS-SCA recently conducted an evaluation of all its insured promotions over the last 10 years, noting that approximately two in every 12 promotions produces an over-redemption (see Figure 4.1). This analysis also demonstrates why promotional risk management is an essential part of any promotional campaign – would any promoter take a near 10 per cent chance that the promotion will cost far more than expected?

Three main promotional risk management services are provided by PIMS-SCA that help promoters plan promotional expenses, eliminate budget overruns and add or increase high prize values while keeping promotional budgets fixed and secure. The first is insured fixed-fee contract. This is the best way of providing the maximum level of protection for a promotion, from sourcing the incentive, the logistical management of the promotion, and the risk of over-redemption through to the handling and fulfilment of a campaign. The sales promotion market has moved on to increasingly sophisticated promotional campaigns, with the result that promoters and their agencies now have to deal with complex handling and fulfilment scenarios that may include a variety of redemption mechanics.

Trying to handle a promotion with an SMS text and web-based redemption ability, combined with a no-purchase-necessary route plus a promotion hotline and the usual prize fulfilment requirements may be too many 'moving parts' for the average promoter and agency. This is where fixed-fee companies can prove invaluable: all are regularly involved in promotions of this type and can easily take on the most

FIGURE 4.1   Typical promotions over-redemptions

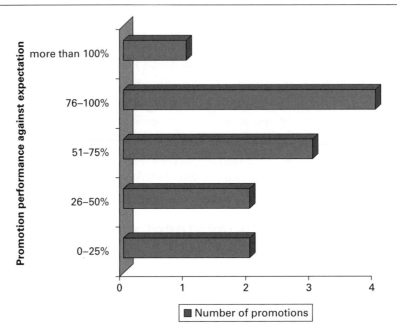

SOURCE: PIMS-SCA

complex promotions with ease. (PIMS-SCA uniquely offers the most financially secure insured fixed-fee product, as each and every promotion is covered by a £10 million insurance policy with 'A'-rated insurers.)

An alternative way of looking at Figure 4.1 is to note that the majority of promotions will not perform to expectation and thus may under-redeem. The majority of promotions perform well in comparison to expectation, but what if it is your promotion that performs particularly badly? As PIMS-SCA demonstrates, one out of every 12 promotions achieves very poor responses against expectations. To remedy this, pioneering the introduction of the under-redemption guarantee to the industry should a promotion significantly underperform, PIMS-SCA will pay back a percentage of the fee on an insured fixed-fee contract. The promoter may be disappointed by the poor response but is not left feeling it has paid way over the odds for the promotion.

The second service is over-redemption insurance. This protects against the financial liability of a promotion redeeming above the expected response rate. This is best utilized when a promoter feels comfortable that the risk is minimal above a certain level and wishes to keep the risk fee as low as possible. For example: a promoter chooses to buy risk protection between 10 and 20 per cent, and is prepared to accept the risk above 20 per cent.

The third is prize coverage. This allows promoters to leverage their existing budget to increase the prize fund available. The risk management company takes on the risk for a one-off fee and, if there is a winner, pays out the prize at no extra cost to the promoter. For example, a £10,000 promotional budget can be turned into an on-pack promotion offering the chance to win £350,000 worth of prizes.

How they work – which coverage is best?

If the promoter is using a tried-and-tested mechanic and is reasonably confident of response levels then probably fixed fee is best. The likelihood is that the response levels will approximate to expectations and thus the promoter will have got good value for money from the fixed-fee company, as most of the fee will have been used to pay for the responses to the promotion.

If the promoter is running an untried mechanic and is targeting a new set of customers, PIMS-SCA would recommend over-redemption insurance. The Great British Public can be a fickle lot and not so easy to predict. Many ideas that look good on a concept board do not find favour with the consumer. The result can be a low take-up; a fixed-fee solution could prove very expensive under these circumstances.

The experience of PIMS-SCA, as a leading industry stalwart, is that less than one in 40 promotions redeem at more than double their expectation; therefore buying a band of coverage is not necessarily such a bad option. Financially, one could argue that it is the most prudent choice for a promoter.

To assist promoters estimating response rates for various mechanics, PIMS-SCA has compiled data on thousands of promotions over the years and created a free-to-use online promotions database. Visit **www.pims-sca.com** to try it.

What to look out for

If another organization is taking on a huge risk for you, be 100 per cent sure that, if required, it is able to pay out in full by checking its accounts. For instance, if it has three £1 million promotions and all require payment, can your chosen company pay out to all?

Ideally, marketers should ensure that an A-rated insurer supports the underwriting of every promotion, for maximum financial protection, guaranteeing payment is possible no matter what. Look at its past experience and the ability to offer actuarial analysis and evaluation and advice on logistical and security procedures, together with proven handling and fulfilment capabilities.

PIMS-SCA produces a 'Guide to promotional risk management' booklet detailing all sales promotion mechanics and the factors to take into consideration plus anticipated response rates; see Chapter 15 for details of how to contact them.

Other insurance products

- Printer's errors and omissions – protects the promoter from the financial consequences that arise if errors are made by a printer when printing promotional game pieces or literature.
- Event cancellation and non-appearance – ensures that if events or promotions are affected by unexpected problems outside of the promoter's control or the star attraction fails to appear, the promoter's financial interests are protected.

Some case studies on insurance are provided later in this chapter.

Specialist printers

Who they are

Many promotions use standard leaflet, brochure and packaging printers. If you are intending to run an instant-win promotion or to use games or scratch cards, you need to enlist the services of a specialist printer. Other printers specialize in the short runs that are sometimes needed for display material or individual-outlet promotions. Others specialize in label leaflets (those that carry a large amount of information in a concertina leaflet the size of a sticker).

How they work

If you are running a game or instant-win promotion, you need to know that the right number of winning cards have been printed, that they are evenly distributed, that there can be no leakage of cards from the printers or distributors, that they cannot be counterfeited and that you can verify the winners. This is a tall order and leads to constant innovation in the technologies involved.

Part of the development is in the inks used. Latex overprints are the standard format for game cards. Developments include heat-sensitive inks that reveal a message on being touched, cold-sensitive inks that respond to a cold drink being put on them, and microwave inks that respond in a microwave. Another development is to replace hidden messages with a crack-open card that reveals another card inside. Special inks can increasingly be used on ceramics, plastics and textiles.

Avoiding counterfeiting has led to the development of computer systems for verifying winning tickets. One process is to mark winning tickets with a security number which, when entered into a database, shows the exact layout of the card. Another is to print winning tickets with codes that only show in ultraviolet light or that can be read only when matched exactly to a template. Holograms and three-dimensional technology are also used; the best techniques, naturally enough, are not disclosed even to promoters.

What to look out for

Make sure you use a printer who really understands this business: winding up, as one retailer did, with 27 winners of its top prize in the first week of a promotion is a cost you cannot afford. Ensure, also, that your printer has errors and omissions insurance that specifically covers games.

Once the material has been printed, look closely at the procedures for packing and distributing winning tickets. If you are including an instant win inside a product (for example, underneath the cap of a bottle), make sure it is safe against tampering, both by retail staff and by consumers. Keep up with evolutions in game technology. Games succeed as much by novelty as by the scale of the prizes being offered. It is well worth using a specialist printer's knowledge to be the first in your field to use a particular ink or game device.

Field marketing and brand experience agencies

Who they are

FM&BE agencies offer a large number of mainly part-time staff as a long-term extension to your own company's staff (outsourcing the sales function, typically at a saving of 15 per cent on in-house provision and with sales targets in effect under contract to be delivered) or to undertake one-off projects. Some 40,000 people are employed part time in the business. A large firm may have as many as 15,000 people on its books (people working in the industry are often on the books of several companies). For further information on field marketing see *The Handbook of Field Marketing* by Alison Williams and Roddy Mullin.

The larger firms are increasingly moving towards full-time staff working on long-term contracts for major promoters. They also overlap with handling houses in offering database, storage and dispatch services as well as staff. You can expect a competent agency not just to provide the personnel, but also to plan geographic coverage, create briefing materials, dispatch and control the items needed in the field, monitor and control the staff, analyse the results and even design and produce special uniforms for them.

Field marketing/experiential agencies can be found at **www.fieldmarketing.com/ agency-directory**. The same principles and selection as given for promotional agencies apply (see above). On the website they are split into field marketing sub-categories. The ones of interest to promotion are: direct sales, sampling, roadshows, experiential events, national and international. The support suppliers, which include venues, stages, stands, roadshow vehicles, signs, screens and interactive media, event management, etc, can be found at: **www.fieldmarketing.com/industry-directory**.

How they work

Field marketing personnel can be employed to do almost anything that needs people out in the marketplace. They can act as a sales force to smaller outlets, install promotional material (this is usually done poorly by many retailers), distribute leaflets and coupons, hand out samples, collect consumer data, undertake mystery shopper calls, staff exhibition stands, sell directly to consumers, provide information in shopping centres and airports, and carry out blind product tests. Their application in promotional campaigns is huge.

Prices vary depending on the nature of the work to be done, but are commonly based on a personnel cost of £13.50 per hour. A typical brief may be to call on independent retailers with promotional material and stock. Taking planning, travel, briefing and supervision into account, you could expect to pay £25 per outlet visited for a contract call service. A tactical call would be less.

What to look out for

The critical point to remember is that field staff are part of your firm as far as the people they meet are concerned. There is a balance to be struck between the cost a firm charges and the level of briefing, training and supervision that your own staff receive. Increasingly, the emphasis is on higher quality, and rightly so. Effective use of field marketing agencies depends, as with every other promotional supplier, on clear briefing and understanding of what you want to achieve. The motivation to sell is probably higher outsourced (to meet the contract targets) than with in-house staff, however incentivized.

Premium sourcing houses

Who they are

Open any promotional magazine and you are confronted by page after page of advertisements for clocks, sweatshirts, electronics, model cars, crockery, books, pens – you name it, it's there. The British Premium Merchandise Association (BPMA) acts as the trade association for manufacturers of premiums, and its magazine is an effective advertising feature for its members' products. For any given product area, there are also endless sources of manufacturer information in trade directories and, increasingly, on the internet.

Why not go direct to these companies to buy the premiums you need? For small quantities and for standard items, it often makes sense. These businesses are not large: few have a turnover of more than £10 million. However, for large quantities, special products and products made in the Far East, it can make most sense to go to a company that is set up to design, source and ship promotional premiums to your specific requirements. These are the premium sourcing houses. They typically have extensive contacts in the Far East, a direct or indirect base in Hong Kong, design facilities in the United Kingdom, processes for quality checking in the country of origin and other developed countries, and extensive knowledge of international customs regulations, product safety legislation, shipping arrangements and trade finance.

The Sourcing Team (**www.sourcing.co.uk**) works hand-in-hand with the BPMA and offers some really useful guidance on ethics and sustainability – nothing worse than discovering your premium merchandise has been manufactured in a non-sustainable way using child labour. Three useful websites on this are:

ETI Base Code, **www.ethicaltrade.org/eti-base-code**

SEDEX, **www.sedexglobal.com** (empowering responsible supply chains)

UN Global Compact, **www.unglobalcompact.org**

How they work

Premium sourcing houses ensure that promotional items are created, manufactured and delivered to the specific needs of a promotional campaign. Examples from the past show the nature of their work:

- Nestlé has a continuing requirement for products that give 'playground cred' to Smarties among 7–9-year-olds. The right premium ensures that Smarties remain an attractive product for this age group and not just something that your kid sister eats. Developments in low-cost consumer electronics meant that it became possible to create the Zapper. This is a Smartie-shaped widget with eight coloured buttons that emit noises of sirens, machine guns and the like, and is cheap enough to offer with five proofs of purchase. The electronics were manufactured in one country, the plastic casing in another. It has been supplied to Nestlé subsidiaries throughout the world.

- Mugs are a promotional evergreen, used by coffee, tea and confectionery manufacturers, among others. Traditionally they have been sourced in the United Kingdom, but UK prices are not competitive in world terms. There are numbers of low-cost producers, but their quality has often been inadequate. There are also increasing regulations governing the toxicity of printing inks. Long-term collaboration between a sourcing house in the United Kingdom and a Far East factory led to the development of the right mug for KitKat at the right price.

- Another high-profile promotion run by Nestlé was themed on magic tricks. The company had identified a series of injection-moulded magic tricks that it could obtain from China, but was forestalled by quota restrictions on imports from China imposed by the EU. Its premium sourcing house was able to identify a manufacturer in India and help the factory meet unfamiliar quality requirements.

What to look out for

You can expect a premium sourcing house to have extensive contacts with manufacturers throughout the world and to have a track record in creating and manufacturing products and shipping them across the globe. Pay particular attention to their quality systems: if you value brand reputation, it is not worth skimping here. Premium sourcing houses registered to ISO 9001 will have demonstrated the capability of their systems. It is seldom worth the risk of dealing with an intermediary company offering products at knock-down prices that cannot demonstrate quality systems.

It is worth bringing up premium sourcing at an early stage of the discussion of promotions. In a number of markets – children's products in particular – the choice of premium may be critical to the success of a promotion. A good premium sourcing house will understand marketing as well as premiums. If you form a long-term relationship with a sourcing house, you will often be the first to hear of innovative products that are right for your market.

The following case studies illustrate how fixed-fee, over-redemption and prize coverage can be insured.

CASE STUDY 4.1 Butterkist

Lime Communications created an exclusive on-pack campaign for Tangerine Confectionery's Butterkist popcorn brand and Universal Films, aimed at attracting and rewarding consumers while enforcing popcorn's association with the movies. PIMS-SCA coordinated and managed the coupon element of the campaign while ensuring total balance sheet protection from the outset.

Objectives: To increase penetration. To build an association with films.

Mechanic: The campaign appeared on over 8 million promotional packs across six Butterkist product ranges. Consumers purchased promotional packs of Butterkist, entered their unique promotional on-pack code at **www.butterkistproductions.co.uk** or via Facebook, to instantly reveal if they had won a prize.

Thousands of movie-related prizes were up for grabs with a £1 million total prize fund; five holidays at Universal Orlando, 10 trips for two to a London premiere, 25 private screenings for up to 50 people, 100 home entertainment systems and thousands of DVDs. Each promotional pack offered consumers a 50p money-off next purchase coupon to be downloaded for print and redemption.

PIMS-SCA's role: E-Demption powered the money-off next purchase coupon element of the campaign including building the promotional microsite, coupon production, coupon processing, web page creation, coupon print notification e-mails as well as providing additional insight into coupon usage. With over 8 million potential 50p money-off coupons up for grabs, PIMS-SCA's fixed fee covered the costs associated with all coupon redemption, including invalid redemptions, therefore removing the potential £4 million exposure from the promoter's balance sheet. As well as providing £1 million prize coverage and incorporating its secure Draw Server into the campaign to allocate prizes, PIMS-SCA liaised with the DVD suppliers to fulfil the thousands of prize winners.

CASE STUDY 4.2   McCain

Blue Chip Marketing developed a free mail-in campaign for McCain Smiles in partnership with the National Literacy Trust and Penguin Books. With over 1 million classic children's books up for grabs, each worth £2.99, PIMS-SCA provided a fixed fee for total balance sheet protection.

Objectives: To drive penetration.

Mechanic: Leaflets featuring a URN, together with reading tips, were inserted into 2 million promotional packs. Consumers collected two unique codes from the packs and visited a promotional microsite to enter them together with their contact details and claim one of six Ladybird Treasured Tales for free. Books on offer included *The Gingerbread Man, Little Red Riding Hood, Cinderella, Jack & The Beanstalk, Goldilocks and the Three Bears* and *The Three Little Pigs*.

PIMS-SCA's role: PIMS-SCA was asked to ensure that all financial risk was removed from the promotion, and supplied a fixed-fee solution accordingly. The fee included managing the availability and supply of the requested Ladybird books along with all the handling, financial and logistical management associated with the promotion. The fixed-fee solution ensured McCain ran a secure, risk-free promotion with complete balance sheet protection as each and every PIMS-SCA fixed fee includes £10 million of coverage with A-rated insurers.

CASE STUDY 4.3   Discovery Foods

Carbon Marketing created a two-pronged in-store campaign for Discovery Foods consisting of a money-back guarantee and a money-off next purchase coupon mechanic.

Objectives: To increase sales of Discovery Foods products.

Mechanic: Promotional staff in selected Tesco and Sainsbury's supermarkets encouraged consumers to buy Discovery Foods products while handing out leaflets featuring a 50p money-off next purchase coupon. If the consumer spent over £3 but wasn't happy with the Discovery Foods purchase he or she was refunded up to £3 by writing to the manufacturers, explaining the reasons and enclosing the till receipt.

PIMS-SCA's role: PIMS-SCA performed a risk evaluation of the campaign and provided a fixed-fee solution for total balance sheet protection. The fixed fee covered financial risk, logistical and administrative management of the promotion as well as coordinating handling services to take care of refund applications. All coupon redemptions and the associated costs were covered to ensure Discovery Foods' budget remained fixed and secure.

CASE STUDY 4.4 PIMS-SCA '£25,000 Santa search winner'

Each Christmas PIMS-SCA sends its clients and suppliers a Christmas card offering the chance to win a big cash prize, as a thank you for their business throughout the year.

Objectives: To reward clients and suppliers with the chance to win £25,000 via the annual online Christmas card.

Mechanic: All clients and suppliers registered on the PIMS-SCA database received an e-mail wishing them a Merry Christmas plus the chance to win by playing a free online scratch card. Players clicked on the link and opened three windows on the advent calendar game to search for Santa. A variety of Christmas themed characters could be found behind the windows as well as three Santas; if just the three Santas were revealed, players won £25,000. Players could have unlimited free practice plays before playing the one-shot £25,000 prize play game.

PIMS-SCA's role: PIMS-SCA designed and created the online scratch card game as well as covering the £25,000 jackpot with its own prize coverage.

CASE STUDY 4.5 Kerrygold win a bag instantly

In a campaign to increase penetration, a bespoke 100 per cent pure cotton Kerrygold shopper bag was offered to one in four purchasers on the reverse of 600,000 promotional sleeves on 250 gm packs of Kerrygold Lighter or Kerrygold Softer butter. Losing packs included a 20p money-off next purchase coupon. To claim the bag winners sent off the promotional sleeve or went online to enter a unique pack reference number. Other activity included promotion in Asda's in-store magazine plus a door drop to Sainsbury's customers. The fixed-fee solution provided by PIMS-SCA ensured Kerrygold's promotional budget remained fixed and secure from the outset no matter how many consumers claimed the bag or redeemed the coupons.

CASE STUDY 4.6   *New Zealand Herald* $25 camera offer

To encourage daily purchase, reward subscribers and increase occasional purchase, readers of the *Herald* could collect six tokens and then send them with $25 plus $5 for postage and package to claim a digital camera that retailed at $79. The self-liquidating promotion was covered by PIMS-SCA to give total financial security for the newspaper. The result was amazingly successful with uptake 18 times more than expected.

CASE STUDY 4.7   Golden Wonder 'Crack the Keycode'

To increase penetration Golden Wonder ran an on-pack promotion to win one of 25 brand new special edition VW beetle cars. PIMS-SCA hosted the promotion and covered the cost of 24 out of the 25 cars on offer should consumers successfully crack the winning eight-digit codes devised for each car; Golden Wonder only covered the cost of one. If no one won a prize then all entries were entered in a free prize draw so Golden Wonder had at least one prize winner.

Summary

Promotion agencies, handling houses, POP manufacturers, promotional insurers, specialist printers, field marketing agencies and premium sourcing houses form an infrastructure of businesses with one common thread: making promotions work. There are others too, including the companies that supply off-the-shelf promotions. The trade press regularly reports on them, not least because they provide a substantial amount of advertising, which makes much of the reporting uncritical. You need to use the trade press and exhibitions such as Incentive World.

If you do any amount of promoting, you are likely to need all of them at some time. It pays to identify a company in each sector with a solid financial basis, to consult with them at an early stage of promotional development and to build up a long-term relationship. No promoter can hope to develop specialist expertise in each of these fields. It makes sense to use them for their skills. If you decide to put all your promotions to a sales promotion agency, it would be wise to establish who they are using for specialist services. One weak link in the promotional chain – whether it is handling, premium sourcing or field marketing – is enough to destroy a promotion. Promoters should be aware of the benefits of promotional risk management and how it can impact on a promotion and ensure balance sheet protection.

Self-study questions

4.1 What issues should you take into account when organizing a pitch among sales promotion agencies?

4.2 What are the main things needed in a brief for a handling house?

4.3 What things can you use promotional insurance for, and why should you do so?

Non-participative promotion – communication with no promotional offer

05

This chapter examines the plethora of ways with which to communicate with the customer/shopper through a wide variety of marketing communications that require no action on the part of those receiving the message, who can even 'switch off' and ignore it.

Just standing on a street corner holding a placard counts as a marketing communication, particularly if a shopper is a tourist looking for somewhere to eat and the food outlet is not on the main thoroughfare! To avoid being ignored, clearly something creative needs to attract attention (see Chapter 3). Shock tactics (smoke, simulated fire, gruesome pictures), movement (lights, changing panels, scrolls), a distinctive smell (aroma), or noise (music, a jingle) is needed to draw attention to this form of promotion.

I strongly advocate that a promotion is used with any communication through any media, if only to attract the shopper/buyer to the message and because the effectiveness of media is greatly enhanced by a promotion, as research by the IPA shows. The opportunity to describe each media in relation to every other media without any promotion, is beneficial.

The media

Today's media environment has characteristics that are radically different from just 10 years ago:

- It is abundant and easy to populate with content, but consumers have become adept at 'switching off'.
- It is cheap to buy, and sometimes free, but it is more expensive to reach mass audiences due to fragmentation and the fact that where once a channel had one platform, now it has many.

- A shift of advertising away from mass media towards personalized forms of marketing including for example, direct mail, the internet, mobile, retail media, word of mouth has seemingly diluted the impact of non-participative media, but as shown by engram research, it would seem to be an important part of initiating the consumer's engram 'hook' and building the 'mind file'.
- All media are under pressure because of issues of accountability and ROI. Financial auditors and CEOs now expect to see measurement of the effectiveness of any media activity.

Measuring effectiveness

Of course those overseeing the marketing communications budget will need to know that they are getting value for money and have some measure of effectiveness: it would seem a no-brainer to find out if the money is being spent to any useful effect. However, it is the case that relatively few people measure the effectiveness of the marketing they pay for. *The Grocer* reported in May 2012 that 61 per cent of retailers do not measure anything. In addition to knowing whether marketing communication works or not, making a comparison between media and channels is important. Only a business can make such comparisons and just for its particular customer segments. (Measuring marketing effectiveness is relatively easy to do and is covered by Roddy Mullin in *Value for Money Marketing*.) The main requirement is the intent – the will to do it. It is of course the only way to find out what works for the customers you target, with the marketing communications you pay for.

What each medium can do perhaps is shown in Table 5.1. Some media are good for coverage, some are liked by the trade, some are intrusive and as for duration – it is said that a cinema ad is impactful, but that the impact only lasts for about 15 minutes.

The persuasiveness of the different media will of course vary by each customer, depending on a number of social and cultural factors. How well developed a medium is in any country will also have an impact, along with the legal environment in which the marketing communications operate. There are enormous variations between urban and rural media in any country.

Again there are general principles that apply; some media are better at making customers aware of brands, their products and services than others. Such awareness, if effective, is stored away in the subconscious by a customer until some need prompts a search of the knowledge stored in the brain and the medium is recalled. How this works is explained through engrams (see Chapter 2). Experience is a powerful reinforcer of memory and so those retailers that allow customers to test or try a brand may really benefit long term (see Chapter 7). This applies to intangibles such as software too: 74 per cent of digital businesses, according to Econsultancy, now recognize that user experience improves sales.

The customer will look at the total offer and the Six Cs will feature in his or her assessment of any purchase (see Chapter 2). Table 5.2 illustrates the way that different media impact on the customer.

TABLE 5.1 Illustrative effectiveness of media (based on a Saatchi & Saatchi idea)

	TV	Cinema	Radio	Print	Outdoor	Internet	Mobile
Visual colour sound movement	✓✓	✓✓	✓	✓	✓->✓✓	✓->✓✓✓	✓->✓✓✓
Intrusive	✓✓	✓✓✓	✓?	✓	✓		✓?
Detail				✓✓		✓✓✓	✓
Interactive	✓?		?			✓✓✓	✓✓?
Time flexible	✓?		✓✓			✓✓✓	✓✓
Duration			?	✓		✓✓?	✓?
Coverage	✓		✓	✓	✓	✓✓	✓✓
Profile	✓?	✓	✓	✓✓		✓✓	✓✓
Less cost/'000			✓	✓	✓	✓✓-✓✓✓	✓✓✓
Trade affinity	✓✓	✓	✓	✓✓	✓	->✓	->✓
Customize message				✓		✓✓✓	✓✓

The media and channels

The key to comparing different media and channels may be to use 'share of voice' and here the report from the IPA showing how advertising is improved with the addition of other approaches is helpful. The magic number three (three media is the best number to get hard results) according to the IPA research, recognizes that more than one media is required, but it is insufficient in the holistic overview of the shopper's journey to purchase – six is a better number, allowing for the building up of the engram 'mind file'.

Outdoor (see below) and some research done by the BPS (British Population Survey) show the importance of local media. I suggest that the shopper perspective should be paramount. It is obvious really: examine the shopper's environment, as only there will be presented, messages that are effective on the shopper's journey to purchase.

TABLE 5.2   What the media can do (illustrative; based on an Admap idea)

	Awareness	Acceptance	Preference	Insistence	Reassurance
TV	✓	✓?			
Radio	✓	✓?			
Cinema	✓✓	✓?			
Outdoor	✓✓	✓?			
Press	✓✓	✓	✓?		
PR	✓✓	✓	✓		
House literature		✓	✓✓	✓	✓
Direct mail	✓✓	✓✓	✓✓		
Door-to-door	✓	✓✓	✓✓		
Website		✓?	✓✓	✓	✓
E-mail	✓✓	✓✓?	✓✓	✓	✓✓
Mobile	✓✓✓?	✓✓?	✓✓	✓✓	✓✓
Experiential sales	✓✓	✓✓✓	✓✓✓	✓✓✓	✓✓✓
After-sales service					✓✓✓

Synergy works

The IPA Report, *Models of Marketing Effectiveness* looked at the lead medium – the medium the authors identify as the primary channel with the highest spend or focus. This analysis was restricted to TV, press and outdoor as there were too few cases in the IPA databank where other communications channels were noted as the lead. Using press as the lead medium demonstrates the biggest hard business effects,

TABLE 5.3   Channel combinations effectiveness

	Advertising only %	Advertising and web %	Advertising and DM %	Advertising and promotion %	Advertising and sponsorship %	Advertising and PR %
1. Very large hard business effect	71	71	77	84	74	70
2. Very large soft business effect	57	65	61	68	72	70

SOURCE: IPA

whereas outdoor drives the biggest intermediate effects such as brand fame or awareness. However, synergy delivered the best overall results; see Table 5.3.

The IPA stated that three proved to be the most effective number of advertising media to drive hard business measures but 'the more the merrier' for intermediate measures (see Chapters 7–9 for more on this). As a result of the engram research I now believe six are required.

Advertising coupled with a sales conversion channel such as direct marketing or sales promotion was the most effective combination to drive hard business success such as sales, or market share. Advertising coupled with sponsorship or PR were the two most effective combinations to drive intermediate metrics such as brand fame.

Message location

As discussed earlier, the location of a message has an impact on the way it is received. 'The medium is the message' is a phrase coined by Marshall McLuhan, meaning that the form of a medium embeds itself in the message, creating a symbiotic relationship by which the medium influences how the message is perceived. This is certainly the case for messaging in venues.

Research by the IPM for the British Council of Shopping Centres showed that visitors in shopping centres and pedestrianized city centres were in a much better frame of mind to receive complex messages. Those in high streets with traffic were more concerned with safety. Meanwhile venues such as train stations left people more stressed (too many other messages to concentrate on) while garden centres actually under-stress people. You need to be engaged properly with your surroundings to be able to take in everything new coming your way. So always consider the surroundings at the same time as the message.

Non-direct communication

Advertising is not an individually targeted medium and it embraces many sub-disciplines. The classic mechanisms are outdoor (posters and billboards, static and dynamic), print (newspapers and magazines), broadcast media (radio, TV and cinema) and packaging and the point of sale.

Outdoor advertising

This includes posters, including digital posters which change, or video posters which show a video clip, now common on London Underground). The Outdoor Media Centre (OMC) approach to the customer journey is a four-stage process:

1 absorbing (the shopper becomes aware of the message);

2 planning (considering what to do about the message);

3 obtaining (purchasing a product or service);

4 sharing (telling others about the message/purchase).

Static billboard results show it is rated higher for absorbing. Dynamic results indicate 70 per cent remain at the absorbing stage although two-thirds generated 'feel' or 'do' response. There is clear evidence from the engram research to support the premise that advertising does move people onwards on the journey to purchase, building the shopper's 'mind file'.

By way of comparison and using the OMC approach, TV is best at absorbing stage, online is best for planning, whereas radio and press communicate detail better at the obtaining stage, but TV and outdoor can assist, if there is a driver here giving a call to action. Outdoor advertising is best used locally on routes to venues, shops, outlets, events.

Transport advertising

This can be considered as a part of outdoor advertising, but when displayed on external surfaces of the transport it is in effect a moving billboard. Posters on walls, walls opposite platforms, escalators, steps (all of which can now be dynamic) have a time measured in seconds for people to view. Small posters are also placed on the inside of buses, tubes, trains, trams.

TV advertising

Thirty-second slots are usually sold to appear alongside appropriate programmes. Some programmes can be sponsored, meaning that the advertisements are more suitably linked to target audiences. These advertisements can also be interactive where the customer can feed back a response using the buttons on the remote control (direct response). Remember that a TV commercial can also be used online. (Note that TV advertising with promotions shows a greater response rate than without; see Table 5.1.)

Booz reports that alongside filmed comedy, the Target Corporation offers shop-pable content (it runs outlets similar to Wal-Mart) providing the chance to buy clothes and other items as shown or worn by the characters in the film. The shoppers were linked to the website but also to social media for product reviews by other shoppers. Marketers, in areas including consumer electronics, clothing/apparel, and consumer packaged goods (CPG), are investing in direct-to-consumer relationships to drive value across the path to purchase and close the loop between engagement and sales. Nike, with its Fuelband mobile fitness experience, links with the shopper's personal fitness profile, introducing shoppers to other Nike products that supplement the fitness experience.

Other media are:

- Local radio advertising – slots are offered alongside commercial radio broadcasts.
- Cinema – national and local-only advertisements can be placed on screen before feature films.
- Print – magazines, newspapers, all take advertisements.
- Advertorial – where the advertisement is written in the magazine or newspaper style to look like an editorial.
- Inserts – printed loose-leaf pages inserted into a magazine or newspaper, tip-ons which are stuck onto the relevant page.
- House literature – when a retailer offers (usually free) leaflets proffered at entrances and exits. Supermarkets and department stores, hotel chains often use publishers to produce a free monthly magazine, again offered through outlets.
- Packaging – a key placement for the engram; the product package itself may be the engram.
- POS material – alongside the product or service, it draws attention to the product. It may be hung from the ceiling, stuck onto the floor, on the shelf (adjacencies), a special dispenser or arrangement (ensembles); all can highlight the product.
- In-store video can give advice on using products that help people to buy while on their shopping trip.

Public relations

The CIPR defines PR as follows:

Public relations is the discipline which looks after reputation, with the aim of earning understanding and support and influencing opinion and behaviour. It is the planned and sustained effort to establish and maintain goodwill and mutual understanding between an organization and its publics.

PR is the opposite of advertising: the article that features your company is not paid for. The reporter, whether broadcast or print, writes about or films your company as a result of information he or she received and researched.

Publicity is more effective than advertising, for several reasons. First, publicity is far more cost-effective than advertising. Even if it is not free, your only expenses are generally phone calls and mailings to the media. Second, publicity has greater longevity than advertising. An article about your business will be remembered far longer than an ad. Publicity also reaches a far wider audience than advertising generally does. Sometimes your story might be picked up by the national media, spreading the word about your business all over the country. Most important, publicity has greater credibility with the public than does advertising. Readers feel that if an objective third party (a magazine, newspaper or radio reporter) is featuring your company, you must be doing something worthwhile.

Sponsorship

This is a very broad subject and is particularly useful to indicate a brand dimension. It is a part of PR. Support for a charity (for example the name of the charity appearing on their website, stands or vehicles) can show a caring dimension of a brand. Even police vehicles may now be sponsored in the UK. The Charities Aid Foundation (CAF) has a website that can advise on local charities by category. Contacting the CAF may be helpful as it can align the objective of the sponsorship to a specific charity.

Targeted message media

Direct marketing

Direct marketing is a communication between seller and buyer directly: no intermediary media is used. It is visual and sometimes auditory (telemarketing). It is also to an extent sensual and olfactory. The thickness, embossing and smell of paper can deliver a perception of quality. It is most often in print or text format and originally just used the post; it now encompasses the internet (e-mail), telemarketing and mobile marketing (SMS/MMS). Direct marketing is targeted towards an individual, though not always by name – it is enabled by the customer choosing to open or to activate the message. The original purpose of direct marketing was to get the shopper to buy through the post or ask for a catalogue, to request a demonstration, or to persuade the shopper to physically visit a bricks-and-mortar establishment (for example a store, restaurant, spa or hairdresser) or to participate in some way.

Direct mail

This is the original form of direct marketing. This is when a personally addressed letter is sent making an offer to the individual; software programmes now allow the letter to be personalized. A sample can often be added to a direct mailing in addition to or instead of a promotion. A direct mail should give clear benefit to the recipient and be persuasive and appropriate. The response of the shopper to the direct mail varies according to the attractiveness and creativity of the message and the offer it conveys. Organizations such as Central Mailing Services, British Market Research Bureau, the Royal Mail vouch for the success of such mailshots. Nine out of 10 people open direct mail and 75 per cent like to receive a voucher or offer. A third of the UK population responded to direct mail in 2011 and as a result 6.2 million went online and 7.3 million went to a store. The response rate stands at 3.42 per cent. In 2010, 17.7 million people ordered from catalogues received through direct mail.

Door-to-door delivery

This is when the message, still usually in letter or leaflet format, is delivered to a house but not addressed to the householder by name. The service is offered by the postal service and by other organizations that deliver door-to-door, such as local newspapers or specialist firms that deliver to houses. Samples and promotions are again used to make the unaddressed message of greater interest to the receiver. As with direct mail, success depends on the attractiveness and creativity of the message and the offer it conveys, but the rates of response are usually lower with people assessing such material as junk mail.

Inserts

These are included in magazines or newspapers and are similar to leaflets and hand-outs (see below) but the delivery mechanism is different and depends on the shopper noticing the material and taking action. Inserts can also be glued on to the advert or to a front cover; these are known as 'tip-ons'.

Telemarketing/telesales

Telemarketing is the outbound activity of a call centre. Experience shows that tele-marketing is more effective with B2B messages as long as the offer is both relevant and beneficial. It is even more effective if the telemarketing call is preceded by a letter.

Telesales is where an existing customer is contacted. The call centre can be used to acquire data about the person being called. Codes of practice exist for tele-marketing and 'cold calling' is often not appreciated by shoppers. It has been exten-sively used in the UK for PPI claims calls, energy companies and telecommunications companies seeking householders who are prepared to change their supplier or service provider.

Leaflets/hand-outs

These are normally sheets of paper left in places where people can pick up informa-tion, typically about holiday and tourist venues (available in tourist information centres, hotel and B&B lobbies) and activities or cards that are offered by people standing in the street or in places where there is a high footfall, usually advertising an event such as a store or restaurant opening. Local Councils, concerned about litter, often have by-laws about what may be handed out when and where, and marketers may need to check and obtain permission – this applies on station concourses too. A person holding a placard can be a temporary solution to market communication near the point of sale.

(Econsultancy has produced *Marketing Attribution 2013. A buyer's guide,* suggesting which media to use. The guide describes which firms undertake analytic work.)

Implementation

If you seek to simply educate, inform or just build the brandgram in the shopper/buyer's 'mind file', then non-participative promotion without a promotional offer is sufficient, using any of the media listed in this chapter. However, I advocate that a promotional offer is always added. It does require effort (see Chapter 9) and there is a cost. Insight shows that with TV it increases response by two to seven times the level without a promotional offer. The same probably applies to all media. Think of the rush in a cinema there would be if a free drink was offered (say one in five) in a draw, or a simple BOGOF to those buying a coke or popcorn rather than just the invitation to visit the foyer before the main feature starts.

BRIEF 5.1   The new Argos digital 'bricks and mortar' outlets

Argos, with a turnover of £4 billion (50 per cent from online trading, though 90 per cent end up in store) is trialling six new outlets. Catalogues are replaced by tablets. The walls are all digital with promotional (and scarcity) messages displayed alongside news, weather and local messages. Staff are equipped with tablets for competitor comparison. Delivery has been speeded up both in-store and from orders placed online, with a hub system for items not held in store. Argos is also trialling delivery for eBay and uses for 3D printers. Where special catalogues are in print format (Christmas toys) then Blippar is offered to view them and bring them to life.

BRIEF 5.2 Ford Fiesta

A TV ad shows a young woman driving a car. To exploit the new in-car talking text message feature the young male passenger makes a stupid remark, then texts to the car his apology seeking forgiveness. This is read out and makes the young woman smile – so all ends well. There is no other message than text that it is a Ford Fiesta. This clearly is designed to build a favourable image of a Ford Fiesta added to the engram.

BRIEF 5.3 Gatwick airport

On the London Underground Victoria line, inside the carriages there are now statements advocating the extra runway for Gatwick Airport. There is no call to action.

Summary

The way you stack media does, to an extent, influence the outcome that you get. The engram research supports a stacking of media, both non-participative and individually targeted, but to trigger the tipping point use a promotion.

If you stack hard (promotion) on top of softer lead media such as advertising or outdoor, you are much more likely to get hard outcomes. So if profit is your goal, this is the route to start with. Remember that media also include elements that you might not normally consider, such as point of purchase, as part of the marketing budget. If, however, you are seeking brand fame, image or reputation, just building the brandgram through the engram hook, then opt for other partners, such as PR.

Self-study questions

5.1 What platforms must a promotional video operate across?

5.2 What is the preferred communication that insight has determined shoppers seek? What frequency should a retailer use for such a communication?

5.3 How might augmented reality be used, a) by a shopping mall, b) for a furniture store, c) reading a print magazine?

Shopper/
buyer-activated
promotions

06

Overview

This chapter should really be a media stream (using Layar with a constantly changing text, with video and audio) covering the continuous and exciting developments in technology and its application to communication for the shopper/buyer and how the brand manager, supplier and retailer can fit marketing communication into that stream. Using the Layar app you should be able to wave your mobile over the print here and see an up-to-the-minute description of the latest technology with video clips of what it can do for marketing communication. Read more in the paragraphs on augmented reality that follow.

Nowadays when information on any product, service or brand is sought, the shopper/buyer can access a communication device to find the answers 24/7. The search typically includes visiting websites through mobile, tablet, laptop or PC. It may of course arise while watching TV or be a retailer-generated mobile alert (SMS or e-mail) or from accessing a QR (or AR) symbol in print, or NFC-triggered mobile message that may direct people to bricks-and-mortar outlets with promotional offers or to apps that can be downloaded. This is all dependent on technology that is deployed by the retailer, brand or supplier. It equally depends on the technology available to the shopper/buyers (what they have and whether they choose to use it). The chapter title reflects this: it is the shopper/buyer who leads the action. The future will see consumers constantly able to access information and news from anywhere on the planet. Mark Anderson of the Strategic News Service has coined a term for this: AORTA (Always On Real Time Access).

Another innovation, just in Japan at the moment, is iButterfly. Shoppers scan with their camera/app a retail environment (mall or high street) and geo-targeting responds with a series of butterflies across the camera view. Participating outlets are shown as butterflies on screen; shoppers either catch them in a form of gamification play (recording 'butterfly points' towards future offers) or click on a butterfly when that outlet signifies promotions just for them and which, by entering the store, they can redeem. This is the modern equivalent of the book of store vouchers, except the offers can be targeted to the shopper more precisely.

There are other innovations: SoLoMo (Social Local Mobile) is an incoming technology that combines location with acknowledging presence of a mobile and then ascertains the distance to participating outlets. The system provides extensive feedback to the marketer while acting as a form of companion, for example in the retail area. Triumph, which sells lingerie, used a body scanner in a launch at Selfridges and then screened the body shape so that shoppers could see what they would look like wearing the lingerie as the body shape moved around on screen. Over 100,000 tweets resulted and a hike in sales. Taking 'selfies' is all the rage; women taking photographs of themselves without make-up raised large amounts of money for a charity (without the charity being involved); men followed suit by taking selfies with themselves wearing make-up. Inviting people to participate in such promotions seems a sure-fire way to achieve considerable brand involvement.

What are the facts?

TV

Consumers today watch TV, surf the Internet and check new e-mails simultaneously – though 64 per cent of 55+ year-olds stated they have never participated in this modern habit. (Trust PMS, http://www.trustpms.com/Documents/Pin/Responses_30_seconds_or_less.pdf)

The average family home contains 10 different devices, with almost six (57 per cent) of these connected to the internet. These devices are encouraging family members to second screen, with three quarters (73 per cent) of those surveyed saying they use a separate smartphone, tablet or laptop while watching TV. (Econsultancy, https://econsultancy.com/blog/63566-10-interesting-internet-marketing-statistics-we-ve-seen-this-week#i.m2putjp6zevcxf)

Mobile

Families in the UK are using instant messaging and video calls to talk to each other in the home. Almost one in three (30 per cent) said they use devices such as tablets and smartphones to let each other know when dinner is ready (rather than shouting up the stairs), or ask for help with homework. (Fresh Business Thinking, http://www.freshbusinessthinking.com/news.php?NID=20194#.U2y7tIFdXgW)

Mobile ad spend in the UK grew to £429.2 million in the first half of 2013, an increase of 127 per cent compared to the same period last year. (IAB report, reported by Econsultancy https://econsultancy.com/blog/63534-mobile-adspend-up-127-to-429m-in-first-half-of-2013)

In 2012, 36 per cent of advertising spend in the UK was on digital. This is up from 19 per cent in 2007. (OFCOM's 2013 International Communications Market Report, reported by Econsultancy, https://econsultancy.com/blog/63993-ofcom-reveals-uk-digital-advertising-trends-stats)

Some 27 per cent of all online sales, worth £3 billion, were placed on a mobile device. Of those mobile sales, 82 per cent were from tablet computers. The figure was up by 131 per cent on the same time last year. Meanwhile, sales from a smartphone rose by 186 per cent. (Internet retailing, http://internetretailing.net/2014/01/uk-shoppers-spent-91bn-online-in-2013-and-look-set-to-spent-107bn-in-2014/)

US mobile retail sales are estimated to grow from $12 billion in 2013 to $27 billion by 2016 – a $15 billion increase in only 36 months. (Forrester Research, reported by http://contentz.mkt3416.com/lp/38068/308100/media/BC_Q4_mCommerce.pdf)

Smartphone usage in the UK has increased from 62 per cent in 2013 to 68 per cent in 2014. (Consultancy, https://econsultancy.com/blog/64511-32-of-uk-consumers-make-purchases-on-a-smartphone-stats)

Watching online video content has become increasingly popular, rising from 61 per cent in 2013 to 66 per cent in 2014. (Internet Retailing, http://internetretailing.net/2014/03/uk-consumers-do-more-online-shopping-than-rest-of-europe-finds-google-as-it-launches-site-to-help-brands-exploit-mobile/)

Twice as much was spent via mobile devices as was spent using them in December 2012. The figures beat IMRG's original estimate last January of 12 per cent growth. (Internet Retailing, http://internetretailing.net/2014/01/uk-shoppers-spent-91bn-online-in-2013-and-look-set-to-spent-107bn-in-2014/)

In fact, people walking through store aisles with a smartphone in hand are 14 per cent more likely to purchase. (Forrester Research, reported by http://contentz.mkt3416.com/lp/38068/308100/media/BC_Q4_mCommerce.pdf)

MMS has three times the engagement of SMS.

In the United States the Government's FEMA offered 'text message shelters' which directed users to the nearest shelter for hurricanes and earthquakes once their zip code was entered.

Social media

Social media is a means to provide feedback or complaints directly to brands. Visiting social networks has also gained popularity (72 per cent in 2014 compared to 64 per cent in 2013). (Internet retailing, http://internetretailing.net/2014/03/uk-consumers-do-more-online-shopping-than-rest-of-europe-finds-google-as-it-launches-site-to-help-brands-exploit-mobile/)

The merging of social and mobile is the perfect combination for food and drinks ads using fun and witty videos.

Internet, websites and e-mail

Tablets now account for more web traffic than smartphones, concluding that although smartphones are more common, tablets offer a far more convenient browsing experience. (http://econsultancy.com/blog/62307-tablets-now-account-for-more-web-traffic-than-smartphones-stats)

Looking more broadly at internet usage across devices, it was found that 83 per cent of UK online consumers use the internet daily in 2014 and 64 per cent several times a day, compared to 75 per cent and 57 per cent respectfully in 2013. (Internet retailing, http://internetretailing.net/2014/03/uk-consumers-do-more-online-shopping-than-rest-of-europe-finds-google-as-it-launches-site-to-help-brands-exploit-mobile/)

30 seconds or less is the average length of time that consumers spend reading or listening to online marketing communications. (Responsys report, http://www.responsys.com/land/download-how-marketers-can-reach-the-distracted-consumer)

More UK online consumers purchased on the internet in 2014 than 2013 (77 per cent compared to 72 per cent). (Internet Retailing, http://internetretailing.net/2014/03/uk-consumers-do-more-online-shopping-than-rest-of-europe-finds-google-as-it-launches-site-to-help-brands-exploit-mobile/)

Advertisers online spent a record six-month figure of £3.04 billion in the first half of 2013, an increase of £435 million or 17.5 per cent on the same period in 2012. (IAB Digital Adspend report, http://www.theipm.org.uk/documents/digital-ad-spend-breaks-3bn-for-h1-2013.aspx) The report shows that the increase has largely been driven by a massive take-up of online and mobile advertising by the Fast Moving Consumer Goods sector.

UK shoppers spent £91 billion online in 2013, according to new figures. The internet retailing market grew by 16 per cent during the course of the year. (IMRG-Capgemini e-Retail Sales Index for December, http://internetretailing.net/2014/01/uk-shoppers-spent-91bn-online-in-2013-and-look-set-to-spent-107bn-in-2014/). It was capped by a final month in which online sales rose by 18 per cent, with £11 billion spent, up from £9 billion in December 2012. The IMRG now forecasts 17 per cent growth in 2014, and estimates £107 billion will be spent online over the year.

It is estimated that 21 per cent of retail sales now take place online. (Retailing trade association)

61.8 per cent rise in Click & Collect orders and a shift to traffic from PC to mobile devices making up over half of traffic to johnlewis.com. (John Lewis, reported by http://www.uk.capgemini.com/news/uk-news/ps91-billion-spent-online-in-2013-imrg-capgemini-e-retail-sales-index)

Internet advertising expenditure to almost double between 2013 and 2017, growing by 56.5 per cent over the 5-year period. (Key Note forecasts, reported by http://www.businesswire.com/news/home/20130719005316/en/Research-Markets-Internet-Advertising-Market-Report-2013#.U2zQC4FdXgU)

The channel on which consumers spend the longest time interacting with marketing messages is e-mail – 50 per cent of consumers spend on average between 5 and 30 seconds on incoming marketing e-mails. This suggests that the unobtrusive, opt-in nature of e-mail continues to reign supreme. (Trust PMS, http://www.trustpms.com/Documents/Pin/Responses_30_seconds_or_less.pdf)

Typically (49 per cent) receive between 2–10 e-mails per day from all brands they actively subscribe to, almost one-fifth (19 per cent) of consumers receive 11 or more marketing e-mails per day, only 8 per cent of consumers are reading every marketing e-mail they receive, compared to 43 per cent who are reading less than half of e-mails sent by marketers. (Trust PMS, http://www.trustpms.com/Documents/Pin/Responses_30_seconds_or_less.pdf)

Consumers are most likely to look at or read marketing content from brands on weekdays, between 5 pm–11 pm (23 per cent) – 32 per cent of consumers have liked a brand on Facebook, while just 12 per cent claim to follow a brand on Twitter. (Trust PMS, http://www.trustpms.com/Documents/Pin/Responses_30_seconds_or_less.pdf)

A third of consumers (33 per cent) expect brands to contact them with relevant incentives and discounts within a day of registration or subscription to a website or service. To the consumer, this isn't an unrealistic expectation – they are savvy to the fact that marketers collect data on them. They expect this to be used to provide quick, highly relevant discounts, services and products based on the behaviours they have shared with the brand. (Trust PMS, http://www.trustpms.com/Documents/Pin/Responses_30_seconds_or_less.pdf)

A third of UK internet users in 2013 are accessing the internet using a tablet. This is up from 24 per cent on the previous year. The 2012 figure was double that of 2011.

Giving staff tablets helps overcome showrooming.

The impact on marketing

Consumers are becoming more selective about which brand messages they pay attention to, rapidly hopping from one device to another. Marketers need to orchestrate individualized customer experiences across the digital channels, with the most relevant offer for that particular moment. Mass marketing techniques no longer pay off. Consumers are looking for quick, digestible content that is highly relevant to their wants and needs and delivered across their preferred digital channels.

Internet and mobile direct marketing spend

In 2012 the DMA reported that 40 per cent of marketing e-mails were opened on a mobile device. Table 6.1 shows online retail media predicted spend and indicates that marketers seem to change their budget little, year on year. An earlier survey for

TABLE 6.1   UK source trending

Marketing budget source for online retail media	2 years out	5 years out
The same budget	53.2%	43.3%
A different existing budget	21.3%	22.1%
A mixture	20.2%	21.7%
A new budget	5.3%	12.9%

Kingston Smith on web spend and trends found that marketers left media spend to agencies and often did not control the web spend, which came from a different budget. Hopefully a survey now would find that marketers control internet and mobile budgets and each year re-evaluate this increasingly key area of communication.

On the upside, a new Crimson Hexagon survey of 170 digital marketing and advertising professionals found that 72 per cent of respondents said that they now consider social media to be a more reliable source of public sentiment than traditional focus groups. When discussing social media as a research tool, 11 per cent of brands and agencies surveyed say they consider their market research to be 'very thorough'.

Social media

Social media consists of many alternatives, the principal ones in 2014 being Facebook, Twitter, Pinterest and Instagram. Google and YouTube have featured. Pinterest is now offering an app that can be integrated with supplier and retailer software packages, giving a smooth transfer to websites. This allows the shopper to move to make a purchase from the non-purchase Pinterest site. Instagram is probably overtaking the others for marketers as it offers to cross-fertilize a brand's most loyal fans, visually enhancing through genuine real-time content, all of which is more relevant to shoppers. Instagram was not intended originally for commercial use but offers lifestyle insights of other shoppers and can be linked both to a brand website and to Facebook. Mobile social is another increasingly popular way to communicate with a mobile audience. There will also be HTML5 push notifications, giving marketers a way to message users who are on their mobile websites.

A dedicated team is required to be able to respond in near real time, both to pick up and use plaudits and correct misunderstandings or misinformation. Kellogg's reported at the 2013 Industry Insights Summit how, as traditional partnership marketers, it uses real-time marketing to drive results. Kellogg's maximized its 2012 Olympic partnership, producing an on-pack overnight when Gabby Douglas won gold; she appeared on the front of a Corn Flakes box and the image garnered a million tweets in one day.

Why is social media useful? Booz (May, 2013) reports that understanding social sentiment that differentiates between positive and negative feedback helps marketers establish the shoppers' pulse, but also allows the marketer to harvest and to use the shoppers' language in subsequent messages. More important, it is one of the six media that need to be used to build on the engram the shopper's 'mind file' – the brandgram. It is a trusted source of independent recommendations or otherwise of a product, brand or service.

In an interview with the *Harvard Business Review* in 2013, Sir Martin Sorrell said that he thinks Facebook and Twitter are for PR, not advertising. He believes they are a branding medium and about developing the brand over the long term. Someone saying something nice on Facebook about your brand is probably not going to drive an instant purchase! The impact of social media on shoppers is immense and marketers need to somehow direct shoppers to social media sites.

So which retailers use what social media online? An analysis of McDonald's social media activity by EConsultancy found McDonald's had not touched its Google account. IKEA and Wal-Mart have done the same; while ASOS and John Lewis are active with daily updates. On Pinterest, McDonald's has one single account but runs no competitions, and because it operates in 119 countries and the rules vary in each country, it is not very active and simply copies content from Flickr on to Pinterest; it only has 2,000 followers there. By contrast Red Bull and Wal-Mart are very active on Pinterest. McDonald's is active on Twitter in some countries but not others. It posts a lot but only responds to about 20 complaints daily in the United States. Facebook is the social media where McDonald's is most active but only locally: there are 500,000 fans in the United Kingdom; globally there are only about five posts a month. McDonald's does record a high 'liked' ranking, possibly because it is a global corporate. If the intention is to maintain a presence in people's minds (see Chapter 2 on engrams) then its wide coverage has maintained that.

Websites and e-mails

Websites and search engines

The search engines are now remarkably responsive and shoppers can rapidly access websites. There is now enough professional support for a website to become an excellent marketing and sales tool (the messages it should carry is covered later in this book). In addition search engines such as Google take advertisements on a pay-per-click basis that appear alongside the results of search and alongside web pages. As an aside, research by Sponge (April 2013) finds 78 per cent of UK retailers do not offer Wi-Fi free in-store to shoppers. Half of the shops that do are collecting valuable information and benefitting from the opportunity to engage with shoppers while offering them something of value. The best experiences the survey finds come from John Lewis and Warehouse with Debenhams and Pret A Manger providing a more involved experience. According to EpiServer, Debenhams meets shoppers' demands in terms of speed, key functionality and ease of use. One in 10 log on to free Wi-Fi at restaurants and cafés daily – so the shopper demand is there.

User initiation is key; when someone chooses to engage, that's the opportunity for marketers to really deliver an experience that is favourable and welcomed. Where a lot of advertisers go wrong is creating experiences that are disruptive and jarring, forcing people to leave the page. It's essential to keep users on the page so they can easily go back to their original content at any time.

Ecommerce appears to have reached a tipping point, as new figures suggest that mobile devices are now behind all online sales growth. Analysis from e-retail trade association IMRG and Capgemini has found that sales via desktop computers have been steadily declining since the first quarter of 2011, with all online growth now coming from sales through mobile devices. In the second quarter of 2013, desktop sales flat-lined; while mobile devices accounted for 23 per cent of all online retail sales. The forecast for online sales in 2013 is for 15 per cent growth, thanks to the fast growth of mobile commerce.

E-mail

Advertising can also be placed alongside e-mail messages, if the shopper/customer has agreed to this. Usually this is after registration with the originator. Companies no longer need dedicated staff responding to e-mails but can use e-mail automation. It is estimated in a Gartner report that by 2020 customers will manage 85 per cent of their relationship without talking to a person and that such nurtured leads will, according to DemandGen, produce on average a 20 per cent increase in sales opportunities. Companies that excel at lead nurturing generate 50 per cent more sales-ready leads at 33 per cent lower cost (Forrester Research). It has been found by GetResponse that e-mails that include social sharing buttons have a 158 per cent higher click-through rate. Nucleus Research, giving an overview of marketing automation, says it drives a 14.5 per cent increase in sales productivity and a 12.5 per cent reduction in marketing overhead.

RedEye reports that personalized e-mail automation should be used for registration, reactivation, chasing abandoned baskets, conversion, thank yous, cross-selling and social 'shared/liked' messages. RedEye also recommends a frequency or timeliness of e-mails, in effect providing a lifecycle of e-mails that acquire, convert and develop a relationship. Making offers with promotions is an additional consideration. The e-mails are based on customers' online and e-mail behaviour. It is now possible to extend that automation to website direction, sending a text message and receiving a call from a call centre.

E-mail marketing list segmentation is undertaken by 85 per cent of e-mail marketers (DMA report, 2012). However, mobile users are also increasingly using their devices to check for e-mail messages, making it imperative for marketers to ensure their e-mails are optimized for mobile.

BRIEF 6.1   Top e-mails

Here in a book, for obvious reasons, it is difficult to portray what are good practice e-mails. ETDEsign found these in 2013 (visit **www.exacttarget.com** or .co.uk. to see the e-mails in detail):

- Kickstarter (simple, provokes interest and directs to rich landing page);
- Toms shoes (responsive design where the shoes change on the mobile);
- Moosejaw (effective plain text e-mail);
- Reiss (navigation bars easy to use);
- Jetsetter (homes in on preferences for travel but also addresses subscriber's e-mail preferences);
- Fitbit (summarizes and rewards fitness achievements weekly);

- Lowe's (clever profiling of subscribers);

- IVCi (rtf format conversational style);

- Zulily (a five e-mail welcome series promoting its app);

- Foursquare (responsive design for highly mobile subscribers);

- Twitter (e-mail draws you in);

- JCrew (opposite of content first; draws in subscribers with advice);

- Pandora (infographics example);

- Levi's (seeks photo uploads);

- Havaianas Australia (delightful animation);

- Jack Spade (clean, simple, with call to action);

- CB2 (fun, interactive gift decision-tree);

- Anthropologie (easy pictures and advice on what to wear);

- Bendon Lingerie (clever image blocking mosaic).

Mobile marketing

Marketers are almost overwhelmed just trying to decide which to use and when with a staggering number of options when it comes to messaging mobile users. There are push notifications, which are becoming a popular way to reach users who have downloaded a brand's app. These can include local push notifications, app-originated notifications and in-app alerts. But the choices do not stop there on mobile alternatives.

Adaptive designed sites will detect the device that the person is using and serve a design specific to that device. Responsive design is where e-mails and websites are designed to be responsive and will expand, contract and rearrange themselves based on the space available to them. Mobile-first is a strategy for approaching the design of sites and e-mails encouraging consideration of the smaller screens first. The result is very streamlined designs, where the content and accessibility take priority over design-heavy elements and eye candy. In the mobile inbox, some mobile-first e-mails are super skinny when viewed on a larger screen.

There are two other considerations: proactive and reactive. With proactive the mobile user is required to register to receive messages. These usually make offers. When an offer is taken up a further offer (bounce-back) should be made to retain involvement. Registration can be achieved through the offer of a game or app. Reactive is responding to shopper queries without the need for registration.

Mobile is an important way to send a message to consumers, who increasingly have their smartphones and tablets within arm's reach 24 hours a day. 'Mobile has become the wiring and the plumbing of retail, with impressive progress in integrating mobile calls to action in-store and in the vicinity', according to *Mobile Marketer*, adding that agencies (in the United States) are not keeping up and budget needs to be allocated to offer more than just porting PC web creative. Catalina Marketing suggests that:

> By combining in-store location, past purchase history, purchase intent, purchase cycle and numerous other points, Consumer Packaged Goods (CPG) marketers have an unprecedented ability to influence the consumer the instant before they make their purchase decision. It's cool, it's the future of retail.

However, it is easy for marketers to fall into the trap of sending too many messages and annoying users, especially when the same message is being delivered across multiple messaging platforms. The challenge for marketers is, that because mobile is such a personal medium, users have a high expectation that messages will be relevant and add value to their lives. There are ways for marketers to address these issues, including increasingly sophisticated user analytics that provide customer context alongside traditional methods used in advertising such as A/B split testing. This is where two versions, A and B, which are identical bar one variation that might impact a user's behaviour, are compared. Typically version A might be the one currently used (control), while version B is modified in some respect. As with any direct marketing strategy, testing and learning is key. One of the challenges for marketers is aligning the channel with the target user experience on mobile. Marketers need to think about mobile as being interactive. Generation X, Y is hugely driven by instant gratification and the fastest way to reach them with an interactive message is SMS – they send something and get it back right away.

Today the marketing funnel has never been more important. According to Econsultancy, 46 per cent of consumers research on a smartphone before making a purchase in store; it's therefore not surprising that 62 per cent of companies believe understanding how mobile users research/buy products is very important.

On the whole, banner ads are ubiquitous yet often ignored. While many mobile ads are ineffective, research (and, arguably, profits) has shown that those built for the small-screen that allow users to choose whether or not to activate the ad, drive more interaction and deliver a far better experience than standard banners. Econsultancy reports:

> The pursuit of new ways to grab a little attention has littered the web with a dizzying array of ads that test the patience of readers as much as they challenge the notion of user-friendly page design – particularly on the small screen of mobile.

The question, then, is how to serve up ads that are not unwelcome guests, whose messaging fits the medium. Ads can only be effective if readers aren't thinking about them as ads. They have to be noticed, but not noticeable, in the context of what they're reading or searching for but not interruptive. Optimizing for this kind of experience on mobile presents unique challenges, chief among them the amount of space at one's disposal, which is miniscule by web standards. That single limitation alone requires a new way of thinking. Mobile has pitfalls and opportunities for publishers and marketers alike. The smart ones will try to imagine what could be and adapt rather than imposing their will. At their finest, mobile ads should feel like part of the experience, using the precise form of non-linear story-telling that web hyperlinks made possible.

We're in the midst of a great migration to portable devices and the opportunities for marketers are immense. It will be much tougher to cultivate a relationship with users than it was on the web, but if handled properly we'll find the perfect balance between the ultimate user experience and advertisers' agenda.

QR codes, augmented reality and apps

Three useful technologies are described here.

QR codes

A QR code (quick response code; see Figure 6.1) is a type of 2D bar code that is used to provide easy access to information through a smartphone. The QR code is offered on any photographically available media. Print is the most common form – on packaging, on posters in magazines and newspapers. It can also be produced on dynamic media; the only requirement is that it can be photographed by a smartphone.

FIGURE 6.1   Example of a QR code

Using a QR code through mobile tagging is described as follows:

> In this process, known as mobile tagging, the smartphone's owner points the phone at a QR code and opens a barcode reader app which works in conjunction with the phone's camera. The reader app interprets the code, which typically contains a call to action such as an invitation to download a mobile application, a link to view a video or an SMS message inviting the viewer to respond to a poll. The phone's owner can choose to act upon the call to action or click cancel and ignore the invitation.

Static QR codes, the most common type, are used to disseminate information to the general public. They are often displayed in advertising materials in the environment (such as billboards and posters), on television and in newspapers and magazines. The code's creator can track information about the number of times a code was scanned and its associated action taken, along with the times of scans and the operating system of the devices that scanned it. Note that in US markets they are finding QR codes take up valuable space and affect creativity, while on the shopper 'minus side' the app has to be loaded before the shopper can use the QR code. Activating a QR code should be engaging for the shopper but many are not.

Dynamic QR codes (sometimes referred to as unique QR codes) offer more functionality. The owner can edit the code at any time and can target a specific individual for personalized marketing. Such codes can track more specific information, including the scanners names and e-mail address, how many times they scanned the code and, in conjunction with tracking codes on a website, conversion rates. (*Mobile Marketer*, April 2013, **http://whatis.techtarget.com/definition/QR-code-quick-response-code**)

Augmented reality (AR)

Augmented reality is no longer just for enhancing advertising campaigns; there are now many more practical applications of the technology to improve the customer experience. In camera mode the mobile is used with messages or pictures imposed on the screen.

BRIEF 6.2   IKEA app

An example is the IKEA AR app, available to download from Apple's app store and Google Play, which will work with any smartphone or tablet. Econsultancy reports that 'all the customer needs to do is place the 2014 catalogue in any space within their home, activate the app, and they can see exactly how a virtual Billy bookcase or Ektorp sofa fits into the real-time environment'. It also reports that IKEA states the app 'resolves the problem of 14 per cent of customers who say they've bought the wrong-sized furniture for their rooms and over 70 per cent who say they don't really know how big their own homes are'. This is of particular importance to the UK customer as our houses are the smallest in Western Europe:

The App is by Metaio software company, which also developed the VW and Audi interactive owner's manual apps, and is:

> designed to replace the weighty paper tome taking up valuable space in the glove-box. The app allows the user to point their device at any feature of the car and the app gives quick assistance to any query identifying more than 300 elements and quickly pulls up maintenance guides in a 3D overlay. (Econsultancy, **https://econsultancy.com/blog/63574-augmented-reality-the-ikea-catalogue-and-beyond**)

BRIEF 6.3   Layar

The first company to develop an augmented reality app for mobile for use with the first digitally shoppable magazine (published in November 2012) was Layar. Econsultancy reports:

> In the September 2013 issue of Seventeen, it was possible to scan over 220 pages with a mobile device and add any item to a shopping basket. It was also possible to create an in-app mood board to pin favourite clothes or styles, unlock discounts when scanning certain adverts and the ability to unlock bonus content such as videos and playlists. Zappar recently teamed up with Pedigree to add augmented reality to children's annuals making a compelling case for augmented reality's effectiveness in engaging with the consumer and in helping traditional print media integrate itself into the digital market. (Econsultancy, **https://econsultancy.com/blog/63574-augmented-reality-the-ikea-catalogue-and-beyond**)

Applications

An app is a downloadable piece of software that allows a user to carry out actions without the need to understand the software workings. An app can be used to display items in a supermarket and allow people to place an order; an app can be used to read QR codes. In today's hyper-competitive app marketplace, simply creating a great app isn't enough. You need a solid app marketing plan to make sure you can bring in the users you need to meet your goals. The best approach is to validate your marketing strategy with testing and benchmarking. Firms such as Fiksu offer a benchmark service, which test-markets your app and provides a detailed report that compares your likely costs to others in your app category, plus concrete recommendations for improvement.

BRIEF 6.4   Barclays turns payment app into one-stop shop

Barclays has revamped its peer-to-peer payment app, PingIt, to allow consumers to use the service to pay utility bills and to buy goods direct from billboards, magazine adverts and TV. In Barclays' words, the app aims 'to bridge the gap between advertising and sales by enabling consumers to purchase advertised goods and services'.

BRIEF 6.5   Mobile site building

Internet Retailing reports (**http://internetretailing.net/2014/03/uk-consumers-do-more-online-shopping-than-rest-of-europe-finds-google-as-it-launches-site-to-help-brands-exploit-mobile/**):

> *With consumers increasingly shopping and browsing on mobile, the new Google Multi-screen resources website offers advice, case studies, tips and insights to help businesses looking to set up or improve their mobile site: adapting or creating a website to work seamlessly across smartphones, tablets and desktops – it is a significant and on-going undertaking.*

Examples of success:

- Autoglass®, the vehicle glass repair and replacement specialist, invested in a mobile-optimized site in 2010 to reach more customers on the go and increase sales leads. Overall, mobile bookings are up by 11 per cent and clicks are up by 53 per cent year on year.

- Plusnet, a provider of broadband and phone services, built a website using responsive web design to facilitate site conversions on all devices and improve user experience. The business has seen online sales via smartphones and tablets grow tenfold year on year.

Multi-screen

The brand manager, retailer need to ensure they provide a multi-screen capability for the shopper. Google's top 10 tips for multi-screen site development are:

1 Be sure of search: make sure mobile users can easily access your site through search.

2 Focus on speed: smaller images and careful coding can help.

3 Design for key tasks: re-evaluate the key tasks for your mobile users and design for them.

4 Identify users' needs: your homepage should guide users to the right place.

5 Aid moving between screens: give ways to share and save content to revisit on another device.

6 Be touch-friendly: users should never feel the need to pinch and zoom.

7 Simplify checkout: use default inputs, user data and good error design for easier-to-use forms.

8 Don't rely on mouse overs: users on touch devices simply can't see them.

9 Customize, don't cut: offer the content and capability of the desktop, but customize, don't overload.

10 Prompt calls: provide buttons to start phone calls at potential conversion drop-off points.

According to Bronto:

> This expectation of mobile friendly content extends beyond site experience. With 48 per cent of e-mails opened on mobile devices (according to Litmus), the inbox needs to be able to make the transition between devices. This can be tricky considering the coding limitations of e-mail messages. Google are forecast to change this. (Bronto White Paper, **http://www.slideshare.net/digitalpymes/responsive-design-31304232**)

Implementation

The discovery that shoppers build a 'mind file' of a brand and products in their subconscious and, as one message element, seek peer reassurance through social media/verbal communication before purchase, a brand manager, supplier or retailer needs to make it easy for shoppers to click through or to be directed to social media. Genuineness of content is essential and attempts to influence comments will be discovered. The WauWaa brief below highlights how this can be achieved directly, otherwise general forums such as Twitter, Pinterest and Instagram will suffice. A website, app or any other new technology should be designed to allow 'browse and discover' rather than 'search and buy'.

CASE STUDY 6.1 Unilever Peperami 'Fanimal'

Objective: The purpose was to increase trail around the 2010 World Cup.

Strategy: To build relevance with the key 18–24-year-old bloke audience and appearing cool and engaging for under-16s.

Solution: To offer 1,000 impact-activated rubber shouting mascots with a repertoire of comically insulting phrases about rival teams, communicated on 10 million packs with entry via SMS and winners redeeming online.

Results: Sales uplift was nearly four times target with entries 50 per cent higher. Brand penetration increased from 13.6 to 14.4 per cent in a crowded marketplace. IPM Award 2013 Gold winner.

BRIEF 6.6   New model 'shoppers provide content' start-ups

WauWaa is a UK start-up that uses social media as content; the company targets first-time parents. The website allows users to share parenting emotions, problems and experiences; for both mums and dads it is engaging, interesting and compelling. The company describes the model as 'browsing and discovering' (as you would shop in a store) rather than the old 'search and buy'. The company offers products (the website is changed three times a week) that are suggested by parents; 51 per cent of first-time visitors to the site buy. Parents are encouraged to upload photos of the products in use (the products supplied are, however, photographed in a studio). Of those making contact with the site, 51 per cent do so via mobile (not tablet). The company aims to give a loving experience. It is real parents, with real topics, with a multi-cultural, multi-ethnic mix and a genuine passionate interest that cover topics such as pregnancy, birth and rearing children. Some 7,000 bloggers create the content, with more joining weekly. It is an engagement channel, not one seeking followers. The company describes this type of start-up as for millenials only. (Craftsy uses a similar model for making items in wool and material – users share experiences and advice and the company supplies the materials and tools. Brit is similar but covers a range of categories including cooking, DIY, crafts, technical items that are all uploaded and recommended by users then sourced and sold by Brit.)

BRIEF 6.7   New model for online fashion shopping: Dressipi

The challenge: How do you personalize recommendations for emotional purchases like fashion?

The solution: Dressipi offers free access to the digital equivalent of a personal stylist. By combining proprietary technology with the know-how of a team of expert stylists, Dressipi allows women to discover and put together the clothes, accessories and brands that fit their shape, style and personal preferences. It works when customers are purchasing new products and/or wanting to better utilize their existing wardrobe. The service is easy to use. Customers create their personal Fashion Fingerprint © which identifies their body shape, style, size, colour and brand preferences and the recommender then searches the universe of clothes to identify the products and combinations of products (outfits) that best match the individual's Fashion Fingerprint and the occasion for which they are dressing.

At point of purchase, Dressipi determines their best size for each individual brand and style of clothing. The Dressipi Size Finder app is also available to download as a Smartphone app.

Dressipi assigns between 30 and 50 consistent features/meta data to each garment of clothing (with varying levels of automation). For each customer there are approximately 70 data points and for each brand about 30. Using a number of algorithms, Dressipi then narrows down the hundreds of thousands of products available to a smaller unique set and the final 10 per cent of preferences are captured.

The Dressipi solution (combined with its data insights) is clearly delivering both efficiencies and real margin improvement (see Table 6.2).

TABLE 6.2   Dressipi vs the industry

	Dressipi Av	Industry Av
Conversion rate	5%	1%–3%
Av garment return rate	10%–15%	30%
Av email open rate	45%	18%
Av basket value	£91	£35.09
Sell-through	N/A	60%

Summary

Marketers must assume the speed of technology change will continue and should employ millenials (those under 30) to keep ahead of the competition. Communication is clearly heading towards a domination of mobile over all else. Who knows though: the Google glass or the mobile watch or indeed devices inserted into clothing may replace the mobile. A focus on social media content would seem to match the needs of the next generation, allowing the recommendation of peer users to highlight the products to buy for any group (segment) of customers as shoppers and buyers. This fits in well with the discovery of the need to build the shopper's 'mind file' and the requirement to receive messages from distinct sources.

Self-study questions

6.1 Describe new uses for the following in your company: a) NFCs, b) QR codes, c) augmented reality – download Blippar and Layar and try them out.

6.2 Why is mobile becoming the preferred communication channel?

6.3 What are its technical benefits?

6.4 What are its relationship benefits?

6.5 What are the pros and cons of e-mails vs text messages?

Active promotion: field marketing, one-to-one sales and the brand experience

07

This chapter is about delivering active promotions (see Chapter 4 for a discussion of suppliers). A key benefit of using suppliers is that they are aware of the law (see Chapter 13) as it affects active promotions, such as the Clean Neighbourhood Environment Act 2005.

There is some misunderstanding about the term 'field marketing'. Technically it is outsourcing the sales function (see *The Handbook of Field Marketing* by Alison Williams and Roddy Mullin). What is outsourced in detail is sales, experiential marketing, demonstrating, sampling, merchandising, audit and mystery shopping. If a firm's primary purpose is not selling but only promoting the recall, why not out-source it, just as many firms now outsource catering? FM staff are totally focused on ROI and the bottom line.

Field marketing has many sub-disciplines; the specific interest in this book is FM as a means of putting a message across. Some 34 companies operate within the sector in the UK; it is sector worth over £1 billion a year.

One-to-one sales

These can be experiential, a roadshow, events or exhibitions, and field marketing offers an instant fix, providing short-term extra staff for a product launch, providing brand experience, managing price changing, training your own staff, event management, crisis management, running an active promotion, manning a stand to provide brand presence at trade shows or professional shows. Credit card companies use FM staff to sign people up at Eurotunnel terminals. Companies such as Mars, BT and IBM use FM staff for selling.

The Experiential Marketing Committee offers this definition: 'Experiential marketing is a live and interactive marketing discipline, which builds positive emotional sensory engagement between a brand and its consumers.' It was Confucius who said, 'Tell me and I will forget; show me and may I remember; involve me and I will understand.' In the past few years there has been more emotional and sensory involvement of the audience by the introduction of theatre and creativity to gain their buy-in to the brand. This has become known as 'live brand experience' or experiential marketing. Although this FM discipline is not new, it is an interactive development of the events discipline and it is becoming increasingly recognized as such as more companies choose to specialize in it.

A roadshow is when a promotional activity moves around the country, for example when a radio station has promotional trips to different seaside resorts in the summer. An event is an activity that does not move; it may be promotional activity in a shopping centre, at an exhibition, in a car park or at a county show. Events can be conducted at more than one venue across the country, so the difference between a roadshow and an event is blurred. Roadshows and events can be truly experiential when they appeal to the consumer's senses and involve them in the brand and the activity.

The purpose of experiential marketing, roadshows and events is to generate brand awareness and brand loyalty in a lively and engaging manner through trial, sampling and interactive involvement that reflects the brand image and values. It is an entertaining way of putting a product or service in the public eye, generating positive awareness and drives sales. Clearly it has an impact on a brand's engram. This can also be a lively part of any integrated campaign, and events are becoming one of the key methods of attracting the consumer to participate with the brand and associate it with enjoyment. Interestingly, many venues such as shopping centres that have been used for years by field marketers are now actively looking for interactive, lively events on their premises. They wish to see their visitors entertained (and not hassled) as part of the pleasurable experience in the venue.

Experiential marketing at its best is a very creative event that will reflect the brand being experienced. It is creative in every sense of the word – in conception, visually, emotionally and in its execution. Obviously a balance has to be found between the impact and excitement of the activity and the logistics and safety aspects that must be in place before it goes live. Location, location, location – the venue is key to successful shopper participation.

Where to hold the event? Whether the event is a roadshow or a live brand experience, it must be held where the target consumer market is to be found in numbers, so that there are many positive experiences. For example, events held at music festivals and rock concerts will target young people (OK, except Glastonbury where there are lots of old too), events at popular seaside resorts are held to meet families, events on railway concourses target commuters. Car dealers use a new car launch event to offer test drives to existing customers of previous versions of the model, possibly adding excitement by arranging for the event to be held at a racing circuit.

Sampling and demonstrating

These are always face-to-face; that is, in the presence of an FM staff member, who guides the customer through the sampling or demonstrating process, notes any customer reaction and responds to it. Sampling is straightforward and often is a simple taste or smell opportunity, whereas demonstrating can be a more complex exercise where the consumer is shown how a product operates. While carrying out sampling or demonstrating, the FM staff will be communicating, describing the product or service, its features and benefits while informing and educating the listener. The FM staff person is the brand ambassador. A key difference between sampling and experiential marketing is that the latter uses the five senses to involve the customer, who is frequently a hands-on participant.

Sampling allows the consumer to trial the product or service. Food and drink, perfumes and aftershaves fit this sampling category. With 85 per cent of business in the UK coming from the service rather than the manufacturing base, many services also use sampling as an effective means of trial; the brand ambassadors will introduce the product to the customer by giving or showing them the sample, explain the benefits of the product and its USP, offer trials and raise brand visibility. During the sampling a short brand message can be delivered, and a leaflet can accompany samples where appropriate. The more memorable, lively and involving the activity that surrounds the trial, the better the product recall, and the greater the affinity between the consumer and the brand. By sampling the product, end users are not only made aware of the product, but they also know that they like it. They have knowledge of that product and this understanding will translate into future purchases. Samples may be handed out for later consumption, such as shampoos, newspapers, printed materials or software. There is a cross-over between sampling and experiential marketing.

Demonstrating is when the product or service is shown, explained and demonstrated to consumers: the consumer observes and sometimes has a go at using the product; for example mobile phones, tablets, vacuum cleaners or coffee-making machines. The value is that people who have sampled or been demonstrated to, now understand the product. People will always talk about a product and use it when they understand it and feel comfortable with it.

Merchandising

If a brand is not on the shelf, or not visible, it cannot be bought. This makes merchandising a crucial part of proclaiming product or service presence, and in ensuring good placement, correct pricing and product availability in sufficient quantities to meet demand and drive sales. Merchandising is also a very important part of brand awareness and the purchasing environment for the consumer – 70 per cent of purchasing decisions are made in-store. It involves making sure that the brand is obvious and available and it will generate sales by:

- placing POP or POS material in an outlet to promote the product;
- stacking the shelves with the correct number of products or varieties and number of facings so that availability is obvious;
- placing self-talkers advertising the product;
- building a secondary display, for example a free-standing display in an aisle, or a display on a gondola end in-store;
- installing a special promotion and placing all the communication for the activity;

- meeting with the staff in-store and promoting the brand to them, checking their ordering procedures and ensuring that systems are in place to avoid running out of stock.

The amount by which sales will be uplifted by merchandising activity will vary according to the product, position and environment but, as a guideline, a secondary display in a grocery multiple can lead to a minimum of 25 per cent uplift in sales and frequently much more. Merchandising can be a tactical or a strategic ongoing activity with POP materials regularly replaced and updated, which ensures that promotions and products are communicated with impact. If you have followed the process so far, you will understand the crucial ingredients in devising a well-considered merchandising campaign and its value in the sales journey.

FM merchandising discipline has become somewhat of a hybrid, borrowing parts of the elements of other disciplines, to include:

- visiting a retail outlet, establishing a rapport with the retailer (CRM), training the retailer's staff;
- discussing the retailer's stocks of the brand, the presentation of the brand and the profit the retailer can expect from the brand (sales);
- van and car sales: selling some of the product to the retailer, either from the merchandiser's car or by taking a transfer order (sales);
- conducting an audit to highlight the status of the brand in that outlet on entry and exit, defining the achievements of the call (auditing).

If merchandising calls of the hybrid type are conducted with the same retailer on an ongoing basis as part of a strategic contract, the rapport becomes stronger and more brands or product variants can be sold in to the retailer, extending the reach of the brand. By including so many steps in the visit, the outputs from the visit are maximized, which makes the best use of the merchandiser's time and, therefore, the budget.

Sales by a salesperson

This is more than 'order taking', which is when a person just takes payment and perhaps packs the item purchased. 'Sales' is selling, when a salesperson engages with shoppers to obtain their trust and confidence in the knowledge held by the salesperson. A trained salesperson will qualify the shopper and fact find. He or she will also discover where the shopper is in the buying process to match the sales process to the shopper. Only when the salesperson is assured that the shopper is ready will a 'sales close' be attempted.

After-sales service

A follow-up to a sale will discover useful feedback on the product or service and allow an opportunity to sell in more associated products and services and accessories. It builds the relationship and reinforces the engram.

Brand manager/retailer implementation

From the marketing plan the need for active promotion will have arisen. This could require experiencing the product or service, seeing it demonstrated, sampling it or extra sales support. This might also be considered as a contingency – plan for a crisis.

Consider how best this active promotion can be carried out and who you want to do what – the creativity element is key to attracting the shopper to take it up (see Chapter 3). Remember also to attract forward-looking shoppers such as 'future shapers' (see Chapter 2). Prepare a brief based on these considerations; general points from Chapter 11 may help here. Then consider next whether you need a supplier. Such additional professional sales assistance will make up for any staffing limitations that you have. They have a wealth of experience from which you can but benefit.

CASE STUDY 7.1   Dave's Man chair

Agency: Mediator

Client: Dave (TV)

Partner: Burton

Objective: Sample new content on Dave by showcasing new shows in truly memorable ways.

Strategy: Create a Dave brand experience; take it off air to interrupt the target audience in their non-viewing time.

Solution: Dave's Man chair celebrated men's dislike of shopping and provided a respite area for men across the United Kingdom to take a break from shopping and enjoy some new and world-class entertainment from Dave. Sited in 15 flagship Burton stores, the chairs housed a tablet containing exclusive Dave content, competitions, quizzes and podcasts to fully immerse customers in the Dave experience.

Results: An industry first achieving heavy-weight exposure for Dave's new shows in flagship stores nationwide over six months: 70,000 video views, 90,000 participants, 33 per cent uplift in ABC1 male 16–34 viewing, £1.4 million worth of media value generated year on year. Shows on the app performed 90 per cent above slot average. The campaign picked up an IPM Award 2013 in Commercial Partnership Marketing.

CASE STUDY 7.2   Classic FM

Agency: Mediator

Client: Classic FM Global Radio

Objective: Sample Classic FM to new audiences, promote the new breakfast show and remind existing listeners to tune in.

Strategy: Identify moments in the target audiences' lives when classical music complements their environment and activity.

Solution: Mediator negotiated a partnership with Hotel Du Vin to celebrate the launch of John Suchet's new breakfast show with a breakfast takeover in 14 hotels. The two-month campaign saw a specially mixed CD being played at breakfast time in restaurants and hotel lobbies and distributed to guests as a free gift during their stay. TVs in rooms were also tuned into the station, targeting guests on arrival. Both brands supported the campaign through their CRM communications

Results: 1.8 million people reached, 6:1 ROI, 100 per cent of respondents to a survey said they would take the CD home to listen to, 97 per cent of non-listeners said they were now more likely to tune in, 17,000 competition entries (70 per cent higher than average), 6.6 per cent increase in listeners during January–March 2011 while the partnership was live.

(**SOURCE:** Rajar/Ipos-MORI/RSMB, Q1 period ending March 2011)

BRIEF 7.1   Dyson product recall

Dyson has recently recalled some 1 million space heaters to install a safety cap. Think of the additional staff required to manage call centres, send out packaging, receive and fix the safety problem, return the heaters, as well as just promoting the recall. Dyson also gave a new 2-year warranty as an after-sales promotion.

BRIEF 7.2   'Unbelievable' Pepsi

In 2014 PepsiCo UK and Britvic are launching a three-week sampling campaign for Pepsi Max supported by TV sponsorship, in-cinema electronic displays, digital communication, and augmented reality outdoor advertising in city centres which will encourage fans to submit six-second videos of something unbelievable. The online content will be acquired from 'unbelievable talent', supported by an experiential sensory stunt in central London. It is being described as a bold and striking campaign designed to encourage cola users to try Pepsi Max.

BRIEF 7.3   The new Thompson/TUI digital holiday outlet

The shopper is invited, as a brand experience, to come and play with a large touch screen global map wall. Shoppers can examine where they have been and where they might want to go and describe their holiday preferences and the experiences they seek. Supporting screens show videos of facilities and bring to life the experience. The proposed holiday can then be e-mailed to the shopper for take-up later if he or she so wishes. Already some feedback has arrived from customers who have been on their bespoke holiday sending blogs (including selfies), which further encourages new shoppers featured on a community wall. The shop allows customers to take home a tailored brochure rather than a pile of catalogues (saving costs). The décor simulates a pool environment with golden lilos as seats. The staff are hand-picked and trained to make the experience fun, exciting and caring. As a result the brand appeal has improved.

BRIEF 7.4   New magazine launch

Shoppers were invited by brand ambassadors onto a stand in six different shopping centres to receive a shoulder and foot massage from trained masseuses. On completion, when they were relaxed after a pleasurable experience, they were offered a copy of the new magazine. Word spread. Local shops were well stocked with the new magazine and sales were recorded and reported as very good indeed.

BRIEF 7.5   Increasing professional body membership

A stand at an exhibition where there was a large number of potential members was staffed with a team who approached visitors asking if they were members. If not they explained the benefits of joining as members. The return was assessed as high.

BRIEF 7.6 Targeting independent off-licences for brands such as Stella Artois and Tennents

A bi-monthly visit by a team of 22 carrying stock achieved 3,200 new distribution points, with 26,542 POS items placed in store and 13,951 cases sold in six months. The aim was to show distribution, visibility and quality of alcohol brands not previously held. One off-licence went from selling zero to more than 20 cases per week.

BRIEF 7.7 Sunsilk product launch

To support the launch of a Sunsilk frizz control cream, eight women on four branded scooters with trailers visited 35 towns and distributed 1 million product samples over 20 days. The campaign was supported by advertising. Brand awareness increased as did brand recognition. The launch started the engram building of the 'mind file' process.

Summary

If you are offering a new product or service, an active promotion is probably the fastest way to get shoppers and buyers to learn about it and understand its benefits and features. If it is possible to encourage social media activity to obtain feedback on the product or service, this adds to the engram of the shopper.

Self-study questions

7.1 Write down the reasons your company might need an active promotion. Whom would you target and how would you communicate the active promotion to them?

7.2 What location would you select for what active promotion: a) a station concourse, b) a racecourse, c) a flower show, d) a shopping mall?

7.3 Why is merchandising important for a promotion?

Everywhere – promotions

The key point about a promotion is that it can be effective in every part of the promotional mix and can be used for every element of the offer. If used well, it can spice up any element of the Six Cs alongside any promotional tool.

Promotions within the 'promotional' mix

How does a promotion fit with the rest of the mix? The promotional mix describes the seven marketing communication alternatives that are available: To recap:

1 *Packaging/the engram:* the importance of having a unique hook on which a shopper or buyer can build their 'mind file' has been realized. A product packaging, logo, etc used as the engram has to be distinctive and readily recognized. A promotion is easy to add to a pack.

2 *Advertising:* paid-for space and time in broadcast, print media (including Point of Sale) or the new media (websites, interactive TV and mobile) and other paid-for communications; material can also be presented to the shopper as video or audio. The purpose is to inform, educate and build the 'mind file'. A promotion adds the extra excitement and fun.

3 *Publicity as an addition or speared to advertising:* information and opinion about your products or services carried by third parties. This is very powerful if you can get it. Celebrity chefs are excellent at raising sales of ingredients, utensils or 'gadgets'. Health and beauty correspondents are recommending anti-ageing creams; when they did this with a Boots own product described as 'the best', men were arriving in the United Kingdom from abroad with the product high on their shopping list from anxious beauty-seeking partners. Public Relations is when you pay an agency to stimulate publicity; a promotion alongside publicity makes it memorable. Social media is free, but is customer/shopper-generated publicity. A promotion stimulates the activity.

4 *Direct relationship marketing:* personal presentation to customers or prospects to which they can respond directly through filling in coupons, posting tip-ons, contacting call centres, e-mails, and using the new media – interactive TV, mobile advertising, text messaging and e-mails – all are a part of direct marketing. The promotion is a call to action; remember 55 per cent coupon response!

5 *Experiential marketing:* personal selling face-to-face where a personal presentation of products or services is made to customers, prospects or intermediaries carried out through a shop, exhibitions or demonstrations, allowing the shopper to 'test drive' or sample the product or service; personal selling at customer premises and merchandising. A promotion adds to the brandgram.

6 *Promotion:* incentives and offers that encourage people to behave in a particular way at a particular time and place, usually delivered by one of the other promotion tools. When it is a promotion in the retail space it is known as a sales promotion.

7 *Social media:* this could be considered as a sub-tool of publicity but as it is of importance to the shopper/buyer as one of the six message media it is included here separately. A business can respond to, stimulate and generate social media that has an impact on the 'mind file' of shoppers.

This division within the promotional mix helps in a number of ways. It gives a rough-and-ready definition of what each is able to contribute to the mix and helps companies decide which will be most useful in achieving particular marketing objectives.

Comparisons of the effectiveness of different types might help and Tables 5.1 and 5.2 should give you an idea at least. Mobile marketing of course depends on the permission of the customer. Table 5.1 shows that cinema ads are best at getting attention but the impact does not last. The internet and mobile marketing are moving ahead of the other media which reflects reality. Table 5.2 perhaps illustrates why experiential marketing is doing so well. The two tables if nothing else are designed to make you think about your target audience and how effective your planned promotion is likely to be with different media. Just how effective are promotions? Table 5.3 illustrates the difference when a promotion is added. So what can a promotion do?

The 12 core promotional objectives

There are 12 core promotional objectives that a promotion typically addresses:

1 increasing volume;
2 increasing trial;
3 increasing repeat purchase;
4 increasing loyalty;
5 widening usage;
6 creating interest;
7 creating awareness;
8 deflecting attention from price;
9 gaining intermediary support;
10 discriminating among users;

11   restoring brand perceptions and deflecting attention from complaints after operational mishandling of customer accounts;

12   retaining brand perception on service failure.

1. Increasing volume

The volume of product or service that you sell is, in the long run, dependent on a range of fundamental marketing factors defined in customer terms as 'the offer'. Promotions geared to increasing volume can never overcome deep-seated weaknesses, but they can be of considerable value in meeting short-term and tactical business needs such as to shift stock of an old model prior to a new introduction; to reduce inventories prior to their financial year end; to increase stockholding by retailers prior to the introduction of a competitor's product and to lift production to a higher level. Volume-generating promotions invariably bring in the marginal buyers, those who only buy when a product or service is 'on offer'. These buyers tend to be regarded by many companies with the distaste as promiscuous, but they do not form an exclusive group. The more people buy of a particular product category, the more brands within it they tend to buy. We are all promiscuous purchasers to some extent. A volume promotion can bring in marginal buyers to an improved product or service who may well stay with you thereafter.

Almost any promotion that provides an incentive to buy will help to increase volume. Price promotions used to be the most effective in the short term, but recent and continuing experience suggests this is no longer the case. They can be aimed at triallists, regular users or new markets; they can put the emphasis on intermediaries or on the final customer; and they can use a very wide range of the offers described in this book. What must be provided is a real and genuine incentive: a low-budget self-liquidator may massage consciences, but it will do nothing to shift volume. Two case studies in this book are examples of non-price volume promotions: Maxwell House (Case study 8.3) and Faber & Faber (Case study 9.25).

The variety of techniques available to increase volume carries its own weakness. It is better to be specific about where you expect to find the extra volume. This means linking the increased volume objective with one of the other objectives listed below.

2. Increasing trial

A major source of extra volume is those who have not used your product or service before or have not used it for a long time. For retailers, they would be people who have not visited their premises before. Increased trial is also a self-standing objective that is fundamental to the growth of any business.

Potential triallists have, by definition, no personal experience of your product or service. They may be using one of your competitor's products or services or none at all in your category. A number of offers are particularly effective in gaining increased trial:

● providing a free sample or a trial coupon so that people can try out your product or service;

- providing an additional benefit so that your product or service seems superior to others on the market;
- providing short-term financial benefits, such as good credit rates, so that it seems better value than others;
- doing something different and imaginative, such as an open day or special event that lifts it out of the general run.

Among the examples of trial promotions in this book are Bovril's sampling programme (Case study 8.4), and the 'Tango Bash' (Case study 9.1). These both focused on giving reasons for people new to (or lapsed from) the brand to try. Offers such as free extra product or those that require the purchase of large quantities of your product or service are unlikely to attract potential triallists. They will not, after all, want to buy it in volume until they know they like it.

3. Increasing repeat purchase

Repeat purchase promotions overlap considerably with volume promotions, as existing customers are most likely to be prepared to bring forward their regular purchases and buy in bulk. Repeat purchase promotions are also effective in achieving other marketing objectives, such as spoiling the launch of a competitive product and getting your customers into the habit of using your product to the exclusion of others. This can be particularly important in markets such as the pub trade and confectionery products where people habitually use a range of different brands, chopping and changing between them from day to day (a pattern known as 'repertoire purchasing').

Here are some of the offers that are particularly effective in increasing repeat purchase:

- coupons on the product giving discounts off the next purchase;
- specific incentives for multiple purchases, for example, 'buy three, get one free';
- collector promotions, such as collecting 10 tokens and sending for free merchandise or a cash refund.

Maxwell House (Case study 8.3) and Gale's honey (Case study 9.11) are both imaginative examples of promotions that target the need to increase repeat purchase. Promotions that are unlikely to be appropriate for increasing repeat purchase include door-to-door coupon drops and straight money-off flashes. They simply give the regular purchaser a discount without requiring a multiple purchase, which is very nice for the purchasers, but of no use to the promoter.

4. Increasing loyalty

Loyalty to a product or service is a much more subjective and personal quality than repeat purchase. It is possible to buy something on a regular basis because it is the cheapest and best, without feeling any loyalty towards it. Loyalty keeps you buying when (perhaps temporarily) it ceases to be the cheapest and the best.

An example of loyalty occurred in the early 1980s, when Ford replaced the Cortina with the Sierra. The early Sierras suffered from a number of teething troubles, and although Ford lost market share to Vauxhall's Cavalier, its extent was limited by Ford's high level of loyalty among motorists and fleet buyers. To paraphrase Winston Churchill: anyone can support you when you are right; friends are there to support you when you are wrong.

Most supermarkets in the United Kingdom have adopted loyalty promotions. They are designed to achieve a high level of personal identification and involvement with a company's product or service beyond the collection of points. They tend to be long running and to become integral to the way purchasers think about the product or service.

There are a number of types of promotion that work well in building loyalty:

- long-term collector promotions, where a wide range of merchandise branded with the product or service can be collected;
- clubs that people can join that offer a range of special benefits – these are particularly effective for children's products;
- factory visits, roadshows and other direct-contact promotions, which bring purchasers into personal contact with the people behind the product or service.

A good example of a loyalty promotion is Shell's Smart card (Case study 9.6); the two 'Music for schools' promotions run by Jacob's Club and the Co-op (Case study 11.4) are also relevant. In their different ways, they link closely to the interests of their consumers.

Immediate cash discounts to those who are not members of the scheme have no place in loyalty promotions. Their objective is to supersede immediate cash considerations by appealing to longer-term benefits. This is one of the major ways in which value promotions can contribute to long-term brand value.

5. Widening usage

Very often a product or service will be widely used in only one of the many possible ways. For example, many households buy honey, very infrequently, to use as a spread. A minority of households use it in great quantity as a cooking ingredient. Telling people how to use honey in cooking is therefore an important objective for honey processors.

Sometimes a company will have to widen the usage of a product or service because its original use is fast disappearing. The transatlantic shipping companies had to do this when people stopped seeing ships as a mode of travel, and had to be persuaded to start perceiving them as a form of holiday. Promotions can be very effective in widening the usage of a product or service in a number of ways:

- by physically linking the product or service with something else already in the new usage area, for example issuing trial samples with another product;
- by offering books or pamphlets that are of value in themselves and explain new ways to use the product or service, for example a cookbook offered by food brand;

- by creating a non-physical link with something else already in the new usage area, via coupons or joint promotions with another company, for example coupons from a travel agent for winter ski gear.

Widening usage will almost always be achieved by a combination of promotional tools, including advertising and publicity. There is often huge consumer resistance to overcome, for example to the idea that you should put Mars bars in the fridge or drink sherry with a mixer. The Lee & Perrins promotion for Worcestershire sauce (Case study 9.12) is a good example of extending usage of a very distinctive product.

Money-off or other cash-related promotions will not help at all in this. The right kind of value promotion can encourage purchasers to make the leap and try out the new usage of your product or service. Only when they've done that will they be convinced that what you have said in your advertising is true.

6. Creating interest

This can seem a very woolly objective, and is often avoided in favour of something that seems more specific, such as 'increasing volume'. Many consumer markets are mature and offer limited scope for product differentiation. Providing a reason to buy one product rather than another can be as simple as creating interest and excitement.

It is no accident that our ancestors punctuated the year with a series of festivals, fairs and holy days. Life becomes very boring if it proceeds at a regular, uninterrupted pace. Purchasing products and services is exactly the same. Out of sheer boredom, purchasers can decide to buy something else or go somewhere else. Creating interest in your product or service by means of a promotion is a way of keeping purchasers with you. It is a matter of ringing the changes, having something fresh to offer, and keeping interest and enthusiasm on the boil.

The principle has long been understood by people who run successful businesses. One of Jesse Boot's colleagues recalled the early days of what became the Boots chemists chain in the 1880s: 'Always, Mr Boot had something striking, something to make people talk about Boots.' Richard Branson of Virgin has similarly had people talking about his companies as a result of a constant stream of striking innovations, stunts, offers and promotions.

Value promotions that create interest are characterized above all by their humour, inventiveness, topicality and style. Examples include:

- being the first to offer a new product or service as a promotional premium;
- linking up with a celebrity or relevant charity;
- finding a totally new way to do something that people enjoy doing.

British Airways' offer of tickets on Concorde in spring 1997 achieved a massive 30 million responses. Older examples include the treasure hunt for a buried hare featured in the book *Masquerade* and later copied (with disastrous results) by Cadbury's Crème Eggs; the telephone Trivial Pursuit game run by Heineken lager; and the enormously successful 'tiger in your tank' campaign by Esso in the 1960s, which had millions of cars driving around with a tiger tail hanging from their petrol cap. Case study 3.6 on Eversheds shares these qualities.

7. Creating awareness

For new or re-launched products, creating awareness is a key objective. This is a different challenge to that faced by mature brands, where the aim is to maintain interest. It is often assumed that creating awareness is a job for media advertising. In fact, there are a number of promotions that are very effective at making people aware of products:

- joint promotions with another product or service that is already well known in a particular market;
- link-ups with charities or voluntary groups that have a relevant image;
- the production of books or educational materials for schools and the general public.

Generating awareness is a wholly legitimate business objective, particularly in industries where purchases are infrequent and for new brands. Major brands, for example the Body Shop, Häagen-Dazs and Swatch watches, were launched and developed largely through promotional activity. In the case of the Body Shop, it included the active engagement of customers in campaigning against animal testing. Häagen-Dazs used placements in leading restaurants and selective arts sponsorship. Swatch hung giant watches from buildings and early on built a customer club. The 'Tango Bash' (Case study 9.1) is also an example of this kind of promotion.

Crucial to such ideas is the understanding that people are selective in the attention they pay to advertising. There are more than 9,500 brands in the United Kingdom that advertise enough for their advertising to be recorded by MEAL. How many can you name? Most people run out of names after a few hundred. Promotional activity can cut through this selective attention.

8. Deflecting attention from price

An obsession with price on the part of your customers is dangerous. It can readily lead to price wars, which have a destructive effect on company profitability. Price wars are a form of mutual masochism into which many industries fall from time to time until, finally weary and impoverished, they find more sensible ways to compete with each other.

The purpose of a great deal of advertising is to replace price considerations with a focus on features such as quality, brand identity, performance and loyalty. That way companies can compete effectively and achieve attractive margins.

Both price and value promotions are part of the armoury companies have at their disposal to do this. The key is to offer benefits that justify a higher price and cost less than an equivalent price cut. If your product is priced at 10p more than your competitor's and that differential cannot be justified on intrinsic grounds, you can either discount by 10p to achieve price parity or offer an extra benefit that costs you 9p or less and looks at least as attractive.

A very wide range of promotional offers can achieve this objective. Among the main ones are:

- variations on price cuts, ranging from 'pence off next purchase' and 'buy three, get one free' to cash-back or cash share-out offers that appear more valuable than a straight price cut;

- making price comparisons less direct by offering extra-fill packs, short-term multi-packs, joint packs, or part of the product or service free, for example;

- long-term collector promotions, such as Shell's Smart card promotion (Case study 9.6), which can seem more interesting than price cuts.

SMP's promotion for Gale's honey (Case study 9.11) is a good example of deflecting attention from the premium price of branded honey. In 2007 the forecast shortage of honey was likely to push the price up further, and the need to deflect attention was likely to be greater. It is a constant challenge for manufacturers of brands in markets in which retailers' own-label products have taken a significant share. Part of the success of Kleenex facial tissues in the last 10 years has been the extent to which its active promotional campaigns have limited the market share of cheaper own-label tissues (Case study 11.1).

9. Gaining intermediary support

Some products and services rely very heavily on the support of wholesalers, distributors, agents, retailers and other intermediaries. Others, sold directly to the end user, still benefit from the support and recommendation of other businesses. And every business benefits from word-of-mouth recommendation from one satisfied customer to another.

All these people can be regarded as intermediaries. Gaining their support ranges from being absolutely crucial to simply important, and there are a number of sales promotion techniques that businesses can use to this end. Among the key ones are:

- specific programmes directed at wholesalers, retailers, agents and distributors to gain distribution, display and cooperative advertising;

- 'member get member' schemes, which reward customers for introducing new people to you;

- promotional events aimed at the media and other decision-making influencers.

Gaining display is a central objective for promotions run by manufacturers who sell via retailers, wholesalers, distributors or other intermediaries. It is often the display that results in extra sales, but it is the promotion that secured the display in the first place.

Display can take many forms: extra shelf space, a gondola end (the end of a shelving rack), a window bill, the display of door stickers, the use of point-of-sale material, the presence of leaflets or the installation of a dump-bin or special display rack. It is all about achieving extra prominence for your product or service.

A number of promotional offers are effective in achieving display:

- incentives directed at store managers and sales assistants, or free offers targeted at those who make the orders, as in the direct ordering of stationery items, where the person placing the order is offered a personal gift;
- price offers that enhance the margin to the intermediary;
- the production of attractive, compelling offers of every kind that the intermediary believes will provide it with an advantage – tailor-made promotions, which run only in one store group, are particularly effective.

There is a close relationship between trade and consumer promotion in the retail trade. If a promotion succeeds with the trade but lacks a strong consumer element, it may still succeed with the consumer simply because of the display and volume support of the retailer. However, the reverse is not true: a promotion with a strong consumer element that does not appeal to the trade is unlikely to succeed with either.

Examples of effective promotions to intermediaries include Zantac 75 (Case study 11.2) and the Electrolux campaign for the X8 (Case study 9.17).

10. Discriminating among users

A large number of businesses, such as hotels, airlines, train companies and leisure facilities, face three unavoidable market factors: 1) they have high fixed costs in providing the service, which do not vary significantly with the number of people using it; 2) usage varies considerably from time to time; and 3) different people are prepared to pay different amounts for the service and accept different levels of restriction. This has been particularly true of air travel.

This last factor enables businesses to manage fluctuations in demand. The price paid for an airline ticket varies depending on the time and day of the flight, the degree of flexibility allowed, how long in advance the ticket was booked, the type of seat purchased, the purchaser's participation in a loyalty scheme and the outlet where it was booked. The objective that airlines and similar businesses share is to maximize the revenue per seat – and that means avoiding giving better terms to those who do not need them at the same time as giving the optimum terms to those who do.

For these businesses, promotional thinking is at the heart of marketing strategy, and they use a number of mechanisms:

- Customers who are motivated by price are self-selected. They book early or via particular outlets and so on, while those who are less motivated by price do not.
- The difference between business and leisure travel is marked by requirements to spend a Saturday night away to qualify for leisure pricing. Business users are, in turn, given special discounts on leisure flights.
- Particular groups are given additional benefits not available to others. For example, families and the retired can buy train tickets at a price not available to others.

Taken to its logical conclusion, discriminating among users allows companies to develop particular packages of product, price, distribution and promotion for different categories of user. The major challenge is to keep the boundaries between them clear, so that those prepared to pay higher prices do not take advantage of lower prices. This in turn means that offers are often deliberately short term, focusing the benefits on those most motivated to take advantage of them.

11. Restoring brand perceptions

Some of the more astute banks, utilities and communications companies that typically charge customers automatically on a monthly basis are finding a new way to handle customers who complain. They offer a promotion. The complaints are often justified, particularly from a customer perspective. Automation of the operation is usually the culprit. For example, bank (and bank credit card) customers have found that if they omit to pay a few pence on a £100 charge they will still incur the full late payment charge because the response is automated. Where a mobile telephone company offers three months' free insurance cover on purchase, automation adds the insurance cost to the invoice for subsequent months and, as there is a one-month notice requirement for termination, customers end up at minimum paying for two months' cover they did not ask for. It is unclear that acceptance of the free coverage at the time of purchase implies acceptance of the insurance terms. On takeover of a telephone business, a telephone company adds in a handling charge for non-direct debit customers or fails to provide a 'payment by' date so that late payment charges are raised unwittingly through automation of which the customer is unaware. What some banks, offering their credit cards to third parties, say a petrol retailer, have yet to realize is that they can damage the third-party brand at the same time as damaging their own brand.

When a customer complains, a way to mollify the customer (particularly to avoid the involvement of regulators) is to offer additional services but at a reduced overall cost (say one that is being offered to new customers anyway). Or when an insurance product is accidentally run on, despite customer cancellation, to keep the door open to a customer returning in a future year a financial reward is offered to maintain the brand perception as favourable. The key is to balance the time and resource following up complaints with a recognition that the offer of some form of sales promotion deflects the person complaining. It also saves the often huge investment in a brand, which may have taken years to grow, from a dissatisfied customer's potential adverse perception of the brand, all arising as a result of automation and a failure to handle a complaint.

12. Retaining brand perception on service failure

The borderline between what is a contracted service and what is implied or an expected extra service is no longer straightforward. Passengers expect a refund if a train is cancelled. Airlines offer free drink and food when there are delays. To attract customers, garage servicing companies offer courtesy cars. But what happens if there is a shortfall, say in the case of the garage? The customer can be distracted with the offer of an alternative to retain the goodwill, for example a voucher to allow free entry to an event or attraction. It is simply offering a promotion at a different point in the cycle. The key is contingency planning and training of staff in what to do when a hold-up or disaster strikes, with the sales promotion immediately on hand to restore customer faith in the brand.

Value and price promotions

The key phrase is 'add value'. 'Value promotions' essentially give an extra benefit. Ways to add value are to offer extra features, such as a free mail-in item, a chance to win a prize, a special container or some other benefit over and above the normal product offering. They often have a positive impact on brand value. Value promotions include:

- free draws;
- mail-in premiums;
- container promotions;
- competitions.

There are promotions that cut price, called 'price promotions'. These offer the concept at a reduced price, or with a favourable finance deal, or on a buy-now, pay-later basis, or with a coupon against the present or future purchase. In doing so, there can be a negative impact on brand value, particularly if it is a 'me too' price offer. Price promotions can seriously undermine the added value that years of advertising have built up. A study has shown that most price promotions, though helping in the short term, end up lowering the price people are prepared to pay for brands. Many advertisers believe that a price promotion is a short-term fix that detracts from long-term brand building. On the plus side, a price promotion can put your product in the hands of customers for them to experience. This can affect behaviour positively and of course during that time they are not using a competitor's product. Price promotions include:

- money-off coupons;
- money-off flashes;
- buy one, get one free;
- extra-fill packs.

There is some doubt over where some promotions lie; for example, some believe extra-fill packs ('33 per cent extra free') belong in the 'value' not the 'price' category. If you want to put them there, you will be in good company – but remember that they can reduce the price people are prepared to pay for the standard size and that can come to the same thing as a price cut.

The logic of value promotions is clear to see. There is evidence that these contribute not only to short-term sales, but also to long-term brand value. The 'Hay Fever Survival' campaign (Case study 11.1) is an excellent example. The case for price promotions is more difficult, and they have been criticized by eminent industry people.

Why do companies use promotions that can undermine brand value? The reason is competition. For most of the last half of the 20th century, the detergent manufacturers Procter & Gamble and Lever Brothers were locked in a titanic battle. Their leading brands competed for performance superiority, communicated by single-minded product-performance advertising. The classic 'side-by-side' comparisons of clothes washed in Daz against those washed in another powder were once considered a definitive form of TV advertising. Product innovation has been far-reaching and relentless.

These two giants also spent massively on price promotion. In the early 1960s, 95 per cent of packs of Procter & Gamble and Lever Brothers' detergents carried a price promotion offer of one kind or another, from a money-off flash to a discount off the next purchase. The situation was mad – and known to be mad. One day it stopped: Daz launched a 'near-pack' premium promotion involving plastic flowers (Case study 9.15). Millions of families collected plastic roses from Daz in the following years. By the late 1970s, however, the majority of detergent packs once again featured money-off flashes and coupons. Retailers have also veered between price and value promotions. Case study 9.10 looks at 20 years of Tesco's promotional activity, which has swung between the two. Unbelievably Tesco in 2014 has initiated another price war, with Morrisons following suit.

Sometimes price promotions can be catastrophic for the company concerned. In 1996, the electrical retailer Comet made an offer for its competitor Norweb. Norweb held out for more, which was refused, and then began an extensive campaign of 0 per cent finance offers. Comet decided not to match them. Instead, whenever customers asked about finance, it directed them to Norweb. Comet's margins went up, and Norweb was crippled by the cost of its promotion. Soon afterwards, Comet was able to buy Norweb at a lower price than it had offered before.

What do these stories tell us? Price promotions can drag a company or a whole industry into penury. However, they are not the cause of penury. Rather, they are the symptom of competition that is so intense that it lays hold of every tool at its disposal, even if some of them are self-destructive. Price promotions are not the ideal way of competing. They are sometimes seen as unavoidable in the marketplace, which makes it even more important to understand how they work, and the circumstances in which they can be less rather than more destructive. The work on the engram indicates that price is not the key shopper mover, though it is high on the list.

One of the things to watch is the evidence from opinion polls that people prefer price cuts to any other form of promotion. Sometimes companies make use of this in their advertising. During the spate of petrol promotions in 1986–7, Jet ran a series of poster ads with the slogan '98 per cent of motorists prefer cheaper petrol'. Not for us, they were saying, all those tacky gimmicks; we just offer lower prices. Shell meanwhile achieved huge gains in market share with its 'Make money' promotion. People may say they prefer cheaper petrol (attitude), but they often buy more expensive petrol supported by promotional offers (behaviour). In 1997, Shell and Esso were taking two very different approaches to this – one with a value promotion, the other with a price promotion (Case study 9.6). It's interesting to note that Jet was also actively engaged in value promotions, winning a European sales promotion award for its non-price collector promotion.

Keeping the distinction between price and value promotions clearly in mind is essential to making sense of the subject. The core of sales promotion is the attempt to influence behaviour here and now, and these are the two ways you can do it. It may contribute to a change in attitude, but that is not its primary task. A definition you may like to consider would run like this:

> A promotion is a range of price and value techniques designed within a strategic framework to achieve specific objectives by changing any part of the offer, normally for a defined time period.

Promotions vs social media

In March 2013 research by Atom reports Unilever has confirmed that it is reappraising its approach, having found that in-store promotions beat social media ROI, delivering a 50 per cent higher return on investment. Unilever had shifted large parts of brand budgets to social media but a recent evaluation has shown it is undertaking more in-store promotional activity too! Promotions using vouchers, coupons and discount codes for shoppers to present at the time of purchase tend to support the Atom findings: effectiveness is covered in reports by Valassis (who manage 86 per cent of UK coupons) which show a 14 per cent rise in redemptions year on year (2011 versus 2012) with retailer issues beating manufacturers' redemptions. (There is more on promotions in Chapter 12.)

The following case studies illustrate the central points made in this chapter about relationships, behaviour and the capacity of sales promotion to change every other part of the offer.

CASE STUDY 8.1   Henkel Off Guard Gigs

Right Guard, after its acquisition by Henkel, targeted a younger male audience around music, to give them the opportunity to experience the brand. Off Guard Gigs, with focused online content and social networking, were created in collaboration with Yahoo music to provide an exclusive brand experience, alongside a competition to win a seat in the campaign's VW camper van at festivals. Winning a gold award at the ISP 2009 awards, the judges praised the repositioning of the brand in such a unique and creative way through taking ownership of music.

CASE STUDY 8.2   MasterCard World Cup on-trade activity

With the objective of increasing usage of its card in pubs (changing behaviour), MasterCard (Arc Worldwide) capitalized on World Cup fever. Despite having no established relationship with the on-trade it succeeded in recruiting 903 bars. High-impact POS encouraged customers to pay with MasterCard, entitling them to an instant win game card. One in five cards rewarded the customer with a football-related prize (including foam hands, face paints, *Crap Teams* books and World Cup DVDs). Win or lose, they could text their details to be included in a prize draw to win tickets to football matches at five top European stadiums over a two-week holiday. Awareness was raised with TV screen and washroom media.

MasterCard's share of transactions increased by 39 per cent, and 42 per cent of customers said that they would be likely to use their card in this environment in the future. Mystery shoppers reported that 58 per cent of outlets visited were 100 per cent POS and TV screen-compliant. MasterCard was a gold award winner in the ISP 2007 awards.

CASE STUDY 8.3   Maxwell House

Maxwell House is the number two brand in the highly competitive instant coffee market, dominated by Nestlé's Nescafé. How was it to persuade repertoire purchasers (those who buy Nescafé and other brands from time to time) to buy Maxwell House? And how was it to persuade existing users to buy the brand more often?

Agency Triangle Communications' answer was a major promotional 'Out of the blue' event that took place on-pack, on TV and in events around the country. The basic mechanic was a free draw. Consumers were invited to win £500,000 of cash prizes by entering via on-pack coupons or 'plain paper' (ie who had not bought the product could enter by writing in on a piece of paper). Noel Edmonds phoned 100 winners 'out of the blue' from the Maxwell House hot air balloon. The phone calls were featured on TV ads as a live dialogue, giving viewers the responses of winners to hearing they had won cash prizes of £2,000 to £10,000. Meanwhile, the balloon made a series of visits to events around the country, creating a direct link between brand, balloon and offer. The novelty of the delivery of the free draw created extensive PR coverage: 500,000 entries were received, the brand achieved its highest market share for six years, and in the promotional period its share was 50 per cent more than it had been the previous month.

This was a free draw on a massive scale, but the mechanic was simplicity itself. What characterized it was the involvement of Noel Edmonds, the novelty of the means of contacting winners, the use of live dialogue on TV and the close link with the brand's mainstream advertising. The promotion won two ISP gold awards.

CASE STUDY 8.4   Bovril

Everyone knows Bovril. It's one of those brands you can't remember not knowing. It's not constantly in your mind though, and people lose the habit of drinking it. For some years, Bovril has had a strategy of reminding people that, when you are cold or wet or in flagging spirits, a drink of Bovril cheers you up and sustains and nourishes you. It is one of those messages that can be put across by advertising, but is very much more powerful when it is experienced.

Agency Promotional Campaigns Group, acting for Bovril, arranged to offer samples of Bovril at 467 bonfire night parties, which are cold, damp and often wet. Bovril linked with local radio stations and charities organizing firework displays. Kits of paste, cups and promotional material were supplied free. Charities could raise funds by accepting donations for cups of Bovril. Local radio stations were offered the opportunity to provide roadshows at the largest events and to trail the events with both DJ plugs and paid-for advertising.

Two million people attended the sponsored bonfire nights, over 5 million were reached by radio coverage and 520,000 people were sampled with Bovril at a fraction of the cost of door-drop methods. Sales rose by 4 per cent over the year. Bovril did not have to create bonfire night – it was already there. The ingenuity of the promotion was recognizing it as a perfect sampling occasion at exactly the right time in the year to promote sales. The executional skill was to provide charities and radio stations with a reason to be involved in the delivery of the promotion. Extended over time, the promotion offered Bovril a direct link with a popular annual tradition.

CASE STUDY 8.5   Sainsbury's

A promotion's capacity to impact directly on consumer behaviour can be used to good ends and bad. Sainsbury's 'Schoolbags' promotion is an example of a promotion that achieved business objectives along with social and environmental ones.

Sainsbury's faced two unrelated challenges: it needed to increase its appeal to families; and it needed to tackle the financial and environmental cost of nearly 100 million carrier bags issued every year at a cost of £20 million. These challenges were brought together by the agency Promotional Campaigns Group in a promotion that provided a reason for families with children both to shop at Sainsbury's and to reuse their carrier bags. The link was raising money to buy equipment for schools. The mechanic was simple. Customers were offered a 'Schoolbags' voucher at the checkout for every carrier bag they reused. These vouchers could be used by schools to obtain equipment, starting with a pack of crayons for 120 vouchers. Schools were recruited to the scheme via direct mail, and the promotion was advertised in store, on TV and in the press.

The promotion succeeded in all its dimensions. Over 10 per cent of Sainsbury's carrier bags were reused, saving 900,000 litres of oil in their manufacture and £2 million in cost. A total of 12,000 schools (about half the total in the country) and a million families participated. The nature of the mechanic will have ensured a substantial incentive to making repeat visits to Sainsbury's. The schools benefited too: they claimed about £4 million of equipment.

This promotion is a good example of hitting more than one objective at the same time, and doing so with a simple mechanic that is easy to communicate via a multiplicity of media.

CASE STUDY 8.6   Scrumpy Jack rural retreats

Erosion of market share arising from rival new products entering the category led to the campaign, described as the quintessential on-pack promotion that affirmed Scrumpy Jack's premium credentials and winning the ISP's 2009 Gold Award for Small Budget Campaigns. Scrumpy Jack's on-pack promotion offered prizes of weekend retreats with an SMS and online entry mechanic. An existing on-trade creative was used to keep costs down, while each retreat supplied visuals free. The campaign achieved a 37.1 return on ROI with a 26.3 increase in off-trade sales.

Summary

Promotions are primarily tactical in nature, but can be part of a long-term strategy. They must be understood in the context of the functional, economic and psychological benefits with which firms seek to meet customer needs. Promotions are a means of influencing behaviour, and alter every part of the marketing mix to do so.

This chapter has set out how a promotion fits into the central business challenge of building relationships that confer differential advantage. It does so as a process that focuses on behaviour and in two different ways: price promotions and value promotions.

There are reasonable criticisms of certain types of promotion that undermine rather than enhance brand value. Tacky and dishonest promotions have no place in long-term relationships. The manager who understands the place of promotion in the firm's strategy will be best placed to manage the risk of using the many techniques available.

Self-study questions

8.1 What are the 12 promotional objectives that sales promotion tackles? How many does and should your organization use?

8.2 You are a newspaper retailer selling at stands outside the Chelsea Flower Show in May, when the weather is likely to be hot and dry, or cold and wet. What promotions as a contingency would you consider offering alongside the newspaper?

8.3 What complaints do customers make most often in your organization? What sales promotion might you offer to restore your brand's values?

The five standard promotional offers

There are five standard promotional offer types. Each of them is described and summarized in this chapter, relevant case studies added and self-study questions asked. For all the variety of promotional objectives, there are some offers that come up again and again, because they work again and again. There is an entire industry that creates and supplies these offers to promoters; the voucher market is worth around £5 billion (UKGC & VA, 2014). Vouchers are a 'stored-value or prepaid solution' in print or electronic form. Many of them revolve around travel, hotels, theatres, theme parks, films and insurance.

They often offer a benefit out of all proportion to the cost to the promoter, such as something worth £50 to your customers that only costs you £1. Of course, the £49 has to come from somewhere. An immense amount of ingenuity is put into devising offers of this kind, and most of them are largely funded by a third party. There are some very good offers as well as some distinctly dodgy ones. Before using any of them, it is essential to understand how they work, what the people supplying them are getting out of them, and what conditions apply to their use.

Off-the-shelf offers

The leading off-the-shelf offers that businesses can use are included here, along with what to look out for and the questions to ask anyone selling you the latest 'unmissable' offer. By following the rules, you can snap up excellent deals and avoid leaving behind you a trail of disappointed and angry customers. Remember, promotions are constantly changing so you should make your own enquiries before using any particular offer.

Free accommodation

The offer
Free hotel room offers date back to 1971 and have been going strong ever since. The concept is simple: you purchase a number of free-room vouchers from a specialist

operator, which can be used by your customers to obtain free accommodation at a specified range of hotels. The stipulations vary. In the past the standard requirement was that consumers bought breakfast and dinner at the hotel, but people became wary of overpriced hotel meals. The offer now tends to be 'two nights for the price of one'.

How it works

The logic of this offer is strong. Hotels have a high level of fixed costs: whatever their occupancy rate, they still have to pay their capital costs and most of their staff. An empty room is revenue lost for ever. The 'free room' concept meets the needs of hotels to fill rooms rather than leave them empty. Satisfied guests can also be expected to return at a later date, paying the full rate.

Of course, if a hotel offered deals of this kind to everyone, it would soon go out of business. So the offer must be restricted to people who would not otherwise come, those who genuinely are 'extra customers'. Free-room deals are therefore communicated by companies that put together a list of hotels on a national basis and make the offer available as a promotional tool. A newly opened hotel may also supply very low priced or free rooms, particularly suited to those with time on their hands – and money to spend on extras. SAGA, for example, and its members, is a user here.

What to look out for

Some operators are better than others, and the concept is still getting a bad name as a result of some cowboy operators. All this rubs off on the companies that use such a promotion. Giving your customers a duff promotion is bad business, and ignorance is no excuse. The answer is to select a reputable company that has been operating free rooms for some years, has a well-controlled and regularly inspected hotel network and adopts a long-term and professional approach. The characteristics that distinguish a good operator from a bad one are straightforward:

- Does it operate a central reservations system?
- Does it ensure that bargain breaks offered by its hotels outside the free-room service do not devalue that offer?
- Does it recommend (and insist on) a description of your promotion that accords with the industry codes of practice?
- Does it provide evidence that the list of hotels is regularly inspected and updated?

Three-night offers are typically valid in small-chain hotels, longer breaks in medium-chain hotels. Some operators also offer a 'club membership', which costs more but is for any number of three-night breaks in a 12-month period. Others offer a 'holiday bond' that gives £500 or £1,000 worth of accommodation costs and amounts to much the same over an extended period. Costs to the promoter for all these offers are substantially discounted for large quantities.

Free rooms have deservedly been working successfully for years and have been used to enormous effect by a range of companies, from banks to motor manufacturers. Usage of the vouchers is often as high as 30 per cent, which indicates the high regard consumers have for them. The secret of successfully using this offer, and most of the others in this chapter, is an accurate match to promotional objectives.

Holiday vouchers

The offer

Holiday vouchers give customers a saving when they book almost any package holiday. The saving can be given in a variety of ways: as a cash discount, a shopping voucher, or any other item of equivalent value.

The advent of cheap flights and booking everything online has meant these sorts of offers are probably taken up less, but for plenty of people a holiday offer is still a great opportunity.

How it works

Customers achieve the savings by posting their holiday vouchers to a nominated specialist travel agent, together with the completed booking form from the back of a tour company's brochure. The travel agent deducts the value of the vouchers from the cost of the holiday.

What to look out for

There are very few drawbacks to this offer. Most people are quite capable of collecting their holiday brochures, making their choice of holiday and completing the operator's form at the back. Most websites show views, videos and 360 degree aspects of accommodation, facilities and attractions, so travel agents have little else to offer unless they have personal knowledge of the destination.

There are six main things to look out for in these firms:

1 Are they ABTA, IATA and ATOL bonded to act as travel agents?

2 Do they have experience of running this offer? It is very easy for an inexperienced firm to get its margins wrong and end up going out of business, leaving your customers high and dry.

3 Is it the best deal available? Working this out requires some simple calculations to establish the level of discount being offered. If it is not a very good deal, it is not likely to motivate your customers.

4 Are the conditions realistic? Some operators insist on at least two adults booking. This may be restrictive if you are selling to single people. Others insist that people take out holiday insurance; you should check that their price for insurance is reasonable.

5 What upfront price are you paying to participate? This varies greatly and should be in proportion to the value of the saving to your customer. The nearer a holiday voucher operator gets to rebating the whole discount, the more it is reasonable to charge you. Some will, of course, try to charge you at a high level as well as hanging on to a large chunk of the discount.

6 Are all the relevant operators' brochures included? Almost everyone includes the main brochures, but if your market is young people, for example, you should check that specialist brochures directed at them are also included.

Discount 'coupons' books

The offer

The original scheme was the purchase of books of coupons, revived recently by among others the Westfield Shopping Centre. Several firms create and promote books of coupons that give savings on a range of theme parks, family days out, restaurants, cinemas and services such as dry cleaning and film processing, and some of them are off-the-shelf.

The tourism industry is a great user of vouchers in leaflets and booklets; Tourist Information offices have plenty of them. It becomes economic to overprint a standard product with your own brand name and message in quantities of over 1,000. Direct Line insurance has offered, through door drops, a booklet of vouchers for its own products. The form of the saving varies greatly within each book. The main variants are a 10 per cent discount, a £3 cash saving, children free with adults, one admission free with a full-price admission, or one free course in a meal for two people. They vary as widely as this because each participating outlet determines the deal it wants to offer.

Discount coupon books are different from product coupons redeemable in supermarkets and household shops, and gift cards and store vouchers (both covered later). There are also discount deals and coupon offers from such sites as **www.vouchermole.co.uk** and local deals from **www.groupon.co.uk**.

Most of the discount books are themed on entertainment and leisure. For example, Barclays Bank wanted a reward for 16–18-year-olds opening a bank account. Entitled 'Student cash code', it offered savings with Red or Dead, Fosters, WH Smith, the Youth Hostel Association, Pilot Fashion, Sony Music, Deep Pan Pizza, Warner Bros cinemas and others. On the theme of 'Get together with your mates', Ruddles inserted a 12-voucher book offering over £200 in savings in four-packs sold in the off-licence trade. The vouchers were redeemable in places such as the SnowDome, the London Dungeon and the American Adventure Theme Park. The unit cost to the promoter was (at the time) about 20p. For large quantities, specials can be constructed. The cost has remained surprisingly cheap.

Newspapers (*Financial Times*, *Daily Telegraph*) offer 'lunch for a tenner' and feature a range of leading restaurants. Fundamentally the same offer, these are targeted at totally different lifestyles and are as effective at the top and the bottom of the market.

Online coupons are an alternative to offline media, where door-drop or postage costs are rising. Brand managers and retailers cannot afford to overlook the internet as a means of targeting new customers and motivating them to go in-store and purchase products.

How it works

These are very much two-way promotional tools. Participation is sold to those offering the discounts on the basis that it will bring in extra custom from those to whom you have given the vouchers.

If a holidaymaker seeks out a restaurant or museum on the basis of possessing a discount voucher, then that is certainly true. Everyone is happy – the participating outlet that gets the extra business, the customer who makes the saving and you (the promoter), who have paid very little to give the books of coupons in the first place.

What to look out for

The drawbacks arise in the small print. A big directory can turn out to include only a few restaurants near where any single customer lives; there may be limitations on the days of the week when the offer is valid; the location may offer its own superior offers that make yours look second-rate; and there may be tiresome restrictions, such as on the use of credit cards. And, of course, not everyone wants to plan their leisure time round a set of discount offers.

Consumers can see these offers as a substantial and attractive bargain, but the offers can also be devalued by offers that seem too good to be true and end up being a con. An offer of '£100 of savings' that turns out to be £90 off a £1,000 cruise plus a host of 10p coupons would certainly be misleading. It is important to ensure that any discount coupon really does offer genuine savings and that it is not talked up beyond what it really delivers.

Two-for-one flights

These used to be popular but the boom in internet flight bookings and low-cost airlines has killed off this promotion. A quick check on cheap flight comparison websites often shows that you can buy flights online that are cheaper than those offered in a promotion. The complications imposed by the airlines may also detract from such offers – priority boarding, seat reservation, paying for each item of hold luggage, long delays checking luggage in and the need to pay for fast track security (at Luton) where others are taken through over-rigorous checks. This promotion may return when new forms of air travel arrive – hyper-supersonic in 2024, for example, which is promising a four-hour flight from London to Sydney.

High street vouchers

The offer

Vouchers allow the time to make personal decisions about when, where and how they will be used, as opposed to coupons that can be much more specific. They can be used with employees when they are really motivational: they are viewed as more valuable than cash.

More than 200 retailers and other suppliers produce vouchers for gift and promotional use. The concept started in 1932 with the launch of book tokens, swiftly followed by record tokens. Since the 1970s, it has become a branded business: books, theatres and gardens are the only remaining generic vouchers. According to the UK Gift Card & Voucher Association, voucher use is worth £5 billion a year, and is growing twice as fast as retail sales as a whole.

Discounts for vouchers are very low – nil on small quantities, and up to 5 per cent on quantities of over £50,000. The choice is between a single-store voucher (Marks & Spencer and Boots are the most popular) and one that can be used in a wide variety of stores.

How it works

Vouchers are off-the-shelf products, but cost the promoter their face value or close to it. In this they differ radically from the other promotions discussed in this chapter. So why use them? The reason is that they carry with them the brand values of the retailer. If £10 in cash is given, it may be used to pay a bill. However, a £10 voucher redeemable at a leading store brings with it the anticipation of a pleasurable shopping trip and a purchase that might not otherwise be made.

What to look out for

Vouchers are cash alternatives and they need careful administration. They can be bought direct from suppliers, from producers, or from firms that act as clearing houses for a wide range of retailers' vouchers.

Be aware that many department stores now offer promotional evenings to their store or account cardholders. Debenhams typically gives 20 per cent off everything for an evening open only to those on its mailing lists. Others have followed: Homebase, for example, did the same with its mailing list, offering discounts on some ranges as well as vouchers and additional Nectar points.

BRIEF 9.1   Sky, Red Letter and Virgin voucher offers

Sky offers a £25 M&S voucher if the shopper introduces a friend. Red Letter Days and Virgin offer adventure experience vouchers.

Insurance offers

The offer

Every car owner or mortgage holder is obliged to hold relevant insurance. Take-up of other insurance products, for house contents, legal expenses, personal accident, travel and so on, varies enormously and is very much lower. Every type of insurance can be used as a promotional premium, but the less widespread products are particularly attractive. The growth of websites that find the best insurance offers are testament to how lucrative the business is.

An insurance principle also lies behind assistance and helpline telephone services, whether for legal advice, pet care, travel or household maintenance. In all these cases, the cost of providing the advice (normally by means of a dedicated telephone line) depends on the proportion of those entitled to use the advice line who actually do so. Advice lines can be offered in exactly the same way as insurance. A breakfast cereal, for example, may want to offer a benefit that is attractive to pet owners. Free pet health insurance or a free advice line on caring for your pet could both be provided on an insurance principle.

How it works

Specialist brokers have put together insurance products in a number of areas that (in volume) are far cheaper than the policies consumers can buy from their brokers or insurance companies, thus offering consumers high perceived value. For example, insurance for a £1,000 camcorder could cost the consumer £80 if bought from a broker. Its cost to a promoter is much less, and reflects five areas of cost saving that the promoter can offer the insurer:

1 Take out the selling costs of the broker and the administration and marketing costs of the insurance company, and the actual insurance cost is just £30.

2 Part of the cost of insurance reflects the fact that it is often only taken out by those with a higher-than-average risk. Offer insurance to everyone, and the average cost reduces to reflect low- as well as high-risk customers.

3 You could also give the insurer the opportunity of a bounce-back offer – a second offer sent to those who respond to the first offer. The bounce-back offer will give the insurer the potential for new business.

4 Offer publicity for the insurance firm on your product or in your advertising and it may subsidize the offer from its own promotional budget.

5 Write the policy in such a way that claims are settled with a new camcorder and not cash, and you reduce the level of fraudulent claims.

All these measures can mean that, in bulk, insurance worth £80 to the consumer can cost the promoter less than £10. It's then a real possibility to offer 'free insurance' as an attractive and low-cost incentive. As an example, NatWest bank has offered £1,000 free life insurance for a year. The insurer continues the offer the second year, perhaps doubling the cover as an incentive. And so on. So everyone benefits.

Sometimes, a trial period of insurance can be offered without cost to the promoter. In 1990, the *Daily Mail* offered three months' free pet health insurance in return for a number of proofs of purchase. About 30,000 people responded, and the insurer took the cost of the claims that resulted. It also converted 7,500 people into regular customers, clawing back its costs and making a profit over time.

Insurance products can be varied to suit a range of products and services. Lloyds Bank offered insurance-based benefits free to those who took out loans for cars and house improvements. For cars, the benefit included road assistance; for house improvements, it included home repair assistance.

What to look out for

Like any insurance policies, these policies need to be examined closely for exclusions that limit their real effectiveness. It is essential to use a specialist broker that understands both insurance and marketing, and to make sure that there is a genuine consumer benefit in the offer. The best of them are as good as any policy bought in the normal way, and very much cheaper. This is because they pass on real economies:

● There are economies of scale for an insurance company in providing 10,000 policies in one go, especially for low-cost policies.

- Those who have received free insurance make a good mailing list for insurance companies to sell the same or related products to, and insurance companies make an allowance for this.
- One-off policies with fairly low insurance ceilings distributed widely across the population tend not to be abused by customers making false claims, and the insurance cost can be averaged across high- and low-risk consumers.
- Insurance companies like to achieve retail visibility and be associated with leading brand names.

Because insurance companies are looking for volume, this promotion is more suited to larger than to smaller businesses, although there is no reason small businesses should not get together to make the offer. Insurance promotions have been used extensively with electrical goods, in the motor trade, and with mobile phones, credit cards and leisure products such as bicycles. They could be used more widely.

Be aware of the interest shown by *Which?* the consumer magazine, in electrical goods insurance. *Which?* researched and found that very few electrical 'white goods' such as washing machines failed in the first six years of their use. The customer was being sold a warranty that extended beyond the first year's warranty required by law. *Which?* considered this was a scam and customers were being taken for a ride. Check on social media to see the latest scams associated with insurance offers.

Packaged schemes

The offer

Take free accommodation, two-for-one flights, discounts on cinema tickets, half-price entrance to theme parks, a restaurant privilege card, 50 per cent off household insurance and hundreds of pounds off selected holidays and what do you get? You get the kind of package that is offered by supermarkets, banks, mobile telephone companies and car manufacturers.

These packages are put together by specialists in the customer loyalty market, and there are several suppliers. A promoter could also construct them individually, but there are evident savings in using schemes that have already been negotiated.

How it works

A packaged scheme marks the point at which promotional devices become part of a long-term loyalty scheme. The emphasis shifts from providing a short-term reason for buying to providing a basis for building longer relationships. The contents of the package can be accurately targeted by selecting the particular balance of offers that suits the lifestyle and aspirations of the customers you want to attract. And the benefits to the hotels, airlines, theme parks, cinemas and restaurants included in the package can correspondingly become more long term. The lifestyle package becomes a platform on which different companies can reach each other's customers and strengthen their identification with them to their mutual benefit. EE offers two-for-one cinema tickets with Cineworld and two-for-one meals with Pizza Express.

Nectar and Avios (formerly Air Miles) are used for consumer promotions, trade promotions and staff incentives. Smaller companies, and those wanting to use them in low volumes, can buy them at around 20p each for a minimum quantity of 25,000 miles for employee and sometimes business-to-business use. In moderate quantities, the price drops for large-scale sector-exclusive offers.

What to look out for

Building a long-term incentive scheme is a significant investment. A major scheme may cost as much as 3 per cent of turnover. It is not worth doing unless you are clear that your target audience is going to be more substantially attracted by it than by the lower prices your competitors may offer.

Plants, print and model car collectables

The offer

A long-running off-the-shelf promotion was the offer of collectables, such as model cars (and earlier free film processing) and now plants. These offers are normally made available to promoters for a fixed fee that includes handling and redemption. In the digital age the offers for films are now for producing prints from electronic storage media. It is interesting, if nothing else, to understand the calculation.

How it works

Here is an example of the stages involved:

1 The OTA (Opportunities to Apply) figure is calculated. This is arrived at by dividing the number of packs on which the offer is communicated by the number of proofs of purchase required to participate. In this example, there are 1 million packs and five proofs of purchase. So, a maximum of 200,000 items worth £700,000 at retail price could be redeemed.

2 The predicted redemption rate is calculated. This is the estimate of the number of people who will actually take up the offer. It varies widely but, in the absence of specific information, it is fair to assume 5 per cent. This reduces the likely number of items that will be redeemed to 10,000 with a retail value of £35,000.

3 The offer is linked in with a 'bounce-back' offer – a second offer made to those who respond to the first. Those who receive their item will also receive a letter with other similar items to buy. The money made on the subsequent offers allows the company to subsidize the first offer.

The processing company will add in its administrative and handling costs to arrive at a fixed cost for providing the promotion as a whole. This will be expressed to the promoter in pence per OTA. In this case, the offer will be quoted at £12,000 or 6p per OTA on 200,000 OTAs. This can in turn be expressed as a cost per promoted pack, in this case 1.2p per pack.

Once the promoter has accepted this quotation, there is nothing more to worry about. The processing company will supply the offer, receive the applications, send out the items and take care of all related handling issues. The company will also bear any fluctuations in redemption. Whether 500 or 15,000 people send in for the collectable, the price to the promoter remains the same.

What to look out for

This is a promotion of a type that gives a fixed, all-in cost and brings to bear the interest that producers, rather than promoters, have in recruiting new users, which reduces the cost to the promoter.

This example focused on collectables as a fixed-price promotion. Companies now offer free cameras, free sunglasses, free tights, free model vans, free plants or any other item on the same principle. The common factor in all cases is the bounce-back letter – in the case of model vans, it is often an opportunity to collect more model vans.

When both the offer and the bounce-back are related, it is easy to see the commercial benefit and how this enables the producing company to subsidize the promotional cost. The picture is rather different when the commercial benefit in the bounce-back becomes tenuous, for example when a model car bounce-back is included with a pair of sunglasses.

Fixed-fee promotions then become a version of promotional risk insurance, which was discussed in Chapter 4. It can be very useful for a promoter to insure a promotion against an unexpectedly high redemption rate. There can also be good arguments for paying an operator to take on the whole promotion for a fixed fee, particularly if you lack the time to organize the premiums and handling yourself. However, it may cost more than if you organize the premium and the handling yourself and take out promotional risk insurance. The commercial logic of fixed-fee promotions depends on the degree of subsidy the operator can give the promotion on the strength of the bounce-back.

The case studies that follow offer three successful examples of the use of travel and activity promotions, and a disastrous one. They provide a graphic illustration of the issues discussed in this chapter. After you have read the case studies, ask yourself the questions that follow.

CASE STUDY 9.1   Tango

Tango has grown to be the most successful, imaginative and stylish youth-focused soft drink. It dominates the fruit carbonates market, not least as a result of a radical approach to advertising, packaging and PR.

This led to Tequila Option One's two-stage promotion. The first asked consumers to collect 16 points from Tango packs to claim a 'free goes' directory. This offered a free go at three of 30 activities that included bungee jumping, windsurfing, music workshops and go-karting. It featured on all pack formats, with varying points being required to obtain the directory depending on the size of the pack. Sales increased by 20 per cent during the promotion.

The second stage was a series of three one-day events in August in Scotland, Nottingham and London. Named the 'Tango Bash', each of these was held in conjunction with a local radio station, with tickets available at HMV stores for £6 plus one proof of purchase. Proceeds were donated to The Prince's Trust. They featured high-profile groups and fashion gurus, music and activities, and attracted more than 30,000 participants.

This promotion involved thinking big and building partnerships. Donating proceeds to The Prince's Trust opened doors to celebrities and media coverage. Tango created something unique to itself, but it did so by orchestrating existing networks and resources.

In communications terms, every possible media type was used: regional TV, press advertorials, point-of-sale material, PR, in-store videos in a sports chain, radio, advertising on the tube in London and a roadshow. The events also provided a setting for trade and press hospitality. It is a good example of promotion creating brand properties, and doing a job well beyond traditional definitions of promotion.

Why was a package of activity events particularly appropriate for Tango?

What logic can you see in Tango's decision to have a two-tier promotion, with both an activity directory and a series of outdoor events?

CASE STUDY 9.2   *The Sun*

January is a key time for switching newspapers or stopping buying them altogether. It is also a key time for booking holidays. In 1995 *The Sun* addressed the challenge of locking in existing readers with a promotion that succeeded on a colossal scale. The paper optioned all low- and mid-season capacity in 140 UK holiday parks. It produced a 12-page pull-out brochure in the paper and backed it up with a £220,000 TV campaign. Readers were asked to collect six tokens on six consecutive days and post them in with £8.50 per person per four-day holiday.

Around 1.1 million passenger holidays were redeemed, making *The Sun* the country's biggest UK tour operator. The paper sold 180,000 (3 per cent) more copies during the promotional week. It won an ISP Gold Award and an award for an outstanding contribution to UK tourism. Unsurprisingly, the promotion has been repeated in subsequent years.

This is promotion on a massive scale – an option not open to many brands. However, at the heart of it is a simple deal. It sold off-season breaks for the holiday camps and newspapers for *The Sun* by virtue of a compelling customer benefit that also benefited all concerned.

What package of activities other than discounted UK breaks would have been suitable for The Sun*'s readers?*

If you ran a holiday park, what steps would you take to gain the maximum benefit from The Sun*'s promotion?*

CASE STUDY 9.3   Passport to the millennium

Brief

Bt.spree.com, BT's online shopping site, required a powerful online promotion to drive site registration and encourage return visits. Working in partnership with brandsynergy.com, P&MM's remit was to package and fulfil the promotion, which had to have a high perceived value and appeal to the broadest possible customer base. The ultimate objective was to achieve 50,000 online registrations by the end of the promotional period and to create a database of registered shoppers that would enable bt.spree.com to communicate on a regular basis with future targeted promotions.

Solution

Online vouchers to the value of £2,000 were to be awarded to the first 50,000 customers to register on the **bt.spree.com** site. They received an electronic booklet of 14 vouchers offering discounts to the value of £2,000 against products and services including:

- £150 off theme park tickets;
- £25 off a one-week holiday for two from any ABTA/ATOL tour operator brochure;
- two nights for the price of one at Moat House Hotels;
- £60 worth of UCI cinema vouchers.

Vouchers could be redeemed online immediately after registration or up until the final redemption date.

Communications

Communications included a high-profile launch with an appearance by TV celebrity Carol Smillie, targeted direct mail, national radio and press ads, and banner ads on the web. In addition, fulfilment was supported by P&MM with a dedicated online queries service; customers also benefited from a secure credit card payment system.

Comment

The company wanted something that would appeal to a wide range of people; this promotion worked by attracting the right people to the right site. The advantage of an online promotion is that it takes down all the barriers to entry you get with a mailed response. Visitors can register, claim their vouchers and redeem them instantly online, with no human interaction.

CASE STUDY 9.4   Hoover – the classic!

In autumn 1992, Hoover needed a promotion to pull itself out of the doldrums. Hoover Europe, owned by the US Maytag Corporation, had made a £10 million loss in the first nine months of the year. It launched an offer of two free flights to the United States for £100 or more spent on any Hoover product. The promotion was to dog the company for the next five years.

Within weeks, retailers were reporting that Hoover products were walking out of the door. People were buying two vacuum cleaners at a time to take advantage of the offer. The travel agency handling the promotion reported 100,000 responses by the end of 1992, twice what it had expected. The downside of the promotion was also becoming clear. Consumers were reporting unexpected delays and difficulties in obtaining flights. Industry experts were asking how Hoover could possibly fund two free flights to the United States from the profit on a £100 sale.

In March 1993, an investigator for BBC TV's 'Watchdog' programme took a job in the travel agency's telesales department. The trick, it appeared, was to use the small print of the offer to put off those who wanted to book their free flights, unless they also booked accommodation, car hire and insurance worth at least £300. Some consumers persisted in trying to take up the offer and took Hoover to court. In 1997, Hoover was still paying out to those who took their cases against it to the county courts.

Meanwhile, Maytag had sold the company and provided £20 million for the cost of picking up the pieces of an offer that should never have been made. It was foolish in many ways: the economics of the promotion never made sense; the estimates of redemption were unrealistically low; the procedures for handling were inadequate. Also, when the scale of the disaster became apparent, Hoover did too little too late to put it right.

What would you do to avoid getting into the mess that Hoover did?

What effect do you think the Hoover experience has had on public confidence in sales promotion?

Summary

The offers featured in the first section of this chapter can strike consumers and promoters alike in two ways: it can seem a piece of magic that something worth £50 can cost only £1; it can also seem a sleight of hand in which someone must be losing out somewhere. The truth is straightforward. Offers that sound great but cost little work on the basis of a number of related factors:

- They bring to bear the commercial interests of a third party, whether this is a hotelier seeking to fill empty rooms or a print processing company wanting new customers.

- They use the discount structure available in certain industries (particularly travel and insurance) to create savings opportunities that customers could not otherwise obtain.

- They are created and marketed by specialist companies with immense experience in the field that are constantly seeking to devise new offers; the best of them have been around for 25 years or more.

Avoiding the dodgy schemes and securing the opportunities that the good schemes create depends on promoters keeping their eyes open, asking hard business questions and not being mesmerized by seemingly unmissable offers. It is simply not worth degrading your business reputation by using a dubious offer any more than it is worth tarring all these offers with the same brush. If any of the offers in this chapter strike you as unmissable, be cautious. Remember not to take an offer and find a use for it; always start with your promotional objectives.

Self-study questions

9.1   What do you need to watch for if you are organizing a free flight offer?

9.2   How do free rooms offers work?

9.3   What issues do you need to take into account if you are using discount coupons?

9.4   Why can insurance be offered in a promotion at a much lower cost than the consumer would pay for it from a broker?

9.5   How do fixed-fee promotions work?

Joint promotions

Most promotions involve giving away some of your margin in the form of discounts, cheap interest rates, competition prizes or premiums. Extra business should more than pay for this, but there's no getting around the initial investment. Joint promotions involve sharing that cost with someone else. No company or charity wants to do this for you without getting something in return. The secret of joint promotions is establishing a mutually beneficial partnership.

A joint promotion is excellent for a start-up: entrepreneurs please note. The new service or product is 'piggy-backed' onto the larger, established, brand-recognized company, product or service. There are additional benefits in using established customer lists (which may be shared for future use as well): the existing brand's presumed endorsement and using the marketing expertise of the partner. It is a fast track way to build a brandgram.

Joint promotions are defined by two fundamental factors: they bring together organizations in different markets that share a common set of customers, and they give participants a real commercial benefit that each side is anxious to realize for the other. Any business can do it, and it is one of the fastest-growing and most beneficial forms of promotion. This section looks first at the planning principles and then at four main types of joint promotion: sampling, referral coupons, charities and loyalty schemes. Finally, there is the phantom partnership – using an event in the public domain without a formal partnership agreement.

Planning principles

Most companies spend time thinking about their own market and their own customers. Naturally enough, they think about them from their own business viewpoint and in relation to their own competitors.

Identifying a joint market involves thinking about your customers in broader terms, both in relation to other people who are trying to sell to them and in relation to people you are trying to reach who are customers of someone else. The key to planning a joint promotion is an accurate profile of your existing customers. The key elements in this profile are:

- demographic data – age, sex, social class, geographical distribution;
- their relationship to you – how often they buy, at what price level, with what degree of loyalty;
- their needs, interests and aspirations – other things they buy, what they want from life.

Credit card companies were among the first to spot the opportunity, with the development of affinity cards in the 1980s. Now virtually every major charity and interest group from the Royal British Legion or NSPCC to the Liberal Democrats has its branded credit card, typically rebating the organization concerned 1 per cent of the value of credit card spending.

Many joint promotions are short term, designed to achieve trial or sampling objectives. Others are developed on the basis that there is a long-term customer overlap between non-competing brands. They reflect the development of the idea of 'tribal marketing': we are forming modern tribes, characterized by our purchasing habits. Those who belong to English Heritage, support charities and go to book-shops form a different tribe to those who do DIY, enjoy home entertainment and join discount clubs.

The process has also developed in B2B markets. It is important to profile the size and type of industry, the number of employees and the level of person you deal with. But that is only the start. People in business belong to different tribes as much as consumers. Some feel an affinity to golf, some to charitable work and some to business benefits. Identifying these affinities enables you to seek out partners that are not your direct competitors with whom you share the same customer profile: the closer the fit, the better it is for both sides.

The biggest obstacles to successful joint promotions lie in making them work. The major culprits are greed, misunderstanding and suspicion. However well the customer profiles fit, if your intended partner is not prepared to talk to you openly about its own customers and is determined to get the maximum out of it without putting anything back in return, the result will be as disastrous as any other partner-ship built on false foundations.

Look for those with whom it is possible to establish agreement about each other's objectives and honesty about tackling present and possible difficulties. Even when there appears to be initial enthusiasm on both sides, a number of factors can emerge that could scupper the best-laid joint promotions. It is therefore vital to ensure the following:

- *Involve everyone.* If the deal involves other people in your company communicating details of another manufacturer's products, they will only do so if the promotion is fully explained to them and they share your determination to make it work. Involvement of senior management in joint promotions is particularly important.

- *Make realistic promises.* Everyone is inclined to talk up the number of customers and contacts they have. It is best to be realistic at the start about what you can guarantee to deliver.

- *Avoid unplanned changes.* Circumstances can change in a company for all kinds of reasons. Management must undertake at the start to minimize this risk.

- *Build in good liaison.* Once a deal is set up, it is tempting to get on with the next job. Good liaison is essential to successful joint promotions, and it must involve people at every level of the company throughout the life of the promotion.

- *Bargain realistically.* Everyone wants to get the best deal and negotiates accordingly. Bargaining should be directed at maximizing mutual benefit at an agreed cost to both sides, and both sides must agree to this in their negotiations.

- *Be proactive.* There is a tendency for the company that made the initial approach to be expected to make all the running and contribute most. This is a mistake. Both sides should be proactive.

The only way to establish whether or not likely partners will have the qualities needed for joint promotions is to talk to them.

Joint promotions can meet the following objectives; each side must be able to see the promotion fulfilling one or more of them:

- to gain trial for your product or service from among the customers of another product or service;
- to associate your product or service with someone else's in the mind of your target audience;
- to make a promotional offer that will attract your customers at low cost to yourself;
- to explain to your customers new ways in which your product or service can be used;
- to place your product in an environment where potential customers are likely to see it;
- to reduce the cost of a planned activity by sharing it with someone else.

Sample promotions

The offer

When people buy product A, they obtain a sample of product B. This is often something that they need to buy on a continuous basis to use product A or where there is a clear connection between the usage of the two products.

How it works

A long-established example of sample promotions is a free packet of washing powder in new washing machines. It carries with it the actual or implied approval of the washing machine manufacturer for the particular brand of detergent. The free sample is of real and significant value. Other examples include the banding of jars of Nescafé with packs of Hobnob biscuits, creating a clear link between the brands in a common usage occasion.

What to look out for

This is one of the most effective ways of gaining trial and, if the partner is selected well, it can also be highly cost-effective compared to, say, a door-drop sample. However, the cost of giving away full samples is high, and it is normally necessary to include some repeat purchase incentive as well. Both the cost and the potential of this promotion make it one to test very carefully in advance.

Referral coupon promotions

The offer

When people buy product A, they receive a coupon they can redeem against purchases of product B. These promotions are often called 'cross-rough coupons', a name that implies that they are a hit-or-miss affair. The name has stuck, although there is nothing rough about them, and they are particularly common between non-competing brands owned by the same company.

How it works

An example is a 'kids eat free' promotion, first developed by Persil and Little Chef in the mid-1980s and now widely used by child-related household brands in partnership with family eating and leisure operations.

What to look out for

Referral coupons have the advantage of being far cheaper to run than sample promotions, but lack their level of trial-gaining impact. They have important benefits in that you can measure how many people have been enticed across and they do not require special packs. Run as a partnership between half a dozen or more companies selling complementary products, they can be particularly effective.

Charity promotions

The offer

Charity promotions, or cause-related marketing, take many forms. The evidence is that customers are more likely to buy from firms that are seen to contribute to social and environmental issues they support. Many of the United Kingdom's best-known charities go out of their way to meet both their own fund-raising needs and the requirements of the firms they team up with. It is a commercial relationship, and all the better for it. Charities need funds, new supporters and wider publicity. Businesses need promotions that show their worth in extra profit and also link them to issues that matter to consumers.

There needs to be a close fit between your target market and the market from which the non-commercial organization gains its support. Selecting the market thus involves a degree of lateral thinking about your customers:

- What sorts of charities and voluntary organizations appeal to them?
- What kinds of project would they like to be associated with?
- What sorts of charities and voluntary organizations connect with the usage area of your product or service?
- What are the charitable and voluntary concerns that are likely to have the highest public exposure over the coming months?

Answering these questions makes it possible to draw up a list of areas – sport, arts, children and so on – that look suitable. The Charities Aid Foundation can be a good starting point for finding out which organizations operate in the areas you have chosen.

How it works

There are various types of charity promotion. Among the longest established are collector promotions, which require consumers to post in wrappers or coupons that are designated as being worth a certain amount to the charity. The promoter counts the wrappers sent in and hands over the equivalent sum. Very often, charities will ask for a guaranteed minimum to justify the use of their name and to reflect the difficulty of estimating redemption levels. Collector promotions run with charities can generate a huge response, particularly if schools and youth organizations can be encouraged to collect the wrappers or coupons.

Here are some examples. BT wanted to remove the old, pre-microchip phone cards from circulation. To do so, it offered a donation to Shelter, which collected both a large number of phone cards and £100,000. Van den Burgh supported its London Marathon sponsorship by offering a sports bag as a free mail-in item on Flora and promising £1 to the British Heart Foundation for every bag claimed. The link between the marathon, Flora and the prevention of heart disease was reinforced in the minds of consumers as a result of this promotional activity being used up until 2009. Charity promotional events have taken a wide variety of forms, from the Oxo/Barnardo's Champion Children of the Year to the Jaguar/NCH Royal Gala Evening at the Albert Hall.

What to look out for

The criteria that apply to charity promotions also apply to promotions with voluntary or community organizations, such as sports and arts associations, and are similar to those that apply to joint commercial promotions. There are four additional factors that are particular to non-profit organizations, which need to be taken into account in finding out what they want. Some of them do not apply to the very big national charities, which have their own promotion departments, but they are all-important in dealing with smaller organizations. They are:

1 *Locate the priority objectives.* Most non-profit organizations have an almost limitless set of needs and wishes. Finding out the priority objectives that are within your means to realize takes time, patience and understanding.

2 *Identify the decision makers.* Non-profit organizations tend to be run by committees and have complicated internal processes. It is essential to understand these and to know where the real decisions are made and under what constraints and influences the decision makers are working.

3 *Establish trust.* The ways of thinking in profit and non-profit organizations are not identical, and an element of initial suspicion and distrust is understandable. To establish trust, you must associate with values and aspirations that motivate those involved in a non-profit organization.

4 *Have respect.* The implementation of any non-profit organization promotion must ensure respect for the recipients of the money raised. Considerable sensitivity is required to ensure that raising money is not done at the expense of self-respect.

If the process is approached in this open way, it is possible for companies to sit down with charities and other non-profit organizations and hammer out a deal that meets the needs of both sides.

Loyalty schemes

The offer

From petrol stations to airlines and supermarkets, loyalty schemes are near universal. Large-scale schemes invariably involve joint promotions – there simply is not enough in any one company's product range to cover all the lifestyle needs that a loyalty scheme tries to meet. Research reported by *Promotions Buyer* (March, 2007) found that 70 per cent of business and leisure travellers say being a member of a loyalty card is a key factor in determining the choice of hotel or airline. The offer to the consumer is both simple and endlessly varied: sign up for the scheme, provide purchasing and demographic data, obtain a card and start collecting. From the management viewpoint the concept is equally simple: develop the version that suits your business and you have a loyalty scheme. Or do you?

How it works

There is considerable dispute about how loyalty schemes work. Are they really about loyalty or are they just old-fashioned 'points mean prizes' collector schemes dressed up with electronic cards and relationship language? Alternatively, are they a means of delivering highly sophisticated database marketing on a mass scale?

Supporters of loyalty schemes point to the substantial increase in market share enjoyed by Tesco since it launched its Clubcard in 1995. There is an expectation, fostered by promoters of schemes such as Avios that the present 140 schemes will coalesce into a series of consortia, each comprising a bank, supermarket, airline and utility, telecoms and leisure business. On this reading, the operation of loyalty schemes becomes central to a firm's market positioning.

Doubters accept that loyalty cannot be bought, but believe it is possible to use card-based schemes to target particular types of buyers and increase the amount and frequency of their purchases. Effective management of data is critical to this, and the measure is whether or not the particular incentives you give create additional sales. Managers can cite examples of this happening and not happening – it is far from automatic.

Marketing people hold widely differing views on loyalty schemes, whether they work and what they actually are. The strongest critics of the schemes point to evidence that the more someone buys of a particular product category the more products they will buy within it. Thus, the more you travel by air, the more airlines you will use. The more supermarket shopping you do, the more supermarkets you will use. If there are loyalty schemes available and you like participating in them, you will participate in them all. Of course, market share can change, but that comes about because of an increase in both frequent and infrequent users. What does not change is the ratio between the frequent and infrequent users of your products or services. In fact, across dozens of markets, that ratio is found to be constant. Loyalty schemes are, according to this argument, a complete misnomer. (See Chapter 2 on bonding with a brand.)

So the question remains open: what part did Tesco's loyalty scheme play in the bundle of characteristics (price, convenience, store layout, checkout speed and so on) that influence the consumer to choose one supermarket over another for a particular shopping trip? Tesco is currently suffering a sales drop. Think of it in terms of the six Cs of the offer. Proponents of loyalty schemes often neglect to recognize the progress made by Asda in the 1990s despite its lack of a loyalty card, and the loss of market share by Sainsbury's both before and after its loyalty card launch.

What to look out for

It is essential to recognize that 'loyalty' schemes are not about loyalty, but about providing repeated reasons for customers to use your product or service. They are a bundle of promotional techniques, the principle one of which is a long-term collector scheme. On the back of that, they can be used to convey short-term incentives of every kind and to engage the consumer in competitions and special events. The downside of these schemes is their cost and complexity, and the danger that they can become a substitute for attending to product and service quality. It is best to measure them on a disaggregated basis – not the scheme as a whole, but each mailer and each subsidiary offer. The scheme works to the extent that its separate elements work.

The expectation is that loyalty schemes will come to an end in their present form in due course, just as Green Shield stamps did in the late 1970s. Their demise was predicted in the promotional press within months of the take-off of UK supermarket schemes. It has not happened yet, but there is a cycle in sales promotion, well-illustrated in Case study 9.10 on Tesco's experience over the last 20 years, and Case study 9.15 on a classic Procter & Gamble promotion of the 1960s.

In the meantime, promoters should focus on the detail: if the individual elements are answering the question 'Who do I want to do what?', it does not matter whether they are dressed up as a loyalty scheme or not. If the individual elements are not persuasive reasons for the consumer to act, no 'loyalty' framework will make them effective. Long after the present wave of loyalty schemes have gone, these individual elements – 'buy one, get one free' (BOGOF) offers, special evenings, items to collect and the like – will still be going strong under another name.

Phantom partnerships

The offer

Not everyone can sign up the joint promotional partners they would like such as the World Cup or the Olympics. The 'phantom partnership' can come to your rescue in such circumstances.

How it works

Phantom partnerships are about making a connection with an event in the news without breaking copyright law. McDonald's ran a 'game of two halves' promotion, offering football merchandise and match tickets. Burger King built on its sponsorship of the England, Scotland, Wales and Northern Ireland teams with an instant-win promotion, also offering football merchandise and match tickets. Flymo gave away free branded footballs with selected mowers, produced POP material showing the cherub from its then TV ad kicking the ball, and offered £50 cashback in the event of Scotland or England winning (which seemed more possible as the event progressed than it did at the beginning). Case study 9.7 describes a similar phantom partnership between Sellotape and the National Lottery.

What to look out for

Cross the line into implying a partnership and you will have the full weight of copyright lawyers on your head, and rightly so. Imply a partnership with a charity that you do not have, and the public reaction will be damaging. However, make a legal connection that does not infringe copyright with an event and most people will applaud your imagination. It is an ideal field for enterprising and careful promoters looking to hook their brands on to whatever is uppermost in the public mind.

The case studies chosen here reflect three different types of joint promotions: a B2B promotion, a long-term loyalty scheme and a phantom joint promotion. Other case studies in this book that are relevant here are the Bovril sampling campaign (Case study 8.4), the Sainsbury's 'Schoolbags' collector promotion (Case study 8.5) and the Jacob's Club and Co-op 'Music for schools' promotions (Case study 11.4).

CASE STUDY 9.5   NatWest/BT

NatWest teamed up with BT to offer three concrete telecommunications benefits. In return for opening a small business account, customers could obtain a free business telephone, £35 off a fax machine and 15 per cent off an answering machine. Against its primary objective of driving recruitment of new accounts, the promotion worked well – new account openings were 52 per cent ahead of target. It also worked against its secondary objectives, showing that NatWest understood the needs of small business, and giving its sales force a simple, clear offer to focus on. The promotion won an ISP Gold Award. It couldn't be simpler or more direct in concept and execution, and offered reciprocal benefits for BT.

What other partners could NatWest seek now that would appeal to the start-up business in 2014?

What mechanisms for communicating this offer would you recommended to NatWest?

CASE STUDY 9.6   Shell and Esso

In 1997 petrol purchasers were faced with a complicated choice. From the supermarkets, claiming a 21 per cent market share, there were low prices but often inconvenient locations. From Esso, there was 'Price watch' – the claim of petrol at supermarket prices right on main driving routes. From Shell, and most of the other forecourt businesses, there were various heavily promoted card-based schemes.

Shell's 'Smart card' was launched in 1994 as a five-year programme to take it to the millennium. The background to the promotion, devised by Tequila Option One, was clear: Shell was the market leader, but losing share in the absence of a long-term loyalty programme. It needed to build sales while maintaining premium pricing, and embrace all motorists while targeting high-mileage users. It needed a long-term scheme that still gave the opportunity for tactical promotions.

Shell's Smart card was set up with the participation of third parties. It offered a choice of instant redemption and long-term saving, third-party purchases and catalogue purchases, charity donations and personal benefits. It was promoted via TV advertising, door-to-door, promotional assistants and POP on forecourts, local radio promotions, direct mail and inserts in magazines. The structure of the card offered both security for points and the capacity for detailed analysis of the transaction history. Within a year, Shell had achieved the figure of 3 million cardholders. Shell's Smart card won an ISP Gold Award and exceeded all its early targets. It has continued to develop, with partners changing. In 2007 Shell re-launched the brand along with a new card scheme.

Esso operated a very different price promotion that is estimated to have increased its market share to rival that of the supermarkets, at colossal cost to its margins. In fact petrol companies' real profits now come from sales of other goods and services in garages, so the retail petrol side can almost be run at a loss, with profits from licensing the service station outlet to, say, a supermarket chain. The trade-off between market share and margins is a critical decision for any company. Petrol retailers face a particular challenge in relation to supermarkets: they have high fixed costs in refining and oil exploration, while supermarkets can buy on the 'spot market' without any such investment. Margin calculations are thus very different for supermarkets and petrol retailers. Joining together on the forecourt is perhaps an imaginative way of combining their businesses to the mutual benefit of their brands. Shell's persistence for a time with its Smart card and Esso's persistence with 'Price watch' suggest that it is possible for collector and price promotions to run side by side in the petrol market, appealing to people with different priorities.

Look around at the current range of petrol forecourt promotions. What do they say about each company's answer to the 'Who do I want to do what?' question?

CASE STUDY 9.7   Sellotape

Sellotape is both the generic name in the sticky tape market and the premium-priced brand leader. It's not an exciting product, and the people buying it for office use are often not end users. How could Sellotape underline its brand leadership to these buyers? Tequila Option One saw that an answer was offered in 1994 by the launch of the National Lottery. Sellotape formed a syndicate to buy 10,000 £1 tickets for an early Lottery draw on behalf of office users who submitted a proof of purchase. Entrants needed company permission and could donate their winnings to charity. This ensured the promotion was within the ASA Code guidelines at the time. It also encouraged buyers to discuss with their managers the reason for preferring Sellotape to cheaper brands.

There was no major prize for the syndicate, but the promotion increased sales by 40 per cent in the six-month period of its run. Could it be repeated? Perhaps not with the Lottery, but with any other major event that offers the opportunity for a low-cost promotional piggyback.

What current and forthcoming events do you think could provide the opportunity of a phantom partnership such as Sellotape's with Lotto?

Look at Case study 9.2, which covers a Lottery-related promotion run by The Sun. *What did Sellotape have to do to ensure that the syndicate arrangement did not promise customers more than it could deliver?*

CASE STUDY 9.8   Walkers Crisps 'Brit Trips'

To promote its 100 per cent dependence on British potatoes and retain its leadership in a competitive marketplace, an on-pack collection scheme called 'Brit Trips' offered rewards with key UK tourist organizations, some 32 of them jointly, in the United Kingdom's biggest travel and leisure promotion. Walkers had been reluctant to go for the internet but it was what made the promotion possible, using branded microsites with the partners describing the breaks on offer. It also matched the 2008/9 UK mood and financial climate of recession and credit crunch, which was clever, as well as winning an ISP Gold Award. It was supported by TV ads, national and regional press, together with online; 900 million packs were sold. This led to 4 million sessions on the promotional website and the creation of over 600,000 Brit Trip accounts, worth £5 million.

CASE STUDY 9.9   Kellogg's zookeeper

This was the first unanimous winner of the 2009 ISP Audience Award. Consumers welcomed the imaginative campaign, its premiums, concern for green issues and the move away from licensed merchandise. Kellogg's sought to set the standard with a 'kid-engaged, mum-approved' on-pack promotion. By partnering with aquariums and zoos, Kellogg's gained access to money can't buy premiums – winning a day as a zookeeper, free entry, free animal fact sheets and noise ringtones. The joint promotion partnership delivered £3.8 million of value to participating consumers and increased sales by up to 76 per cent.

Summary

Joint promotions are the staple promotional vehicle of companies such as Procter & Gamble, Unilever and Kellogg's. There is every reason for companies of every size to emulate them. However, it is vital to remember that joint promotions are based on a mutual business-building partnership. The best test of success is if both partners want to run it again. If you have identified your market and likely partners with the necessary thoroughness, and you enter into the process with integrity on both sides, joint promotions will work a treat. If not, you are best keeping away from them.

Promotions with charities and other non-commercial organizations can have enormous publicity benefits, excite tremendous response and associate you with values that are important to your customers. They must be undertaken responsibly and with respect for the needs and feelings of the people you are helping, but they are rightly a commercial operation.

Self-study questions

9.6   What major problems tend to arise in joint promotions?

9.7   What should you take into account in looking for a joint promotion partner? Think of a suitable partner for your own organization.

9.8   What can you do and what can't you do if you want to promote on the back of a major event licensed to another company?

9.9   What particular rules apply to promoting with charities?

Price promotions

Fixing the price as a promotion rather than just fixing the price is one of the most difficult and sensitive parts of marketing strategy. All the other techniques in promotions involve you in costs; a price promotion affects the bottom line – directly. In the light of the engram discovery, do appreciate that price does not mean everything to shoppers. Their subconscious 'mind file' may steer them away from the cheapest item in the category. Much of the purpose of marketing is to remove a firm from dependency on perfect competition, particularly for products that are commodities. This is why so much effort is spent creating superior-quality products, developing brand identities, building distribution strengths, matching the offer to the customer need and establishing unique customer relationships. Why throw this away by getting involved in price promotion?

That is the argument of those who regard price promotion as a destroyer of brand identities. In the present climate, with the knowledge of the brandgram held in each shopper's mind, the price promotion now seems far less effective. In July 2009 some 10 retailers at marketing surgeries were asked about the effect on their brand of price discounting. In one case, 'was their 75 per cent price discounting affecting the brand as it was certainly not providing profit?' Well of course it was affecting the brand: ironically independent research showed that their customers in fact did not need the discounts, but the customers did have other concerns, which is why they were not buying (poor customer service, logistics and distribution were quoted). The firm had never carried out customer surveys, used a marketer, the directors were untrained in marketing – they were discounting because their managers felt they had to match the competition. In 2014 the shop ceased trading!

This section sets out the different ways that companies think about price promotion and the many techniques available. So much discussion of price promotion is hindered by different ways of thinking about price that the section begins with a look at the principles of price setting and price segmentation respectively.

How prices are set

Competition, supply and demand affect price. Some companies have made the absence of price promotion a key part of their positioning. Woolworth (gone) and Marks & Spencer (having a hard time now) both did so in the last century when they pioneered the idea of 'one price for all'. It needs only one company to discount its prices for others to feel the need to respond. In most countries there are laws that prevent manufacturers fixing prices between them. By reducing supply cost by means of superior productivity, firms can achieve the profits they seek and still charge lower prices than their competitors. Being the lowest-cost supplier is one of the main strategies for achieving competitive differentiation. Variations in demand for the same product have a noticeable impact: for example it can cost more than twice as much to travel on public transport at peak times than in the quieter times.

Setting the price of a product or service is not a primary concern of promotion. The normal selling price to final users and intermediaries will be a factor to take into account in planning a promotion, as are the product's packaging and distribution. The approach a company takes to pricing strategy determines, to a large extent, how price promotion can be used and how the firm accounts for the difference between normal and promotion prices. Much of the disagreement about the use of price promotion arises from people not understanding the difference between two fundamental pricing strategies.

In 'target mark-up', a company decides the margin or profit it wants to make, and adds that to the product or service cost. It may be ROI or the standard level of return in the industry; for them a discount equals money given away, but this is only the case if they would have gained the order at the higher price. In the 'going rate' it starts with the competition rather than costs; they are always engaged in promotional pricing, but it tends to be unstructured and they may be giving money away unnecessarily. More sophisticated companies balance a concern with competition and cost with an emphasis on the third element in pricing strategy – demand. This leads to three different pricing policies:

1 *Psychological pricing* – works on the basis that we often think a high-priced product must be better than one costing less. Firms will set a high price and defend it. Perfume companies try to stop discounters selling their products, because the cost of perfume is part of its specialness. Those who go for psychological pricing will often aim at a small section of the market that is looking for the very best and is not sensitive to price. They will regard price promotions as totally unsuitable for them – and they will be right. This is consistent with the quality of life now sought by customers, enhanced by marketing copy such as 'You're worth it' and 'Spoil yourself'.

2 *Value pricing* – based on the idea that top quality and low prices can go together. This works for a company if it can achieve a volume big enough to give it the lowest production costs in the market. The aim is to set a consistently low price and maximize volume. This strategy is reflected in the 'everyday low prices' (EDLP) claims made by Wal-Mart in the United States and Asda, Poundland, Aldi, Lidl, etc in the United Kingdom. Price promotions can be part of this, but not a central part.

3 *Segment pricing* – the pricing strategy in which price promotions really come into their own. It starts with the idea that people are different. Some are sensitive to price and some are not. Some will shop around and others will not. Some will wait to enjoy a service or receive a product and others will not. The argument is that prices should be determined in accordance with the demands of each segment of the market.

Until chains of shops began setting 'one price for all' in the 19th century, the price was always negotiated between buyer and seller. In some markets (for example, the price of shares on the Stock Exchange or commodities on commodity exchanges) it still is. Segment pricing is a sophisticated and modern way of managing individual negotiation on a mass scale.

Segment pricing

What makes a segment is discussed in Chapter 2. Marketing people talk about segments of the market in a variety of ways. There are occupation and income classifications distinguishing ABs from C1s and C2s, and lifestyle terms where aspiring young professionals may be of similar age and income to lager and football fans, but spend their time and money very differently. People can also be segmented by their stage in the lifecycle, from dependency to pre-family and post-family. The theory is that for each segment of the market there should be a version of your product that fits it like a glove. This is difficult to do. Midland Bank's Vector (for the old) and Orchard (for the young) accounts failed because neither the bank nor customers understood the difference. Midland failed as a brand too and was replaced by HSBC, its parent.

For promotional pricing to be effective, segments have to be real. Business travellers will pay more to travel at a convenient hour than leisure travellers. That is a real segment for ticket sales. However, do business travellers want something different to leisure travellers from the catering facilities at a station? One study suggests that for catering services there are two rather different segments: those in a hurry and those not. These cut right across the business and leisure segmentation.

There are three rules of thumb for telling whether or not a segment is real enough for segmented pricing to work:

1 People in each segment must have different sensitivities to price; that is, they must be prepared to pay different amounts for the same service or product.

2 There must be some physical, structural or time separation between the higher- and lower-priced segments, preventing those in the higher-priced segment deciding to buy at the lower price.

3 The segments must be real enough for consumers not to feel dissatisfied and resentful, and for the cost of operating segmented pricing to be worthwhile.

The most common segments are formed on these principles:

- *Time.* Travelling, parking or telephoning at busy times of the day costs more than at quiet times. Buying toys before Christmas costs more than after Christmas. A DVD costs more when it is first released than later on.

- *Location.* Conveniently located shops, hotels and restaurants charge more than less conveniently located ones. Products and services brought to you cost more than those you have to fetch.

- *Conditions.* Buying in volume costs less than buying in small units. A year's subscription costs less than an individual theatre ticket or copy of a magazine. Tickets bought in advance will cost less than tickets bought on the day, except for when there are last-minute seats to fill.

- *Version.* Superior service costs more than the standard. Peace of mind can be bought, but at a price. Fundamentally, the same product or service can be versioned or packaged at different price points.

The promoter is primarily concerned with promotions that last for a particular time period, take place in particular locations, have conditions attached to the deal and apply to some but not all versions of a product. This is what differentiates intelligent price promotion from wholesale, self-destructive discounting.

Immediate discounts

These are discounts off the normal price that are available immediately at the time of purchase. They take six main forms; see below. The thing they all have in common is that the consumer can buy a given amount of a product for less.

Immediate discounts have a number of important strengths: everyone likes a bargain, they are a powerful and immediate incentive to buy – a sales clincher. Seventy per cent or more of purchase decisions are made at the point of sale. Their weaknesses, however, are very serious. Discounting can rapidly degenerate into price wars. Competitors can readily copy it. It does not distinguish between those who would have bought without the discount and those who need it. It is also extremely expensive as an immediate discount tends to cost you exactly what it saves the customer. Discounting can also downgrade the value of your product or service and lead to a situation where no sales take place at normal price. Very rarely do the sales gains achieved by price reductions lead to a sustained increase in market share. Immediate discounts are powerful but, like a strong drug, they can quickly take over and destroy your business. Companies must also be aware of the substantial legislation governing the making of bargain offers that properly constrains the making of unreasonable price comparisons.

1. Seasonal discounts

The offer
These are price reductions designed to boost sales in off-peak seasons, to move outdated lines or heavy stocks, bring forward purchases or improve cash flow.

How it works
In their familiar form of retail 'sales', they are now highly formalized and have become a seasonal sales promotion far removed from their original purpose of moving end-of-season stocks. Some retailers run 'closing-down sales' continuously for several years, a practice that stretches the bounds of legality. In some high streets, shops are 'closing down' for months. Leisure companies use seasonal discounts very widely, charging different prices in their low, mid and high seasons.

What to look out for
The critical issue is the logic of the season. Excessive use of sales ends up with consumers deferring purchases to the next sale.

2. Multi-buys

The offer
These are a particular form of quantity discount offered by retailers (and funded by manufacturers) for multiple purchases of the same item. A long-established variant is the BOGOF – 'buy one, get one free' – that is flashed on-pack, on the shelf or in newspaper advertisements.

How it works

Multi-buys normally work by means of bar codes. The shop's EPOS system counts up the number of items with a particular bar code and applies the discount automatically. Multi-buys have become hugely significant. The leading detergent firms have increased the proportion of their consumer promotional spending on multi-buys from 20 to 65 per cent.

What to look out for

Multi-buys are easy promotions to set up and give quick and measurable results. They can be very effective for a manufacturer needing to combat competitor action. However, there are significant costs. Multi-buys have become the standard mode of purchase for some consumers. The London Business School study found that 95 per cent of multi-buys are bought by just 27 per cent of households, mainly larger families who are, in general, better off. The level of sales increase a brand enjoys when a multi-buy is offered can be between 50 and 200 per cent. The hangover after the party comes later – when the same consumers switch to your competitor's multi-buy.

Used sparingly, multi-buys are an effective way of stock-building in the consumer's home and can encourage greater usage simply by virtue of greater volume. They also block purchases of competitors' products until stocks of yours are exhausted. They have become a millstone around the neck of manufacturers, blocking other forms of promotion. Also, the manufacturer often doesn't get the credit: 56 per cent of consumers think retailers fund them.

Outside retail, an example of this approach is magazines offering discounts for signing up for longer subscriptions.

3. Banded packs

The offer

There are several options for banded pack offers, but they come to the same thing: two or more of the same product are banded together or placed in an additional outer wrap so that the consumer buys them together.

How it works

Drink and confectionery brands are regularly sold in a variety of banded packs, whether of 12, 24 or more individual units. The price normally falls as the quantity increases.

What to look out for

There are packaging costs associated with banded packs. There is also a need to negotiate additional line listings and to hold stocks of the additional packaging variants. The benefits are that banded packs are clearly a manufacturer's initiative and tend to be less under the control of retailers. They can increase the amount of space available to the product in the shops and can encourage stock-building by the consumer. A banded pack can be a powerful incentive to volume purchase.

4. Reduced shelf price

The offer

This is the commonest form of price promotion. A standard product is on sale with a shelf sticker or poster showing a reduced price.

How it works

If a £1 item is discounted by 25p, it can be shown in a variety of ways: 'normally £1, now 75p'; 'only 75p'; '25p off'; 'our price: 75p'; 'save 25p'. Signs of this kind are commonplace in clothes shops, consumer durable retailers, food stores and pharmacies.

What to look out for

The important point is the credibility of the standard price. It is ineffective (and illegal) to claim price reductions against a recommended price that is not actually charged. More generally, shelf price reductions are simple and effective to operate, but give discounts indiscriminately. They can serve to reduce the willingness of the consumer to pay the full price.

5. Reduced price offers

The offer

Reduced price offers (RPOs) are flashed on-pack, offering a saving – '10p off' or the original price slashed through and a lower price given. They differ from shelf price reductions by being printed on-pack.

How it works

It is one thing for the manufacturer to print a reduced price on-pack and quite another to ensure that the reduced price makes sense in all retail outlets. They require an additional line listing and separate stocks and packaging. Many retailers now refuse to take them and will increasingly require that they receive the same margin as if the full price were charged.

What to look out for

For the consumer, RPOs are an attractive offer – volumes of sales certainly rise when an attractive reduction is made. It also gives the manufacturer control over the price charged to the consumer. However, it is an expensive promotion in terms of margins and packaging and increasingly difficult to run with major multiples. Used too often, it can devalue the standard price. It can also lead to rapid copying, resulting in almost all products in a sector being reduced in price.

6. Extra-fill packs

The offer

These are packs flashed '25 per cent extra free' or '550 ml for the price of 440 ml'. They differ from RPOs in that the price remains the same, but the quantity of the product sold for that price goes up.

How it works

Extra-fill appeals to existing users of your product, who can get more for the same price. They can also be useful in trading consumers up to larger sizes. The costs for the manufacturer include packaging origination and carrying additional stock. There can also be difficulties with some retailers in obtaining new listings and shelf space.

What to look out for

The major advantage of extra-fill packs over price reductions is that the perceived value to the consumer is more than the cost to the manufacturer. Once the packaging has been paid for, the cost of additional ingredients is often low. Extra-fill does not devalue the product in the way that price reductions do. However, they are readily copied: in off-licences it often seems as if every major lager brand is an extra-fill product.

Delayed discounts

These are forms of discount that are not immediately available at the point of purchase. The buyer will normally have to do something after purchase to benefit from the saving. The crucial feature of delayed discounts is that not everyone who thinks he or she is going to take up an offer actually does so. Everyone is familiar with buying a product on the strength of a '20p off next purchase' coupon, sincerely intending to make use of that coupon but finding it in the kitchen drawer some months later – normally after its expiry date. This is the principle behind delayed discounts.

Delayed discounts enable savings to be targeted at people who fulfil the range of conditions that you wish to impose. The non-redemption level means that the size of the saving offered can be higher and therefore more attractive. They also allow an opportunity for creativity that is not normally available with immediate discounts.

The weaknesses of delayed discounts include their lack of immediacy: a bird in the hand can be worth two in the bush. They also involve additional handling and postage costs for both the consumer and the supplier. A £10 voucher could well have added-on costs of around £2: postage for both you and the consumer, plus the costs of envelopes, handling and voucher redemption. These costs are great news for the postal service, but can detract from the value of the offer you are making. There is also the danger that an excess of complexity can turn off participants: if a saving is being offered, it should be apparent that that is the case.

The major form of delayed discount is a coupon that can be used against a future purchase; these are discussed below under 'Coupons'. Other common forms are cash rebates, cash share-outs and repurchase offers. Supermarkets are now offering time-limited coupons at the till, with a cash value related to the purchased items.

Cash rebates

The offer

In a cash rebate, the customer is invited to collect tokens from a number of packs and post them in to receive a cash voucher. This promotion can also be used as a variant of the BOGOF, where a coupon is sent for the full cost of another product. The value of the cash rebate can also be varied, as can the conditions of entry, for example: 'Buy a complete set, and we'll rebate you £10.'

How it works

Cash rebates require postage from consumer to mailing house, and from mailing house to consumer, which adds significantly to their costs. They have been overtaken in consumer goods markets by multi-buys, but are effective in sectors where goods are more expensive and where EPOS systems have yet to make their mark. They are particularly popular in financial services – '£500 cashback when you take out a mortgage' is a typical example.

What to look out for

If the offer is less substantial than £500 (which everyone will take up), the cost to the manufacturer of a cash rebate will depend on the number of people who actually take up the offer. As there is always slippage between the numbers of people who are attracted by an offer and those who take it up, this enables a more attractive offer to be made. The size of the rebate must justify the postage and handling involved. In financial services markets, cash rebates are a highly effective way of incentivizing people with their own money.

Cash share-outs

The offer

In this offer, a sum of money is divided among all those returning the requisite number of proofs of purchase from a product or service. It is typically communicated as 'Send in five proofs of purchase for your share of our £100,000 share-out.' Variants can include the option of sending in an unlimited number of proofs of purchase.

How it works

The predicted redemption rate is carefully calculated to ensure that participants will receive a reasonable sum of money, normally equating to that which they would receive in a cash rebate scheme.

What to look out for

The main advantage of the cash share-out is the scale of the sum that can be offered. This can be attractive. However, it involves a substantial amount of postage and handling and can cost more to administer than the benefit given to the consumer.

Repurchase offers

The offer

Purchasers of consumer durables, such as fridges or hi-fis, are offered a commitment by the manufacturer to buy back the product at a specified point in the future (often five years) for the same amount as the purchaser paid for it. A variant is to offer a lower guaranteed trade-in price.

How it works

This offer at first seems like a guarantee of bankruptcy for the manufacturer. It relies on three considerations:

1 A great many people will forget to apply for repurchase in five years' time.

2 Inflation will have eaten into the value.

3 Those who do ask for repurchase form a good market for repeat purchase.

What to look out for

Offers of this kind need to be carefully calculated and insured, and low inflation levels are making them less attractive than they were. They can also seem too good to be true – certainly in full repurchase form. However, as a means of making an offer with a higher perceived value than cost, they have their advantages in markets with repurchase cycles of five years or so.

Coupons

The offer

Coupons are used to provide an immediate or delayed discount on a product or service to end users or intermediaries. They can be distributed in a wide variety of ways, all of which have different redemption rates and vary considerably in popularity over time. They are used so extensively that they form a subject in their own right. As with delayed discounts, the critical factor is the level of redemption and the slippage between being attracted by the offer and taking it up. Mobile couponing is having an impact. This is where consumers see an advertisement or website that invites them to text a particular message to a given number. They receive in return a bar code that can be scanned in at the point of payment and the 'coupon' is redeemed. A number of plastic cards are also being developed for couponing. In principle, all the systems are the same. The manufacturer or retailer 'gifts' a customer with a sum of money redeemable against a specific purchase.

Misredemption, where a retailer accepts a coupon whether the customer has purchased a product or not, is rife in the grocery sector, costing the industry £20 million a year, and the IPM (when it was the ISP) launched a campaign to stop the practice.

How it works

A coupon is, in principle, a straightforward thing to organize: you print your coupons giving a specified saving on the next purchase; you invite people on your website to print out coupons; you distribute them; retailers or other intermediaries accept them in part-payment for your product or service; and you reimburse the intermediary. If there is no intermediary involved it is even simpler: you accept your own coupons in part-payment.

Coupons are the nearest most of us get to printing money, and we do so in huge volumes. It is critical to think through questions of distribution, redemption and format. There are eight main ways of distributing coupons:

1 on or in your product or service;

2 door to door;

3 in newspapers;

4 in magazines;

5 by direct mail;

6 in-store;

7 via a website – printing off the coupon;

8 via an SMS text for a customer who has given permission.

These different ways of distributing coupons are described by the coupon industry as different 'media'. They have different shares of the total number of coupons distributed and there are radically different redemption rates, ranging from less than 1 per cent to over 20. Note that there is also considerable change year on year. Although the general differences between different forms of media are clear enough, there is considerable variation over time.

So how do you decide which way to distribute your coupons? It depends what you are trying to achieve. Different coupon 'media' have very different uses and characteristics:

- Coupons in or on a product or service are primarily a generator of repeat purchases and a reward for loyalty. They can be used for brand extensions – say to trial a new product. They can also attract new customers.

- Door-to-door couponing is most effective for targeting a particular geographical area, for example near a shop. It is effective in gaining new users, particularly when used in conjunction with a sample.

- Newspaper couponing is apparently wasteful (up to 99 per cent non-redemption), but the figures need to be related to the huge size of newspaper circulations.

- Magazine couponing is similar to newspaper couponing, but can be more carefully targeted. Magazines also allow tip-on coupons stuck on the page.

- Direct mail is the most expensive and also the most targeted form of couponing, and has the highest redemption levels.

- In-store couponing usefulness must be tested to establish whether or not it really does generate extra business for your product or service or simply provides a convenient discount to those who would have bought anyway.

Getting the format of a coupon right is vital for something that can be used as money. Clear guidelines have been drawn up for the grocery trade for the design, structure and organization of coupons.

Any couponing activity requires a redemption system. If you are going to redeem your coupons yourself, the redemption systems are a matter for your own internal accountancy. If they are to be redeemed by intermediaries, you need to ensure that all likely intermediaries will accept them and that they will be duly recompensed for their trouble in so doing. The best answer is to use one of the handling houses; the leader in this field is Valassis, which is responsible for 85 per cent of all UK coupons. Its experience is considerable and it has saved many a promoter from expensive errors.

What to look out for

There are three major problems that can arise with any couponing activity:

1 *Malredemption*: large-scale fraudulent redemption. It arises, for example, from a batch of newspapers being systematically cut for all their coupons and redeemed at a friendly retailer or claimed by the retailer. There are ways of coping with it, and handling houses are best able to advise on this.

2 *Misredemption*: this differs from malredemption in that it is the result of individuals redeeming individual coupons against products or services they have not bought. It is almost impossible to act against without the support of retailers.

3 *Fraud*: internet coupons are an example. Ease of printing requires such identifiers as 2D bar codes. The fraud here is not easy to identify.

Despite these difficulties, coupons are a promotional evergreen. They are a good way to provide a price benefit without making it available on every pack sold. The secret is to use coupons in a creative and carefully targeted manner, and to calculate in detail the redemption costs against the extra business you gain.

Finance deals

The offer

Zero per cent finance is one of the great sales-clinching offers of all time in 'high-ticket' markets – those in which the consumer needs to lay out a substantial sum to make a purchase. It has been widely applied in the motor, furniture and consumer durables sectors, and its application is potentially far wider.

How it works

If a company lends money at less than the rate it pays to borrow it, it has to make up the difference from somewhere. While the principle of subsidized finance is fairly simple, the forms it can take are immensely varied. There are four key forms of subsidized finance:

1 *Manufacturer and finance house deals*. These deals are normally set up by major manufacturers that sell through dealers; they most commonly occur in the motor trade. A large slice of money, at say 8 per cent, is borrowed and then a range of interest rate options is constructed for its customers, for example 4.1 per cent (for repayment in 12 months and a 50 per cent deposit) to 6.5 per cent (for repayment in 48 months and a 20 per cent deposit).

Dealer and customer would agree the actual price of the car in the usual way. The net amount owing would then be repaid by the customer at the interest rate selected. The manufacturer would pay the finance company the difference between 8 per cent and what the customer was actually paying.

2 *Intermediary and finance house deals.* Finance companies generally dislike concluding deals of this kind with companies other than major manufacturers. If you want to persuade them to do so, it is helpful to understand their criteria. These are the main ones:

- The item should be durable, identifiable and movable (DIM). This covers products that last, which have serial numbers on them and can be removed if the debt is not paid. Cars, boats and machinery obviously fit the bill.

- The debt outstanding must be less than the resale value of the item should the finance house be forced to repossess it. The answer to that is to have relatively high deposits and relatively short repayment periods.

- You must be an honest, trustworthy, credible business.

If you can satisfy these criteria, and others of a more technical nature, there is no reason for not approaching a finance house to construct a finance deal that you can subsidize.

3 *Personal loan deals.* Items that are not DIM, for example furniture and carpets, cannot be financed by a finance house, because the items cannot provide adequate security against non-payment. One answer is for customers to take out a personal loan, normally secured against their house. The manufacturer or retailer can then subsidize the interest rate in the same way as with a finance house deal. There are many credit providers with which these deals can be negotiated.

4 *Unsecured finance.* The final major form of subsidized finance involves the manufacturer or retailer providing the credit without direct recourse to any external source of money. Furniture retailers commonly use it. Let us assume that a furniture retailer sells a three-piece suite on a no-deposit, 0 per cent interest deal. The cash price is £1,040, and the credit price is £10 per week for two years. Applying discounted cash flow calculations to the repayments, the furniture retailer can calculate the value of the sale on the day it is made. Two of the crucial elements in this calculation will be the company's view of the movement of interest rates and inflation over the two-year period and the expected level of bad debts. Assuming these estimates are correct, it can identify the true value of the sale in profit and loss terms. The repayments then become a matter of cash flow. Calculated incorrectly or with an over-optimistic assessment of likely bad debts, this method of providing subsidized finance is a sure-fire way of going bankrupt. It is a route that only the most hardened, experienced and cash-rich businesses should even think of.

What to look out for

Most marketing people do not need to be experts in consumer finance. Getting involved in 0 per cent finance deals or other subsidized interest rate offers calls for a fairly sophisticated knowledge of the potential, the pitfalls and the economics of our financial system. If you are willing to master the arithmetic and study the systems, the rewards can be considerable. Even so, it is best to appoint a professional to do the job for you or at least to check your calculations. It is also vital to follow closely the requirements of the Consumer Credit Act and other legislation.

Trade price promotions

A promotion that attracts the retailer but not the consumer may work; a promotion that attracts the consumer but not the retailer is unlikely to get off the starting blocks.

The distinction is often made between 'push promotions' (aimed at pushing products via the retailer to the consumer) and 'pull promotions' (aimed at the consumer, pulling products via the retailer). The distinction is not an absolute one: most promotions need both pull and push if stock is not going to sit on the shelves (not enough pull) or not reach them in the first place (not enough push). Here we look at the push element in the mix – the use of price to give retailers reasons to support the promotion of your product or do the promotion themselves. There are five main forms of trade price promotion.

1. Overriders

The offer
An overriding discount is agreed at the beginning of a year between a supplier and a purchaser and is payable by the supplier at the end of the year if the purchaser has achieved agreed targets. Overriders normally relate to the volume taken over the year, but can also cover display, distribution and other business targets. If the targets are not reached, the overrider is not paid. They are heavily used by food and motor manufacturers and holiday companies supplying via retailers. Some motor dealers derive most of their profit from overriders, discounting the normal trade margin to their own customers.

What to look out for
Some purchasing professionals dislike overriders on the grounds that the cost to the supplier is simply built back into the price. Suppliers also dislike them because, over time, the targets can become ritualized and purchasers can expect their overrider as a right. Nevertheless, they are widely used, and in some markets cannot be avoided – they become a cost of doing business. The trick is to make sure that the targets set for the overrider in annual negotiations give some benefit to both parties over what would otherwise have been achieved.

2. Display and advertising allowances

The offer
These are allowances for a retailer to conduct some piece of promotion for the manufacturer. The allowances can pay for media support, stack ends, leaflets, coupons, window bills, display and any other form of retail support.

How it works

Most retailers have a tariff for almost every form of promotional support, from a stack end to a window bill. Increasingly, allowances are charged for listing a product, and investment in the retailer's in-house magazine or advertising is a required cost of doing business. Allowances that used to be at the discretion of manufacturers are increasingly at the command of the retailer. The growth of EPOS systems has enabled even medium-sized retailers to know exactly how much of a product can be sold from a given position in the store and to charge manufacturers accordingly.

What to look out for

Manufacturers need to look closely at the total profitability of each product line in each retailer. Take away the total of all allowances, overriders, volume discounts and other trade discounts from the selling price to the retailer and you have the net selling price. Take your manufacturing and promotional costs away from that and you know the contribution to overheads you are achieving from that retailer on that product line. If possible – and it often is – allowances should be targeted to achieve particular results, such as extra display and advertising. In many cases, allowances have become part of an increasingly complicated calculation of the cost of doing business with a particular retailer. You need an equally complicated financial system to work out if it is worthwhile.

If you are a small or medium-sized retailer, there is massive opportunity for increasing your margins by claiming allowances. The major multiples all have sophisticated EPOS systems that give them the power of knowledge; small retailers still have a long way to go in acquiring it.

3. Volume and case bonuses

The offer

These are short-term bonuses given by manufacturers to retailers. A case bonus is an amount of additional discount given per case bought. A volume bonus is an amount of additional discount given for buying a certain volume of product – more than would normally be bought at that time. Sometimes these take particular forms; for example, a baker's dozen is the practice of charging for 12 cases while supplying 13.

How it works

Volume and case bonuses are used by manufacturers to fill a pipeline into the trade, to make life difficult for a competitor by filling stockrooms or to encourage a retailer to offer shelf price reductions. They also work in some trade sectors as a means of encouraging display and support for promotional activity. The hugely successful 'Bass Nights' developed by Bass in pubs across the country relied on this mechanism. Pubs were offered a kit comprising posters, quiz games, merchandise prizes and other items to run a themed fun night in the pub. These were good news for the consumer. What appealed to the landlords was the offer of a free keg of beer. This put extra margin behind the bar – and encouraged them to run Bass Nights as often as they could.

What to look out for

Nothing is easier than giving the trade additional discounts in the hope that it will increase sales of your product, but it is a slippery slope that leads to increased expectations of discounts and a steady lowering of your average selling price. It is essential to use volume and case bonuses intermittently and only in return for defined benefits. As retailer power grows in most sectors, this is easier said than done. It is one of the main reasons promoters seek alternative promotional mechanisms that do not devalue the brand's price to the trade or consumer.

4. Count and recount

The offer

The term 'count and recount' derives from days when salespeople would habitually go into customers' stockrooms to count the stock. Count and recount gave the retailer a bonus on the difference between the count and the recount – in other words, on the amount that had been sold. In most sectors, it can now be done by EPOS counting the quantity sold through the till, but the principle is the same.

How it works

Count and recount puts the focus of the manufacturer's discount on what is sold to the consumer. It provides a good reason for the retailer to ensure that products are not just taken in but sold on to the customers.

What to look out for

In major multiples, this technique has largely been replaced by mechanics such as the multi-buy, which have a similar effect. In other trade sectors, count and recount is a way of giving trade discounts that do not simply end up increasing retailer margins. It gives an incentive to consumer sales.

5. Credit offers

The offer

The provision of credit is as important to the retailer as it is to the consumer. Providing the trade with enhanced credit terms can encourage earlier and deeper stocking of your range.

How it works

Multiple retailers derive a significant part of their profits and their positive cash flow by taking payment from their customers two months or more before they pay their suppliers. In these markets, the manufacturer is a key source of capital. In other sectors, trade payments can be faster, and the manufacturer can vary the payment period. This is particularly important in seasonal businesses such as garden centres.

What to look out for

The cost of credit can be calculated for trade promotions in the same way as for consumer promotions. It is important to be aware of the risk of bad debts and to be clear that you have the financial resources to carry the delayed payment. If you can do so, using credit is a powerful means of trade promotion.

The first of the three case studies below illustrates the long-range alternation of price and value promotions in Tesco's promotional strategy. The other two are examples of price promotion taking a far more focused form than it is often assumed to do.

CASE STUDY 9.10   Tesco

During the mid-1970s, Tesco became the largest grocery user of Green Shield stamps. These were stamps produced by a third-party operator, rather like a low-tech version of Air Miles. Consumers collected them at the checkout, stuck them into books and exchanged the books for merchandise at the equivalent of Argos catalogue shops. They were widely available at petrol stations and other retailers as well as at Tesco. Green Shield stamps were a central element in Tesco's strategy for customer loyalty but they were costing 2 per cent of turnover and were spiralling out of control. Double, even quadruple, stamps were becoming commonplace.

So Tesco signalled the end of Green Shield stamps and plunged the grocery trade into a bitter long-term price war with the launch of 'Operation Checkout'. Other retailers were forced to respond in kind. The price war continued into the early 1980s, radically increasing the major multiples' market share, depressing their profits and forcing a wave of closures, mergers and rationalizations. Tesco's own market share shot up from 8.5 to 12 per cent. The recession of the early 1990s brought a new spate of price wars, with retailers competing with discount shops and the expected development of warehouse clubs by developing a secondary range of low-priced own-label 'value' lines. The economy improved from 1993 onwards so the threat of the discounters proved to be less serious than commentators had expected. How matters have repeated themselves in 2014!

Tesco rocked the grocery world with the launch of Clubcard in February 1995. It initially offered a 1 per cent saving on a spend of over £10, plus a range of product offers. Clubcard quickly attracted over 5 million customers and was credited with driving Tesco's market share up to 18.5 per cent and producing a 16 per cent rise in sales in the first year. Competitors quickly followed. When in 2002 Sainsbury's dropped Air Miles, Tesco immediately took them up – some would say it went full circle in returning to its Green Shield stamp days. The delight of a promotion is that everything changes, but over a 40-year period some things look much the same.

For a time the huge investment made by Tesco in shopping online proved successful. It matched customers' requirements in terms of time and quality of life. Studies showed that 43 per cent of Tesco's top (high-value) customers were 100 per cent bonded to the Tesco brand, choosing not to even think of buying anywhere else. A bonding to the brand was a new concept in 'loyalty' then. But Tesco has lost ground since 2012. It knows it is not loved. Where does Tesco go next? It is again offering deep price cuts. Perhaps Tesco needs to understand the power of the engram.

CASE STUDY 9.11   Gale's honey

Gale's faced a classic brand squeeze: it was 15 per cent more expensive than own-label honeys. The Nestlé brand manager in 1994 set its promotion agency SMP a long list of objectives – reduce the rate of sales decline, avoid delisting, create impact on-pack, increase distribution, encourage multiple purchase, build loyalty – and keep the cost of the promotion under control. There's virtually everything in that list of objectives, but they boil down to one thing: provide an interesting reason for Gale's buyers to buy more, with one major constraint: keep the cost under control.

Getting to the heart of a long brief is a major challenge in a promotion. The agency built on the idea of buying more by opting for a '20p off next purchase' coupon as the basic offer. The coupon was printed on latex; it could be scratched away and, if you were lucky, reveal a prize of £10. The consumer was then faced with an interesting choice: the chance of £10 or the guarantee of 20p. Once scratched off, the 20p coupon became invalid. The problem then was what to offer the majority of consumers who opted to win £10 but failed to do so. Instead of nothing, they found a beehive logo, which could be collected and exchanged for a range of Gale's pottery items. Asking consumers to have a bet on a £10 prize and not leaving them empty-handed if they lost, hit every part of the brief. The promotion worked: distribution increased from 80 to 85 per cent, delisting was avoided, sales increased by 15 per cent, and coupon redemption was kept to less than 2 per cent. Also, the database of Gale's collectors was dramatically increased.

When you're in a tight corner, promotions need particularly careful thought. The promotion was a very well-targeted answer to the question 'Who do I want to do what?'

CASE STUDY 9.12   Worcestershire sauce

Lea & Perrins' Worcestershire sauce is one of those products more likely to be found at the back of many people's cupboards than in everyday use. Yet a wide range of daily dishes could be spiced up by a dash of Worcestershire sauce if only it could be brought to the front of people's minds.

The agency Lovell Vass Boddey sought to do this with a multi-layered campaign that won an ISP award. Data from previous promotional responders were profiled against a lifestyle database to target 2 million households with a mini-pack containing a sample of the sauce, a '10p off next purchase' coupon and a free mail-in offer for a recipe book.

The result was a coupon usage rate of 10 per cent and uptake for the recipe book of 6 per cent. Responders also received an additional coupon against next purchase and a lifestyle questionnaire, which received a 25 per cent response. The characteristic of this promotion was the intelligent integration and the use of database profiling to increase targeting accuracy before and after the promotion.

Summary

Price promoting is playing with fire. All the surveys show that consumers prefer it to any other form of promotion. The surveys also show that it devalues brands and leads to an expectation of even more price promotion. The same holds true for the trade.

Promoters are most likely to use price promotion effectively if they think in terms of segment pricing, look for concrete benefits from each discount they give and use price promotion intermittently. One of the key challenges of a promotion is to find value promotions that work as well as (or nearly as well as) price promotions and add to, rather than devalue, brand values. However, price promotion continues to be a benchmark for promotional effectiveness and is often made unavoidable by trade pressures and competition.

Self-study questions

9.10 What are the key features of segment pricing and how does it differ from other types of pricing?

9.11 What are the pros and cons of multi-buys?

9.12 What are the pros and cons of reduced-price offers?

9.13 What alternative means of coupon distribution are available, and what are the typical redemption rates for each?

9.14 If a 10p coupon is placed in a newspaper with a circulation of 2.3 million and a readership of 3.9 million, and you expect a 1 per cent redemption rate, how many coupons will be redeemed?

9.15 What are the main types of trade price promotion?

9.16 What key things should you look out for if you are using a 0 per cent finance offer?

Premium promotions

Premium promotions are the most frequently used value offer in which the benefit comes in the form of an item of (often branded) merchandise. Why a 'premium'? The reason for the choice of name is lost in the mists of time. It can cover anything from a potted plant, through a virtual pet, to a magazine. It can be a standard item, uniquely created or off the shelf. Indeed, all merchandise and all products are potential premiums. Case study 9.15 shows how Procter & Gamble moved from value to price promotion and back again. The basis of premium promotions is competing without tampering with the price.

This section looks at the four main premium promotion mechanics: on-pack offers, with-purchase premiums, free mail-ins and self-liquidators. It is important to understand the different characteristics of these mechanics; in practice they are blurred by a fifth category – the brand-extension promotion.

CASE STUDY 9.13   Häagen-Dazs

An example of brand extension is the 'Dedicated to Pleasure' CD sponsored by Häagen-Dazs. Produced by EMI, the CD used the company's distinctive press advertising on the cover and included the Sarah Vaughan track 'Make Yourself Comfortable' used in its TV advertising. It sold over 60,000 copies, gave the brand a presence in 3,500 music stores and reached the Top 20 for compilation albums (which constitute over a third of total music sales).

On-pack offers

The offer

This is a form of premium promotion in which the premium is physically attached to the product. If it is in the product, as with items tucked into breakfast cereals boxes, it is sometimes called an 'in-pack' promotion. If the premium surrounds the product, replacing its normal packaging, as with a storage jar for coffee, it is sometimes called a 'container' promotion. An example of a straight on-pack is a magazine cover-mount – a premium taped or bound to the magazine cover.

How it works

These promotions have similar characteristics to the immediate discounts discussed earlier: they have instant appeal, give an immediate benefit and do not divert resources into handling and postage; they are also quite expensive to run.

Whether it is appropriate to put a premium in, on or around the product depends very much on the nature and size of both the premium and the product, and the characteristics of your packing processes. It would be evidently impractical to include a paintbrush in a tin of paint and unnecessary to go to the trouble of taping a toy to the outside of a cornflakes packet. All things being equal, it is best to put the premium in the product; next best is to attach it to the product. These steps prevent consumers taking the premium but not buying the product. However, there can be considerable costs in creating new shipping containers and in disruption to high-speed packing lines. Retailers can also be resistant to non-standard pack sizes, particularly in the grocery trade. The use of on-pack offers is thus a matter of carefully weighing costs and benefits.

Cover-mounts are universal in the magazine market. (Where the attachment is on an inside page affixed to an advertisement for the product it may be called a 'tip-on'.) Ideal cover-mounts are flat, cheap, attractive and useful, which is why calendars, diaries and books are found on magazines as different as *Vogue* and *Yachting Monthly*. IPC claimed sales increases of 10 to 15 per cent using confectionery as cover-mounts – a Chocolate Orange bar on *Essentials* and low-sugar Canderel on *Healthy Eating*. In both cases, the products were new to the market, so gave their manufacturers a targeted sampling opportunity. Use of on-pack premiums in the child and teen markets includes pens, make-up and badges on magazines and the extensive use of character merchandise on confectionery. Nestlé has used figurines of Disney characters from 'The Lion King' and 'Pocahontas' in the place of caps on larger Smarties tubes. Once the Smarties have been eaten, the figurine forms part of a collection of characters that the child can keep.

The reusable container form of on-pack offer makes the premium the packaging and the packaging the premium. Familiar examples include glass storage jars with instant coffee.

What to look out for

Immediate free premiums suffer from the cost of giving away anything worthwhile on a low-priced product. On-pack offers are best compared with immediate price offers, and here the advantages really show. They do not devalue the product's price and they can develop and reinforce brand identity – the brandgram. If you have selected the right item, immediate free premiums can be a very powerful incentive to buy. The premium should be right and the offer cost-effective in terms of margin.

With-purchase premiums

The offer

These are promotions in which the premium is not physically attached to the product but is available at the point of purchase. They are sometimes called 'near-packs' or 'gift with purchase' (GWP). Examples include a free portable TV when you buy a car, a free personal filing system when you appoint an estate agent and a free carnation at the conclusion of a restaurant meal. These promotions are common in duty-free outlets and at cosmetics counters in department stores, where vanity bags or other items are given away when a purchase of a particular brand is made. They also work well in the pub trade, so long as great care is taken not to overburden bar staff.

How it works

With near-packs, handling is a critical issue because arrangements have to be made for the premium to be available at the point of purchase without being taken by those who do not buy the product. For these reasons, near-packs work best in outlets where there is counter service (as in the case of cosmetics) or where it is possible and worthwhile to use field marketing staff (as in duty-free outlets). It is generally not possible to use near-packs in grocery multiples today.

The premium can simply be a one-hit reward, such as a vanity bag with a purchase of cosmetics. It is also possible to include samples of other products in the bag, and to include coupons to be used against the purchase of full-size packs. That way the gift with purchase feeds into subsequent sales.

What to look out for

Near-packs give a direct and immediate incentive to buy one brand in preference to another without devaluing the retail price. The right incentive can add real value to the brand proposition and enhance the brandgram, but they are expensive, involve careful arrangements at point of purchase and reward those who would have bought without the incentive. They are, in practice, restricted to high-margin products.

Free mail-ins

The offer

Free mail-ins are premium promotions in which the customer collects one or more proofs of purchase and sends them in for the item on offer, entirely free or at no cost beyond postage. The benefit is delayed and not immediate. It is also subject to action on the part of the consumer after purchasing the item. Unlike on-packs and with-purchase premiums, not everyone who is encouraged by the promotion to buy will send in for the premium.

How it works

The word 'free' is one of the most compelling and powerful in our vocabulary. Rightly, it is subject to stringent restrictions. An offer is 'free' only if the customer pays nothing to obtain the item other than collecting the requisite number of proofs of purchase or pays only for postage in one or both directions. It is fair enough to say 'free with 61p for postage' if that is the cost of the postage, but it is not allowable to say 'free with 50p for postage and packing'. Promotions that require a telephone entry can be 'free' only if a non-premium telephone line is used – in other words, if the promoter is not recouping some of the costs by making profits on the telephone service.

A critical question in the structuring of a free mail-in promotion is the number of proofs of purchase that your customers must collect in order to obtain the item. This is a rule-of-thumb exercise and follows these criteria:

- The number must reflect the typical product category purchase frequency. Note that it is category frequency, not brand frequency: for cat food or a visit to a pub, 10 or more would be wholly reasonable.
- The number must also be influenced by whether or not you are seeking to influence triallists, light users, medium users or heavy users of your product or service.
- The level of redemptions is directly proportional to the number of proofs of purchase required. Raise the number of proofs of purchase, lower the redemption level, and vice versa.

The level of consumer redemption is naturally affected by the attractiveness of the premium (which you will want to maximize) and the closing date for applications (which you should set so that no products will be on retail sale after the closing date). You must decide whether or not to make any charge for postage and whether or not to offer a Freepost facility for customers to mail in their proofs of purchase. Note that the lower the postage costs are in each direction, the higher the response rate will be. You must also decide whether or not to restrict the offer to one application per household. Free mail-ins can be used as part of a bigger promotional package. Remember Gale's offered branded collectables as a consolation offer to those who failed to obtain a £10 instant win (Case study 9.11).

CASE STUDY 9.14   SmithKline Beecham

SmithKline Beecham did something similar to Gale's offer with a promotion for Ribena in 1995, themed on the Casper film. Consumers were invited to look under bottle ring pulls or inside cartons to see if Casper had 'spooked' their pack and given them a cash prize or a special Casper bubble watch. If not, they could collect tokens for the watch or, on the bottles, for a Casper beaker that revealed ghostly characters as it was filled.

Using free mail-ins in this way means that a promotion works at two levels: as an instant-win incentive for light users and as a collector offer for heavy users.

What to look out for

The operational planning of free mail-ins is critical. Things can go wrong with the handling, with the design of the premium, with delivery dates and so forth. Getting them right is a matter of sound organization and attention to detail. You will need to organize the system for warehousing the premiums, receiving customer applications, sending out the premiums, banking the postage contributions (if any) and handling any subsequent customer complaints.

Unless you contract out the promotion to a handling house for a fixed fee or take out insurance, you will need to develop a contingency plan to deal with the twin problems of over- and under-redemption. Make an estimate of the likely flow of redemptions over the promotional period, then monitor the flow over the first few weeks to give you early warning of what the final redemption level will be.

If a free mail-in redeems at below its expected level, you have three options: agree a sale-or-return arrangement with your premium supplier at the beginning (difficult if the premium is specially branded); sell off the surplus to a company specializing in the disposal of unwanted premiums (normally at a significant loss); or keep them for another (but probably equally unsuccessful) promotion. If a free mail-in redeems at above its expected level, you may be faced with difficulties in obtaining sufficient extra premiums in time. Clearly, your early warning system should help here. It is also advisable to make arrangements for rapid extra deliveries with your premium suppliers at the beginning. Section 35 of the Sales Promotion Code makes it clear that 'phrases such as "subject to availability" do not relieve promoters of the obligation to take all reasonable steps to avoid disappointing customers'. If you cannot supply the premium you promised, 'products of a similar or greater quality or a cash payment should normally be substituted'. The best option is to order slightly fewer items than your expected redemption level and have good arrangements for rapid resupply with your suppliers.

Self-liquidators

The offer

A self-liquidator promotion (SLP) is one in which the customer pays for all (or almost all) of the cost of the premium and its associated handling and postage. Such an offer cannot be described as 'free'. At best, it can be described as a 'bargain' when the cost is still below what customers would otherwise pay. A typical example of a self-liquidator would be a 'Super kitchen knife – just £3.99, plus 61p postage.'

How it works

A self-liquidator works in exactly the same way as a free mail-in, except that the customer pays for all or most of the cost of putting on the offer.

What to look out for

Self-liquidators work if one or more factors are present: you locate a premium at a radically lower price than that at which it is available anywhere else; you create an image for your premium (enhancing the brandgram) that makes it a desirable, full-price item; and the margins in the category are very large. With these exceptions, self-liquidators are an attempt to run an extra benefit offer without actually giving an extra benefit. It is not surprising that customers may give them the thumbs down.

Brand-extension promotions

The offer

Brand-extension promotions began when companies realized that people would pay high prices for merchandise carrying their brand names. An offer that makes a profit is a particularly attractive form of promotion. It adds to, rather than uses, your marketing budget and turns the normal worry about redemption rates on its head. If each redemption makes you money, the more the merrier! The line between the premium purchased by the company for promotional use, the product manufactured under licence by a third party and the brand extension jointly marketed by both in their mutual interest has become blurred. Film companies license their film names, and products used in films can benefit from such association. When the premium exceeds the cost, it can be questionable which is product and which is premium.

How it works

A brand-extension promotion requires the promoter to think laterally about the brand – not just as, say, a car or a bar of chocolate, but as a bundle of values that can be expressed equally well in clothing, bags, watches, albums and magazines. Changing the product by including things in it or creating new products by putting your brand name on them is a promotional activity.

What to look out for

The critical question to ask yourself if you are considering this type of promotion is: 'What business am I in?' The danger is that managers become overexcited about what are often marginal profit opportunities in branded merchandise and neglect the marketing of their core product. *The Guinness Book of Records* began as a promotional premium for Guinness. It has become an entirely self-standing product that many will not even associate with the dark liquid that gave it birth.

Business gifts

The offer

Business gifts are items given to trade customers to promote goodwill. In the grocery trade, they are often known as 'dealer loaders' – a reference to their historic use in persuading dealers to load up with stock beyond their requirements in return for an item of merchandise.

How it works

Judging by the level of advertising for clocks, calendars, ties and leather goods in the marketing press, business gifts are big business. A business gift is seen as something that has impact, attractiveness, usefulness and longevity and puts your name in front of a business customer as a reminder. The public sector and many large organizations have rules preventing their staff receiving gifts of more than token value from suppliers, and these must be respected. However, 80 per cent of businesses are small operations run by their owners and there is no conflict of interest between owner and buyer. When NatWest wanted to encourage start-up businesses to choose it rather than another bank, it teamed up with BT to offer what was, essentially, a consumer promotion (Case study 9.5).

Examples of items of merchandise being used in imaginative ways to persuade business customers to do something are: Eversheds, which used a highly imaginative premium item to encourage firms to contact it about intellectual property law (Case study 3.6); Electrolux, which used a tape recorder in a special box to encourage buyers to list a new product (Case study 9.17); and the use of a single wellington boot to encourage commercial property agents to visit a new development (Case study 3.2). The key promotional question, 'Who do I want to do what?' applies to business gifts as much as to any other area of promotion.

Approaching business gifts in this way enables you to use them in a cost-effective and focused way. Business gifts can be used to achieve the following:

- 'We want personnel managers to have our telephone number on their desk at all times.' Does not mean they will call you, so you may need something else too!
- 'We want leisure centre staff to carry their personal kit in one of our sports bags.'
- 'We want shipping managers to put a map of the world on their walls that shows our shipping routes.'
- 'We want marketing executives to come to our seminar on opportunities on the internet rather than to those of our competitors.'
- 'We want chief executives to understand that we are at the leading edge of thinking in our business.'

When you are looking for business gifts, there are three sources. The first is to go direct to the many companies that advertise in the marketing press. This can take time, but is the cheapest way of doing it if you know exactly what you want. The second is to use a business gifts catalogue. There are very many of these, often syndicated to local agents. The third approach is to use a premium sourcing house. These used to be only really interested in large quantities or wide ranges of items, but that has changed and they will now supply small quantities. The advantage of using them is that they know about the latest technologies and designs and can search out and design something original for your company.

What to look out for

There are rules governing VAT and income tax on business gifts, particularly those given internally. Make sure you have a copy of the latest HM Revenue and Customs advice and are in touch with your Revenue and Customs office if you have any doubt. Also make sure you have also understood the internal rules of the companies you do business with. Violating a rule that puts the recipient of a gift in an embarrassing position is bad business: no one can have as a promotional objective: 'I want my customer to be embarrassed.'

The promotions in this section specifically focus on near-packs, on-packs and business gifts. Other relevant case studies for premium promotions are Kleenex facial tissues (Case study 11.1), Eversheds (Case study 3.6) and NatWest/BT (Case study 9.5).

CASE STUDY 9.15   Procter & Gamble

Some promotions are remembered for years, if not decades. Test this out by asking someone over 70 if they remember the plastic roses promotions of the early 1960s. This is the story behind it.

In the late 1950s, Procter & Gamble and Lever Brothers were locked in trench warfare. Daz was an innovative synthetic detergent when it was launched by Procter & Gamble in 1953. Two years later, Lever Brothers responded with Omo. By the late 1950s, there was no functional difference in washing performance between the two brands. Price promotion was rife and ultimately unproductive. Up to 70 per cent of packs carried a money-off flash, weakening the perceived value of the brands. There was continuous heavyweight TV advertising. Despite all this activity, market shares seemed locked at 12 per cent for Daz and 9 per cent for Omo. How could Procter & Gamble break through the 12 per cent share ceiling? How could it escape the price warfare? The answer when it came was a classic of promotional marketing. Nearly 60 years on it carries lessons for any brand in any sector facing similar market conditions.

Procter & Gamble tested alternatives to the money-off packs in a panel of 88 stores across the country. Dozens of alternatives were tested and the clear winner was the offer of plastic roses as a near-pack. Rolled out nationally in 1961, 8 million roses were given away and Daz's market share increased to 18 per cent. Costing around only half of the perceived value of 6 d, the flowers made sense both to the company and to the consumer. The scope for retail prominence was immense. The promotion was repeated in the next two years, scoring brand shares of 16 and 14 per cent respectively. By then, Omo had responded with plastic daffodils, effectively turning the detergent price war into a flower war.

Plastic flowers were then, as now, considered naff by many people. They had very little to do with brand values, but rigorous testing showed that they worked. And they did – for a while. Price warfare then resumed and, by the mid-1970s, was again normal. The lesson of the Procter & Gamble roses is that promotional innovation can have massive impact on brand share, but no single promotional technique lasts for ever.

What parallels to the Procter & Gamble and Lever price warfare can you see in the market today, and how could premium promotions change the situation?

In which retail sectors could you now use near-packs, and in which retail sectors would it be impossible?

CASE STUDY 9.16   Clearblue One Step

What kind of promotion is right for a pregnancy test? Different women hope for very different outcomes, and some may approach the test with considerable anxiety. By 1994, the pregnancy testing market was crowded with technically similar products. Clearblue One Step faced a major competitor that had recently been re-launched with a full support programme. In a crowded market, loss of brand share soon leads to loss of distribution and a cycle of decline sets in. Clearblue One Step identified four objectives for the promotion: to offset competitor activity; to add value to the product; to affirm the brand's position on women's health issues; and to offer an item of relevance irrespective of the test result. The product cost £10.75, and the cost of any promotional item had to be in proportion to that price. SMP's promotion had both trade and consumer targets. In pharmacies, it is often the pharmacy assistant who recommends which pregnancy test to buy, so the promotion had to appeal to them. In multiples, such as Boots, consumers self-select, so if the offer was to work it had to be clearly marked on the pack.

The solution was to band a well-woman diary to the pack. This featured relevant and helpful information, irrespective of the test result, and a host of other health advice. It worked: sales in autumn 1994 were up 20 per cent on the same period in 1993 – a volume increase of nearly 12,000 units a month. It deserved to work and won an ISP award for the company and its agency, SMP. What shines through is the clear link between market conditions, brand values, promotional objectives and the promotional solution.

CASE STUDY 9.17   Electrolux

Convincing buyers to stock a product is crucial for any new entrant. These 'gatekeepers' are the first hurdle any new product has to overcome on the road to success. In 1994, Electrolux launched a new micro-cleaner, the X8. The objectives of the trade launch were to create interest and awareness among buyers, gain listings and increase market share. Building on the name X8, Electrolux sent out a series of 'Xtraordinary' mailers to buyers. The rep then visited buyers, carrying a security box that looked as if it were made from stainless steel, and was emblazoned with top-secret messages. On removing the lid, a cassette player played a personalized message to the buyers about the top-secret mission they were about to embark on. After the message was played, the box revealed the X8 in all its 'micro' glory. The cassette player was left with the dealer.

Daft or what? It certainly worked, creating a great deal of interest and amusement in the trade. All existing Electrolux outlets listed the X8, and the firm gained several new accounts. Electrolux's share in the cylinder cleaner sector increased by 50 per cent and overall it moved into brand leadership.

Marketing is a serious business. Electrolux no doubt had a stack of technical and market research reports to show just how successful the X8 would be, but you can't bore someone into buying – amusing people often works better. (What about Dyson now and its complex technical messages?)

Summary

Premium promotions are the most important way companies can compete promotionally without altering the price. There are four main mechanics – on-pack, near-pack, free mail-in and self-liquidator. The boundaries between them are becoming blurred with the growth of brand-extension promotions.

There are considerable opportunities for promoting, enhancing and extending brand value, but companies must be careful to remember their main priorities. Business gifts should not be considered a separate category, but an extension of thinking about, 'Who do I want to do what?' in the business-to-business field.

There are practical and operational issues to consider in sourcing premiums, organizing, handling, and dealing with redemption rates, further details of which are given in Chapter 4.

Self-study questions

9.17 What are the pros and cons of on-pack offers?

9.18 What do you need to take into account if you are planning a near-pack?

9.19 What contribution can you ask the consumer to make if you are running a free mail-in?

9.20 How can a promotion extend a brand into new distribution outlets?

Prize promotions

Prize promotions differ from every other mechanic discussed in this book in that the benefit to consumers depends on whether they win or not. A 20p coupon is a guarantee of 20p off the product specified on it. A free mail-in is an undertaking by the promoter to provide a premium in return for a certain number of proofs of purchase. With prize promotions, there is no such guarantee. Three other characteristics distinguish prize promotions:

1 They are offers where the maximum cost can be predicted in advance and does not vary with the numbers who participate.

2 A far bigger benefit can be given in a prize promotion than in a promotion where it is available to everyone who participates.

3 They are heavily regulated by the British Codes of Advertising and Sales Promotion, by the Lotteries and Amusement Act 1976, by the Gambling Act 2005, and by other legislation that is far from simple to interpret.

There is a difficult balance to be struck in writing about prize promotions. On the one hand they are staggeringly successful, leading promoters to forget the need for caution. The chance to win a car, a holiday or a substantial sum of money at little or no cost is always attractive to consumers. On the other hand they are a legal minefield and some promoters regard it as a no-go area. But Philip Circus, a legal expert on promotions, suggests that the pressure is off and as long as there is no change to the purchase price, then a prize promotion is ok.

There are five types of prize promotion – competitions, free draws, instant wins, games and lotteries. They are distinct in legal terms, are subject to different legal and code of practice restrictions, and offer different mechanisms for winning the prize. The distinctions are not immediately obvious, and it is worth spending some time making sure you fully understand them:

● *Competitions* offer prizes for the successful exercise of a significant degree of mental or physical skill or judgement. Participants may be required to pay or make a purchase to enter.

● *Free draws* make available prizes by distribution of random chances. The selection of the winning ticket is separate and later, not instantaneous with its distribution. No skill or judgement is involved, and participants cannot be asked to pay or make a purchase to enter.

● *Instant wins* offer prizes by distributing a predetermined number of winning tickets. Consumers know instantly whether they have won or lost. No skill or judgement is involved, and consumers cannot be asked to pay or make a purchase to enter.

● *Games* are forms of free draw or instant win that give the appearance of requiring skill but in fact rely on probability. They can be based on brand-name games, such as 'Monopoly' or 'Trivial Pursuit', or on generic games, such as bingo or snakes and ladders. Because no significant degree of skill or judgement is called for, no purchase or payment can be required to enter.

- *Lotteries* work in the same way as free draws or instant wins, but participants pay to enter.

These distinctions become clear if we take an example of a prize promotion a local travel agent might put on. The promotion could be headlined: 'Win a weekend break with Sunshine Travel':

- It would be a competition if it required entrants to identify the capitals of five countries and to complete a tie-breaker. It would be legal to subhead the promotion: 'when you book your next holiday with Sunshine Travel'.

- It would be a free draw if it said 'Just drop your name and address in the box.' It would be illegal to subhead it 'when you book your next holiday with Sunshine Travel'. Anyone walking through the door must be allowed to enter.

- It would be an instant win if Sunshine Travel overprinted its booking confirmation with numbers that could be revealed by scratching off a latex panel, and a particular combination of numbers instantly won the prize. To be legal, anyone walking through the door should be given an equal chance of winning.

- It would be a game if the promotion read: 'Play snakes and ladders at Sunshine Travel and win a weekend break.' The game may require the use of a dice and even a certain amount of skill. The rules for a free draw would still apply to it.

- It would be a lottery if the subheading read: 'Raffle tickets available at just 10p each.'

To all intents and purposes, lotteries are a no-go area for commercial promoters. The only exceptions are small-scale lotteries, held at a single event (such as a dinner) with non-cash prizes below £50 in total value, and where the proceeds are entirely devoted to charity.

The other four types of prize promotion are subject to specific rules relating to the closing date, the judging process, the description of prizes, the announcing of winners and so forth. The key features are described in the sections that follow, and in more detail in section 40 of the British Codes of Advertising and Sales Promotion Practice. Philip Circus, formerly the Director of Legal Affairs at the Institute of Practitioners in Advertising, and legal adviser to the IPM and BPMA, has written an invaluable book entitled *Sales Promotion and Direct Market Law: A practical guide*. Anyone running prize promotions needs to be absolutely clear that they follow the complicated laws that govern prize promotions, and the best way to do that is to have your copy checked by the IPM, the ASA or a specialist lawyer.

Competitions

The offer

To qualify as a competition, and therefore for it to be legal to ask for a purchase to be made, the winner must be determined by the skill or judgement shown. There are many forms of competition, the main ones being:

- Order of merit: 'List the following five items in order of importance.'
- Complete a slogan: 'Complete this sentence in not more than 10 words.'
- Question plus slogan: 'Answer these five questions and complete this sentence in not more than 10 words.'
- Spot the difference: 'Identify 12 differences between pictures a and b.'
- Estimate: 'Estimate how many packs of this product will fit inside this car.'
- Spot the ball: 'Mark the position of the football on this photograph.'
- Identify: 'Identify these famous people from the photographs of their eyes.'
- Be creative: 'Draw a picture, take a photograph or write a story.'
- Treasure hunt: 'Use the clues to find the hidden treasure.'

By far the most common type of test is the question plus slogan. It is the easiest to fit into the limited amount of space available to communicate most competitions, the easiest to explain and the easiest to judge. Its benefit over a slogan-only test is that the questions filter the number of slogans that have to be judged.

That said, there is a simplicity to promotions that do not have a filter to reduce the number of tie-breakers. It makes the competition easier to enter for consumers and can increase participation. Captioning a photograph is a good one-shot test of skill and judgement that many people enjoy entering. The advent of cameras on mobiles and the popularity of the 'selfie' make photographs a probable success.

About 3 per cent of the population always enter competitions; 40 per cent do so from time to time. The scale of competitions used to be enormous. Today, competitions are much less frequent, having been replaced in many cases by instant-win promotions and put in the shade by Lotto in terms of the prizes they offer. Radio stations frequently run competitions that ask a number of simple questions but have no tie-breaker: the winning entry is the first correct set of answers drawn from a hat. These are, in reality, free draws. It is the skill and judgement in the tie-breaker that is the criterion in the competition as a whole.

Competitions are known for attracting professional competition entrants. These are obviously small in number, but it is wrong to think of a clear divide between professional entrants and non-entrants. The secret of good design is to make your competition attractive to the 40 per cent who sometimes enter and not just the 3 per cent who always do.

How it works

Competitions tend to have a low level of entry (0.5 per cent of opportunities to participate would be considered high) but still absorb management and sales-force time. Competitions can also be useful ways of drawing attention to a product's characteristics. The Zantac 75 promotion (Case study 11.2) used an imaginative competition mechanic for exactly that purpose.

There is a major benefit in running a promotion that has a fixed level of costs and makes limited demands in terms of premium supply. Once you have established the competition prizes and paid for the communication materials, you know the limit of your costs. This is a characteristic shared by other types of promotion and is of particular value when a company's budgeting procedure makes it difficult to cope with open-ended costs.

There are various guidelines it is wise to follow when designing a competition. Remember that it is not a Mastermind test. There is no point in making the test obscure and difficult. There is, however, considerable purpose in making it fun and amusing for your target audience. Competitions continue to be attractive to children.

Once you have selected the type of competition you want to run, design it so that there is an identifiable winner. A competition that consists of only a series of questions is likely to result in a great many correct solutions. The winner cannot be selected at random, as otherwise it becomes a draw. This is the reason for the common use of a tie-breaker. Creative tests are also capable of yielding a single winner. Every other kind of test needs a method of judging between those who get the correct answer to the estimate, the identification, the order of merit or the questions.

It is essential to set it up in such a way that a judge is able to judge. The requirement in a competition is for the exercise of 'skill and judgement'. These are prone to subjective interpretation. It is therefore important to indicate on what grounds 'skill and judgement' will be assessed. This is the reason for the inclusion in tie-breaker instructions of phrases such as 'in the most apt and original way' or 'in the most amusing way'. Any independent judge will want to know the grounds on which the selection of a winner is to be made, so it is sensible to build this into the structure of the competition from the beginning.

When you come to write the copy, make sure everything that the entrant has to do, from obtaining the necessary number of proofs of purchase to completing a tie breaker, is as clear as possible. The events that follow, from the judging process through to any obligation to participate in publicity activity, must also be made clear from the beginning. The British Codes of Advertising and Sales Promotion set out what must be included.

The level of response to competitions is strongly influenced by the prizes on offer. The best starting point is to fix the budget available. There are then several ways in which you can think about the prizes you offer. There is an argument that a single major prize creates the greatest interest; another is that the greater chance of winning one of many lesser prizes is more attractive. There is no absolute answer to this. Partly in response to Lotto, there has been a decline in the conventional system of a complicated and graduated prize structure: a big first prize, three second prizes, five third prizes and so forth. This structure dissipates impact and increases costs. The best solution is probably a single major prize and a large number (perhaps 100 or more) of runners-up prizes. It can be possible to use a variant in which everyone gains an item of some value, for example a coupon for money off future purchases. If you are doing this, be careful not to describe it as a prize. Something that every entrant obtains is not a 'prize' but a 'gift'.

Holidays and cars are tried-and-tested prizes, so be special. Try a twist to a standard prize, for example 'Get your hair cut in New York'. This combines a good standard prize with a special that (importantly) relates to the item in question – in this case, a hair care product or similar. Many competition rules specify that there is no cash alternative; if this is not the case, the amount of the cash alternative should be specified upfront. If you intend to use the prize-winner for publicity purposes, it is important to make this point in the competition rules and to specify it as a condition of entry.

What to look out for

There are several things to look out for when running a competition, and some require very careful thought. Asking entrants to predict a future event, such as the outcome of a football match, is considered forecasting and is illegal in a competition. Asking them to predict when the first goal will be scored is also illegal in a competition, but on the different grounds that it is a matter of chance. Asking them to predict the weather at the London Weather Centre on the day the match will be played may not be illegal because the weather is a state of affairs and not an event; its legality will depend on whether or not a substantial degree of skill is required. No wonder lawyers are needed!

Judging is an area of administration that causes headaches, particularly if you are faced with thousands of entries. Resist the temptation to treat it as a draw, choosing the first tie-breaker slogan that catches your fancy. You could find a dozen other entrants providing evidence that they had submitted the same slogan. Be clear before you start judging how you are going to interpret the rules. Is '100' two words ('one hundred'), one word or not allowed because it is not a word? Do hyphenated words count as one word or two? A good guide is to reduce the number of potential winners by making a strict interpretation of the instruction to complete a sentence in '12 words or fewer'. Being strict also protects you against those who may complain that, if they had known that 'words' meant 'words or numbers', they would have submitted a different entry.

Slogans are often required to be 'apt and original'. There is a trap for the unwary here. If two entries use the same slogan, neither can be the most original, for how do you choose between the two? Slogans that echo the long-established advertising of a brand ('I love Cadbury's Roses because they grow on you') are unlikely ever to be original, however flattering they may be to the advertiser.

In a judging session use a team of eight people. The first stage is to take a pile of entries, choose the ones you like and pass those you have rejected to your neighbour to do the same. When the process has been carried out by five of the eight, that is a majority: the short-listed entries have been short-listed by a majority. The second stage is to go through all the individual favourites and reverse the process, putting to one side any that any single judge dislikes. These two stages will have produced a crop of entries that could all be winners. The third stage is to choose the winner or winners by asking the question, 'Is this entry better than that?' This is done by all the judges together. If you need to select one winner, take the entry at the top of the pile as the provisional winner and read out the slogan. Take the next entry, read the slogan and ask, 'Is it better?' If not, discard it. If it is, it becomes the provisional winner. The process continues until all entries that have reached stage three have been reviewed, and the last remaining provisional winner becomes the actual winner. If there are 10 winners to be selected, follow the same process, but select the 10 entries at the top of the pile as provisional winners. If any subsequent entry is better, discard the least good of the 10 and replace it, continuing until all entries that have reached stage three have been reviewed.

The Code of Practice requires that both an expert and an independent judge be involved in the judging process. They can be one and the same person, for example a teacher for an art-related competition or a travel agent for a travel competition.

They can prove a help in managing the judging as well as demonstrating that the process is fair and seen to be fair.

A large number of entries is a reasonable test of the attractiveness of a competition, but not of its promotional effectiveness. The number of entries can be quite unrelated to the promotional objectives. Attracting entries depends on presenting the competition in the most compelling way for your particular audience: offering a free or low-cost means of entry and making the competition easy. Clever word games will be attractive to some groups, if not to most. It may be, however, that your promotional purpose is trade related, for example to gain display. Once that is achieved, the number of entries makes no difference at all. The question 'Who do I want to do what?' is the basis on which you can determine the style of competition you use and how easy and attractive you make it to enter.

Free draws

The offer

In a free draw, winners are determined entirely by chance and it is not permissible to require any payment or proof of purchase from entrants. Free draws differ from instant-win promotions in that people do not know immediately whether they have won or not. Second stages in free draws vary and include: waiting until the closing date to see if your entry is selected; posting a set of numbers in to a handling house to be checked against a predetermined list of winners (a practice much favoured by direct-mail magazines); and hoping to find the matching half of (for example) a banknote on your next visit to the outlet that hands them out.

Why should promoters use free draws rather than competitions and lose the ability to ask for a proof of purchase? What is the advantage of issuing prizes at random to people who may never be customers? There are four reasons for using free draws:

1 They can be highly effective in generating interest, awareness and participation. In particular, free draws are a strong traffic builder for retailers and a proven readership builder for newspapers. The absence of tie-breakers means that free draws attract up to 20 times as many participants as do competitions.

2 They are easy for the promoter to administer, are easy for consumers to enter, involve a fixed prize fund and are a quick and easy way of building a customer and prospect database.

3 They can involve an implicit encouragement to purchase. This needs to be treated carefully. Newspapers invariably state (as they are required to) that consumers can check their tickets without buying the newspaper; petrol stations invariably state (as they are required to) that tickets are issued to all those who visit the petrol station, not just those who buy petrol. This is the 'plain paper entry' route. In practice, between 80 and 90 per cent of those who enter also make a purchase.

4 They allow substantial opportunities for creativity. In comparison with competitions, which are the main alternative for those seeking a mechanic

with fixed costs, free draws require far fewer rules and do not require questions or tests, but do allow free rein for games of every kind.

Free draws share some of the features of competitions: a fixed prize fund; a range of prizes; and the need to make conditions of entry clear. These points are therefore not repeated here.

How it works

The simplest way to operate a free draw is to have a pile of cards on which consumers can write their names, addresses and any other information you want to collect from them, a box for them to make their entries and a declared date on which the winner will be drawn. For business customers it is even simpler – provide a container into which they can drop their business cards. When you make the draw, it is important that it is done by an independent person and that it is done with witnesses so it is seen to be independent.

Another way is to issue consumers with a card printed with a unique set of random numbers. These numbers are openly displayed and not covered by latex. The winning numbers are announced separately, on a board in a shop or in the pages of a newspaper. Consumers have to check the winning numbers against the number of their card and, if the numbers are the same, contact the promoter to claim the prize. Most newspaper cards operate in this way, with winning numbers displayed daily in the paper. There is a clear advantage of a double hit – first obtain the card and then check the winning numbers. Note that, to be legal, consumers must have a no-cost way of checking the winning numbers.

Predetermined number cards are a variant on the random number system. Each card is uniquely numbered but, instead of the winning numbers being announced for consumers to check, cards must be returned to the promoter to be matched against predetermined winning numbers. Direct-mail operators often use this format because it encourages consumers to respond.

A fourth method is to distribute a series of different cards that have to be matched together to create a set. Only a limited number of the cards needed to complete the set are distributed. Once the set is complete, the win is instant. Petrol stations have used this format to good effect with matching halves of banknotes. The left-hand halves were plentiful and right-hand halves very rare.

These are very much the bare bones of each type of free-draw offer. Actual free draws can be very complicated and can have characteristics of two or three of these types. For example, you can have an instant-win card that is also (when mailed in) a predetermined number card and gives the opportunity to match and complete a set. Numbers can be replaced with symbols or words and a whole range of other variants introduced.

What to look out for

Out-of-the-hat draws are perfectly straightforward. They are regularly used by retailers, motor dealers, and by companies holding an exhibition as a traffic builder, as a way of capturing names and as a focus of attention. As long as the guidelines in the Code of Practice are followed, they present no terrors. Indeed, they are one of the fastest and simplest forms of promotion to organize, and highly attractive on those grounds alone.

Other types of free draw need careful attention to the mechanisms that prevent fraud and ensure an equitable distribution of winning tickets. You need to use a security printer to make sure that you do not have multiple winning tickets in circulation. A means of verifying the winning ticket via hidden but unique marks is also advisable. You need to carefully seed the winning tickets so that they do not all turn up in the same outlet at the same time. Also, you need to ensure that there is no one involved with the distribution of winning tickets who can take advantage of his or her knowledge. A good way of doing this is to ask an independent person to do the seeding. That way you are also protected if you are publicly accused of fixing the scheme.

All these factors are manageable if you do three things. First, use a specialist printer (see Chapter 4). Second, consider the use of promotional insurance (also discussed in Chapter 4). Third, make sure your copy is checked by the ASA, the IPM or a specialist lawyer; a good promotion agency can help you with all of this as well. These three golden rules for successful prize promotions apply even more strongly to instant wins.

Instant wins

The offer

Instant wins have been around for a number of years in the form of scratch cards overprinted with latex, or with perforated windows to hide the winning or losing combinations or the winning symbol inside a can, a cap or carton, or a code that can be checked on a website. Only a limited number of winning cards or cans are distributed, and consumers know instantly whether or not they are a winner. There has to be a way for free entry. Promoters are cautious about releasing figures for the proportion of free entries they receive, but a figure of 10 to 20 per cent would be considered reasonable.

How it works

Instant wins work best on low-cost, high-volume products that have relatively low product differentiation. This enables large prizes to be offered and the possibility of winning the prize to be a major factor in the purchase decision. A decline in response to instant-win promotions is seen each time it is used. This is a standard promotional experience, as Camelot found with its 'Instants'. To continue working, the instant-win principle needs constant refreshing with new formats. Among the best people to advise on new ways of delivering the same concept are the specialist printers of scratch cards and games discussed in Chapter 4.

What to look out for

The considerations that apply to free draws also apply to instant wins, notably in respect of security and seeding. An additional issue to take into account is the possibility that the top prize is won early on in the promotion. From then on consumers are, in effect, being misled about the possibility of winning. The same applies if the promoter keeps back the pack containing the top prize until late on. It can be advisable to have two or three big prizes, though this militates against the attractiveness of the mega-prize.

Games

The offer

'Games' in a promotion are anything from a newspaper fantasy football league, a word search with prizes, a scratch-off game of 'Monopoly', to predicting the temperature on Christmas Day. Some require proofs of purchase and some do not. They are distributed variously on-pack, door-to-door, in advertising and as free-standing cards. Everyone knows what these games look like, and they can be hugely successful. They are really versions of a free draw, instant win or competition.

How it works

Most people think of a game as something that involves skill. In fact, English law defines a game of skill very restrictively. Most games, including complicated card games such as whist and bridge, count in law as games of chance. Only in such games as duplicate bridge, chess, darts and snooker does the element of skill predominate over the element of chance. If it is a game of chance you cannot ask for payment or purchase.

Don't people pay to enter games of chance such as bingo, roulette and the football pools? Yes, they do, and these are regulated under the Gaming Act 1968, Gambling Act 2005 and other legislation. The general purpose of that legislation is to restrict the availability and attractiveness of gambling and to subject it to taxation and detailed regulation.

Games used in a promotion are generally of two types. They are a form of instant win or free draw dressed up as 'playing' a version of 'Monopoly', 'Scrabble', 'Trivial Pursuit', 'Cluedo' or snakes and ladders. Alternatively, they are a form of competition dressed up as 'playing' a word game, predicting a future state of affairs or taking part in some other test of skill and judgement. What they are not (because that would be illegal) is the sort of game that the Gaming Board regulates. It follows that 'games' do not really exist as a separate category of prize promotion; rather they are a version of either a free draw/instant win or a competition.

This distinction has been tested in law. In 1995, News International won a case against Customs and Excise, which wanted to charge it pool betting duty of 37.5 per cent or general betting tax of 7.5 per cent on its 'fantasy' promotions. These varied from 'fantasy fund manager' in *The Sunday Times* to the 'Dream team' in *The Sun* and two cricket competitions in *The Times* – a classic case of versioning the same concept for the interests of different readers. Three of the four promotions operated by premium telephone line. The crucial question was whether the payment that this involved amounted to a bet. If it did, News International would have to have paid up. The tribunal held that it did not.

What to look out for

If you are going down the free-draw/instant-win route, games are in practice a clever and interesting way of dressing them up. All the considerations given in the sections on those two mechanics apply. Above all, ensure there is a free-entry route that is genuine and realistic. The opportunities for a great promotion rely on your skill and ingenuity in devising a game theme that is original, simple and exciting.

If you choose the competition route and require a proof of purchase, the considerations in the section on competitions apply. Be careful not to ask for any payment other than the proof of purchase. It is here that you can take advantage of promotions that are based on probability, which are discussed in the next section.

Probability promotions

The offer

Golf clubs have long enjoyed 'hole-in-one' competitions where an enormous prize is made available in the unlikely event of a hole-in-one being achieved. The possibility is insured against by specialists who have calculated the probabilities and are prepared to underwrite the risk for a fee. Exactly the same principle can be used in promotions that require a series of 10 items to be listed in order of priority or the temperature on a given day to be predicted.

How it works

The basic form of this offer requires the entrant to list a number of items in order of importance, such as the world's best cricketers or the factors that make for a good holiday. The 'correct' solution is chosen in advance by an independent judge and placed in a sealed envelope. Skill and judgement must be required on the part of those entering. It would be wrong, for example, to ask entrants to list a series of numbers in order of importance, because that would require only guesswork.

Who can objectively place in order of importance the all-time best cricketers or the factors that make for a good holiday? Objectively, no one can; however, the judgement of an expert amounts to an objective test. It is fair enough, therefore, to ask a cricketing journalist to determine the all-time best cricketers and a top travel agent to determine the list of the factors that make for a good holiday and to use your expert's answer as the correct solution.

The basis of a promotion in which, say, 10 items are listed in order of priority is the probability (or unlikelihood) of anyone listing the set of items in a particular order. The chances of doing so depend on the numbers of items to list; these are as shown in Table 9.1.

The exponential nature of the increase is obvious. If there are 10 items to list in order of importance, the chance of someone getting it right is 1 in over 3.6 million. It should be possible, therefore, to risk offering a prize of £1 million for the inverse of the probability – just 28p. The risk in letting 1,000 people enter is around 1,000 times greater, but should still cost only £278. Of course, an insurance company needs to cover its administrative costs, security, reinsurance and the possibility of more people entering than expected. The normal minimum for insuring a £1 million prize

TABLE 9.1 Probabilities of listing items in a certain order

Numbers of items	Probabilities of being right
2	1 in 2
3	1 in 6
4	1 in 24
5	1 in 120
6	1 in 720
7	1 in 5,040
8	1 in 40,320
9	1 in 362,880
10	1 in 3,628,800
11	1 in 39,916,800
12	1 in 479,001,600

is £25,000. A rule of thumb for working out the insurance cost is to divide the expected number of entrants by the odds, multiply by the prize value and double the resulting number.

Increasingly imaginative ways are being found to integrate high-value prizes with high odds and lower-value prizes with lower odds. For example, an offer with a football theme could promise a huge prize for getting three questions right:

1 the number of goals in a match (odds 4 to 1);

2 how many players will be booked in the match (odds 20 to 1);

3 the time in minutes before the first goal (odds 90 to 1).

The odds of getting all three questions right are several million to one, but you could offer a voucher or merchandise prize to those getting one or two of the questions right. You could also risk – and insure – the possibility of offering more than one huge prize on the basis that fewer than half the people who win a prize actually check that they have done so.

What to look out for

Promoters using this mechanic should remember that these offers can produce substantial negative publicity and give an impression of sharp practice. Case study 9.25

shows how Faber & Faber dealt with this possibility by offering a prize of such high value and high odds that it was unlikely anyone would win.

Particular care needs to be taken with promotions that involve predicting the future. The distinction between predicting an event (illegal) and predicting a state of affairs (legal) needs to be borne in mind if a competition format is being used and a proof of purchase is asked for. Note that if no proof of purchase is required, both are legal. In all these cases, a specialist insurer (see Chapter 4), can quote a price for insuring the prize you want to offer. It can also work the calculation backwards, telling you, for example, what prize and what odds you could offer if you had (say) £30,000 available to pay for the insurance and a reasonable estimate of the likely number of entrants.

The golden rule, as in any other promotion, is to think about the people who will enter the competition as being people with whom you want to build a long-term relationship. People don't mind high odds – they are high enough in Lotto – but they do mind being misled.

An element of prize promoting comes into many of the case studies in this book: the main mechanic in the Maxwell House promotion (Case study 8.3) was a free draw; a competition was used by Zantac 75 (Case study 11.2) and by Rover Group (Case study 3.7); while Gale's honey used an instant-win technique (Case study 9.11). These all give a sense of the wide variety of prize promotions. The case studies selected for this sector focus, amongst other things, on a particular way of integrating an instant win into a product and on an effective probability promotion.

CASE STUDY 9.18   Visit Scotland

A public sector, non-profit-making organization, Visit Scotland was charged with raising tourism revenues by 50 per cent by 2015; it became IPM Grand Prix winner and Brand Owner of the year in 2013. Agency Blue Chip Marketing used prize draws to persuade consumers to participate in a 'winter white' experience; 134 prize partners and 54 channel partners took part in the coverage.

Result: 26.2 million opportunities to see (460 per cent above target) and increased tourism revenue (by 165 per cent) with gross ROI of £311 for every £1 spent. Thirty-four per cent of respondents took a winter break in Scotland and 55 per cent of these booked a spring or summer break thereafter.

CASE STUDY 9.19   Sarson's

Vinegar is not an exciting product. Sarson's, the brand leader, is constantly looking for reasons to maintain its grocery display and justify its price premium over own-label vinegars. Its one distinguishing characteristic is its 'shaker' top, reflected in its advertising line, 'Shake on the Sarson's'. This, plus the emergence of new ink technologies, was the basis for a promotion by SMP that won an ISP award. Collars on the bottles were printed with a special ink that reacted with vinegar. When sprinkled with vinegar, they revealed cash prizes of £1 to £1,000, a £1 McCain's voucher or a '20p off next purchase' coupon.

The promotion had extensive objectives: increase sales, arrest market decline, add interest, justify price premium, encourage repeat purchase, add value, differentiate from own-label vinegars, and reinforce the advertising message. It succeeded in lifting share. Its characteristic was a clever use of emerging ink technology to deliver a standard range of prizes in an interesting and relevant way.

CASE STUDY 9.20   *The Times* fantasy share game

In 2001, PIMS-SCA joined forces with *The Times* newspaper and Bloomberg to run a fantasy share trading game, offering players the chance to become a millionaire. With over 154,000 players and more than 300,000 registered portfolios, the promotion was a resounding success for *The Times*, Bloomberg and its participants. PIMS-SCA helped *The Times* and Bloomberg to achieve their objectives by assisting in constructing the game in a secure online environment and leveraging the budget to maximize prizes, all at a fixed cost.

To be able to play the online game, entrants obtained a password from *The Times*. By logging on to their website, entrants registered their portfolio containing 10 shares with a fund value of £1 million. Entrants were able to register as many portfolios as they wanted, at any time of the game. For the following 10 weeks, participants traded shares, trying to gain the highest profit. The winner increased the value of his or her virtual portfolio by 30 per cent during the 10-week period. Weekly prizes were awarded for those participants who held the portfolio that rose the furthest within the share rankings. These bonus prizes, worth up to £250,000, were insured by PIMS-SCA, and included a Sunseeker yacht, a luxurious gourmet weekend at Hennessy's Château de Bagnolet and a garage full of Lotus cars. The overall value of prizes available in the promotion was £3 million.

CASE STUDY 9.21   Asda's instant reward cards

This is an interesting promotion as the rewards are for staff, described as 'super heroes', who go the extra mile and make a difference for Asda customers. Each manager is provided with a quota of instant reward cards which provide a range of treats, from paid time off to chocolates or flowers. Special Christmas cards are used in the run up to the busiest shopping period with higher value random prizes – one in five offered £200 Asda shopping vouchers. The objective is to provide instant reward and recognition to Asda 'colleagues' who excel, as well as reinforce the Asda Service Hero of the Month award, who also receive a gold reward card with different added value prizes. The simple campaign aligns with the behaviour and company's goals and generates excitement through instant rewards.

CASE STUDY 9.22   Worthington Cup Final kick for £1 million

In February 2001, Worthington beer, the sponsor of the English football League Cup, offered three lucky consumers the chance to win £1 million. At half time, the finale to Worthington beer's largest ever promotion, with prize money cover, construction and evaluation covered by PIMS-SCA, was played out in front of 80,000 spectators. Two contestants had won the chance to participate in the activity via an on-pack promotion on Worthington's Cream Flow Bitter.

To win the £1 million the contestant needed to complete five football skill tests:

Test 1: Kick a football into the net from the 25-yard line.

Test 2: The contestants competed against each other in a sudden-death penalty shoot-out against Chris Woods, ex-England football goalkeeper. The winner of this round automatically won £25,000 and progressed to the third test.

Test 3: The contestant kicked the ball through a target to win £50,000.

Test 4: This was identical to test 3, but the diameter of the target was reduced and the prize increased to £200,000.

Test 5: The contestant needed to score five penalties, against Chris Woods, out of five, to win the £1 million.

With the spectators' support the contestant won £50,000, and Worthington beer generated huge awareness and PR for its brand.

CASE STUDY 9.23   Cadbury's Txt 'n' Win promotion

When Cadbury decided to run an on-pack promotion on its chocolate bars, moving away from the traditional promotional techniques and incorporating new technologies, it approached PIMS-SCA and Triangle Communications. Cadbury was one of the first large companies to take advantage of text messaging and incorporate it into its own Txt 'n' Win promotion. Contestants simply purchased a Cadbury chocolate bar with a promotional wrapper and sent off the text message that appeared inside the wrapper, from their mobile phone. Winners were notified of their prize via an SMS text message.

Cadbury was able to maximize its brand awareness while minimizing costs and taking away the financial risk. Not only is this mechanic a fun promotion to enter from the consumers' point of view, but it also firmly positions Cadbury's brand at the tech leading edge.

CASE STUDY 9.24   Diageo

Diageo has carried out promotions of its Guinness and Smirnoff brands using SMS advertising. These have included a three-question competition with the prize as free drinks or 'two for the price of one' at certain bars between set times on particular nights. The prizes are awarded on presentation of the text message sent to the winning competitors on their mobile phones at the bar.

These can in future be tied into a code reader kept behind the bar. Many promoters are content to allow much wider broadcasting of offers through viral activity and are happy with the extra trade generated.

CASE STUDY 9.25   Faber & Faber

Some sectors are relatively low users of sales promotions and so give an opportunity for the creative use of techniques that are familiar elsewhere. One of those is the book trade. Publishers face the challenge that 60 per cent of bookshop visitors leave without making a purchase, that consumers buy on impulse and that the saliency of individual titles on bookshelves is low. The solution is to provide a range of key titles with maximum in-store prominence and encourage consumers to browse among them and make a purchase.

Triangle Communications addressed this for Faber & Faber with a self-assembly 'book tower' containing four copies of each of 25 titles, heavily flagged 'How to become a millionaire'. Consumers were asked to enter a competition based on clues among the books and complete a tie-breaker, which was to come up with the title for a book with a given synopsis. The winner was guaranteed a £10,000 prize and the opportunity to turn this into £1 million at a prize-giving event hosted by Melvyn Bragg. At this event, the winner was asked to select from a tower containing 100 books, 99 of them containing £10,000 cheques and one a £1 million cheque.

The need to get intermediaries on board was not neglected and followed the theme of the promotion. Retailers were invited to submit photographs of their displays for a £500 reward, which they could turn into £10,000 by means of the same mechanism used with consumers. The highest-achieving rep also won £500 that could be turned into £10,000.

The promotion increased Faber & Faber's sales during the period of the promotion by 15 per cent. Support from both independents and multiples was considerable, with Dillons featuring it for a two-month period. It also received extensive PR coverage, including speculation about whether or not TS Eliot, one of the featured authors, would have approved of the promotion (his widow said he would have done).

Competitions are a relatively unusual mechanic today, as consumers are considered not to enjoy the literary effort involved. However, book buyers are among those for whom writing tie-breakers is a pleasure. Using a competition enabled a proof of purchase to be required. The mechanic required people to both browse and make a purchase – central to the promotion's objectives.

Faber & Faber made no secret of the low probability of anyone winning £1 million. The press carried stories of how the risk was being offset by the company having placed a bet with Ladbrokes. The firm was right to be upfront about this: book buyers would have worked it out anyway, with potentially negative PR coverage. Being upfront avoided this and added to the positive PR coverage.

In many sectors, this promotion would have seemed old hat. In the book trade, it was both innovative and effective – and closely focused on the firm's objectives at every point.

What other retail sectors can you see using the type of promotion Faber & Faber used, and in which ones would it not work?

Do you think an instant win would work with books, and a tie-breaker competition with vinegar?

Summary

Each type of prize promotion has its strengths and can be used to achieve different promotional objectives. It is vital to be clear about the differences between them. They are among the most powerful promotional techniques, but are subject to quick wear-out. Prize promotions offer particular opportunities for creativity and have the major advantage of largely fixed costs.

The administrative rules are well covered in the Codes of Practice and should be followed in detail. Copy should always be checked, and insurance is often a good idea. The law in this area is particularly complicated and uncertain. Parliament has legislated separately for gaming, lotteries and betting, and in none of this did it specifically address the needs of sales promoters.

Prize promotions are an enormously successful promotional device, as major national newspapers including *The Times* and *The Sun* have discovered. Like them, you should take specialist advice before using all but the simplest forms.

Self-study questions

9.21 What are the main differences between a competition and a free draw?

9.22 What types of prize promotion do games actually consist of?

9.23 What sorts of lotteries are legal for promoters to run?

9.24 How can companies offer a £1 million prize without having £1 million to give away?

PART THREE
Implementation

In-house activity in support of implementation

If the premise of this book is accepted – that the customer is the start point on which everything depends to operate a successful business – then there is in-house activity that should be considered by the board of directors or the owner that will impinge on the running of marketing, including sales, and marketing communications and in particular promotions and promotional offers.

First, the structure and organization of the business needs to truly serve and match the customer need (this may need to be geographically based with delegation of responsibility) and have a customer focus (not just lip-service) in all operations; the resource (funding and providing staff who are carefully selected and trained) must be in place to fully understand the customer (obtain insight) and the support service be just that, supporting. There needs to be a process in place for planning, implementing and measuring the success or otherwise of such plans. Finally an analysis of potential risks and opportunities should produce contingencies and crisis plans (for promotions) that are ready to run.

Organizing and structuring the business

Separate functions, such as finance, production, sales and marketing continue to exist in firms and they can be managed well or badly. Whether people buy a product or work for a firm, they are all engaged in relationships that satisfy their needs to a greater or lesser extent. This dependency on relationships is across all the internal and external boundaries of a firm. What characterizes these relationships? Money plays a large part, whether in salaries for staff, dividends to shareholders or invoices to customers. However, there is much more to it than that: loyalty, expectation and human feeling. The task of business is to maximize the value of those relationships.

The work of a business is a process that takes place every time someone buys or uses its products or services. Relationships are created and strengthened in the process by which the customer and other stakeholders' needs are satisfied and contribute to the success of the business. The successful firm is one that creates a distinctive character in these relationships and operates in an environment that maximizes the value of that distinctiveness. A good marketing department does not create a competitive advantage on its own: production made it, finance sorted out the payment, and dispatch delivered it to the customer. The customer, if well satisfied and with ongoing relationship communication reminders, will return, probably bringing others, and purchase more. The engram research supports all this. Customers use their subconscious 'mind file' and the messages it receives as part of deciding whether to buy or not.

This means a business needs to examine its internal and external relationships and develop a structure, an organization, that makes relationship-building easy. IBM, for example, advocates unifying all customer-facing functions under one person: sales, marketing, stocking and delivery immediately fit with this, but what if you have a number of geographically separate operations? Each core store or outlet needs to be a unified team with a manager who has access to data on local customers and the authority to act locally. The centre of the business then takes on a supporting role to staff, training and providing the budget to obtain customer insight. The power delegated to the team has to include the building of relationships between each outlet with their suppliers and sharing insight so that stock levels and working together on promotions is part of the local operation. The capability to be agile can then become reality, re-ordering stock to meet local demand as necessary.

'Core stores' are those that are surrounded by more people who are likely to buy; for some companies, the difference between core and non-core may be slight, for others it can be vast. Pick your core stores and stock the brands, products and services preferred by the customers you have identified through insight. In other words, by segmenting people and the stores they use, limiting your communications to the local area with some direct and general promotion and in-store preparedness and communicating the product promotion in-store and on-pack, you become a focused shopper marketing organization.

Delivering insight

Facts

Three-quarters of enterprises now say they use big data for strategic decision making, with 65 per cent of finance heads confirming this to be the case. However, the Stibo Systems survey revealed that, despite being used across different business units, 61 per cent of senior managers said their company's data was held by the IT department, 7 per cent saying it was the property of marketing, 21 per cent saying finance, and 9 per cent admitting to not knowing who owned their business's data.

One part of an organization or its operations can have information that would help another to succeed, but it is not always shared. An example of that is in the United Kingdom where under half of all FMCG marketing managers make use of the store-by-store EPOS data that is freely available to their companies to measure marketing impact. So what does a core team need to consider to develop relationships? The following can help in building trust and data capture on shoppers.

Local outdoor signage or advertising reminds shoppers approaching an outlet of what is potentially available in-store, building their engram recollection. Local advertising needs to be in place for events, roadshows, demonstrations or promotions. The retailer needs to increase the store presence locally to increase the share of voice level.

In-store the retailer and supplier can have a field day with on-pack, on-shelf and surrounding POP displays, and retailer or supplier initiated promotions. Remember that 70 per cent of purchase decisions are made 'in-store', so failure to stock and place your products on the store's shelves offers the shopper a chance to pick alternative 'on promotion' products or the services of competitors.

Gaining insight

Carrying out research that provides insight is complex and marketers tend to shy away from it, or rely on agencies to do it for them or just repeat the formula used in previous years. Marketers need to 'bite the bullet' and think about what they need to know. Research that provides insight is further complicated by the fact that shoppers can be influenced by the retailer: shoppers/customers may change their mind in-store or online at the point of sale as the result of some retailer activity.

Research is, or should be, designed to bring communicable insight, which gives you a new view of your problem that allows you to move forward. Insight is a function of the interpreter and of the user and not inherent in the research: judgement brings you insight, research delivers facts. There are basically three types of research that companies could undertake:

1 consumer/customer research per se (who is your customer?);

2 in the shop (the consumer/customer in the shopping/purchasing environment, both in-store and online); and

3 retailer research (information gleaned by retailers from their own data about shopper preferences and purchases).

The first research type is to do with individual shoppers/buyers, and revolves around their view of the product, the usage experience, the advertising messages they have seen and their future intentions. This is something only a business can investigate from its knowledge of who its customers are, what they want by way of products, services and delivery, and how best to establish a relationship with them (the offer; see Chapter 2). To gain insight the research needs to cover: 'before entering the store' or going online and the way shoppers go about their search; their experience of the purchase; and then their experience of the service or product itself once bought.

The second area to look at is the in-store behaviour or the way shoppers react to their shopping environment in-store/on the website, through observing how they react to the layout, the positioning of product, etc. The retailer can influence this.

A third area is to look at the store's EPOS data. This information is generated as a result of the sale and is not, per se, research into the shopper. On top of this you have information from shopper actions, such as social media reporting, or on-pack promotion take-up with data on stocking and availability issues.

Insight on the shopper

It is now possible to track people by their attitudes and actions as well as their demographics. Such targeting can have real impact on both the marketing budget and the sales targets. One of the downfalls of conventional research is that the questions are provided by the researcher and sometimes issues customers encounter are not properly understood simply because the right question is not being asked.

How can the plethora of opinions on websites such as Twitter and Facebook be used to produce a reliable and consistent picture of what real consumers and shoppers actually feel? What is needed is to turn the mass opinions you can find into something more tangible and measurable that you can really work with. There are a number of search engines and companies offering feedback on these opinions. Twitter data is captured by web crawlers that develop real-time feedback on a brand and a related emotion. Emotions can be identified in Twitter data using a computerized content-analysis tool called the Regressive-Imagery Dictionary (RID); see Table 10.1. The RID tool was developed and verified by academics several decades ago. (Note: Other companies use eight categories.)

Furthermore, as each Twitter comment is date-stamped it is feasible to match aggregated Twitter data with aggregate behavioural measures at specific points in time. Plotting these measures over time allows us to draw conclusions about the impact of consumer feelings and perceptions on brand performance. All the Tweets on a particular theme, such as excitement, bad service, high prices or executive pay, are then divided into time periods, such as weeks or days (or even hours of the day). Increasing or decreasing volumes of Tweets can help spot critical trends such as the

TABLE 10.1   Seven emotional categories related

Emotion	Example words
Positive affect	Cheerful, enjoy, fun
Anxiety	Afraid, fear, phobic
Sadness	Depression, dissatisfied, lonely
Affection	Affectionate, marriage, sweetheart
Aggression	Angry, harsh, sarcasm
Expressive behaviour	Art, dance, sing
Glory	Admirable, hero, royal

SOURCE: Martindale, 1975

failure of a new marketing campaign or a potential PR crisis boiling up. This data on important qualitative themes can then be matched statistically with measures of brand performance, such as brand consideration and sales to see how much these trends matter.

BRIEF 10.1 Developing a time-based tracking system

Cranfield took as its basis Aakers' (1997) five dimensions of branding, shown in Table 10.2. With two independent measures of Waitrose success – sales and Twitter contemporary feedback – Cranfield first built a picture of what was driving the average Waitrose shopper. It found that the lead emotion was excitement, followed by competence. Interestingly, competence was not closely associated with the Tesco profile. Given that Twitter feeds have the main objective of bringing friends and followers up to date, and not as grist for the researchers mill, it may be expected that high quantities of praise relates to a shared good experience. Meanwhile, bad experiences also travel well. Experience and self-esteem were negatively correlated to sales. So poor service, making you feel small, and not finding what you wanted would reduce sales.

TABLE 10.2 Five dimensions of branding

Brand personality dimension	Traits
Competence	Reliable, responsible, dependable and efficient
Sincerity	Domestic, honest, genuine, cheerful
Excitement	Daring, spirited, imaginative, up-to-date
Sophistication	Glamorous, pretentious, charming, romantic
Ruggedness	Tough, strong, outdoors, rugged

SOURCE: Aakers, 1975

Communicate and promote

Follow the seven simple rules for marketing established by Byron Sharp (in *How Brands Grow*), reproduced here with permission:

1 Reach all shoppers/consumers of the brand's service or product category, both with physical distribution and marketing communication. All these people are potential buyers of the brand.

2 Be easy to buy. Brands need to be where people would expect to see it – getting it onto the right shelves and keeping it there is an ongoing responsibility.

3 Get the message across. In an age of multimedia getting the message out has never been easier, but getting it across, never harder. Shoppers regularly avoid advertising et al media. So embed an engram.

4 Refresh and build appropriate memory structures. Re-invigorate and remind, enhancing the engram.

5 Create and use distinctive brand assets. Shoppers navigate by what they instinctively recognize – the brand images they are familiar with (the engram).

6 Be consistent, yet fresh. Brands outlive people, and companies. They do this by delivering a consistent message across generations. However, this consistent message needs to be constantly re-imagined to get through to new generations of potential users/consumers.

7 Stay competitive – don't give a reason not to buy. Brands need to focus on getting the best value for money from their discount events, while making sure that their core users – the loyalists who would buy at full price – are not disappointed in discount availability.

Install planning and implementation processes

There needs to be in place a process for planning and implementation (see Chapter 3). Business objectives need to be considered and a business plan produced. From this will follow marketing objectives and a marketing plan. Promotions arise from the marketing plan. The elements of all plans need to be translated into responsibilities for staff with the appropriate delegation of the powers to implement them. Job descriptions, of work objectives and appraisals set out what is required and perform-ance can be measured (KPIs are covered in Chapter 14). Teams can set about the implementation of the plans and running the day-to-day operation, making adjust-ments to accommodate the feedback gleaned from insight (big data and analysis of social media, etc).

The measurements of success or otherwise of any marketing activity including promotions should be stored in a corporate memory facility. Part of the process of implementing a promotion should be the examination of previous promotions to see what worked and what did not.

Assess risks and opportunities to produce contingency and crisis plans that are ready to run. This should include promotional offers that can be implemented at short notice.

Summary

Some would say that the contents of this chapter are simply the application of common sense. My business experience suggests that this is not what happens in reality. Too many silos exist; business politics gets in the way; greed, fear and poor leadership harm the building of relationships that make for business success and hundreds or thousands of happy customers.

Self-study questions

10.1 Assess your firm. Is it a customer-facing business? What needs to be done to improve that?

10.2 Are the means to obtain real customer insight in place? How could that be improved?

How to use and implement promotions

11

From promotional objective to promotional brief

Nobody in business likes giving away something for nothing. So how do you decide on the objectives for a promotion? Remember you have also asked for creative input: 'Who do I want to do what?' (Chapter 3). How do you work out what it can and cannot achieve, and how do you choose between the many techniques available? The promotional planning cycle looks like that shown in Figure 11.1; as you go round the cycle in your promotional career, you'll find that you get better at each of the six elements.

Once you have the business and marketing objectives established and know what promotions you are going to undertake as marketing activities within a campaign, you need to write a short brief. Whether you intend to devise a promotional offer yourself or to brief someone else, the first stage is the same; it is just as valuable to draw up a brief for yourself as for someone else. It should be short (any more than two sides of A4 is long-winded) and involves setting down the answers to these six questions:

1 What is the strategic nature of the brand – its positioning and differential advantage? This will have come from the offer (Chapter 2).

2 What is the promotional objective? Pick only one – see Chapter 8.

3 Define how you will know it has been a success. Find the particular KPI that you need to measure whether you have achieved success. Remember to allocate resource to measure the KPI. Chapter 14 explains why you should set a KPI.

4 Who are the people whose behaviour you want to influence? What are they like and what interests them? What is their preferred 'communication canvas'? Revisit Chapter 2 if necessary.

5 What behaviour do you want them to reinforce or change? In other words, what exactly do you want them to do?

6 What are the operational constraints of the promotion – budget, timing, location, product coverage and logistics?

FIGURE 11.1 The promotional planning cycle

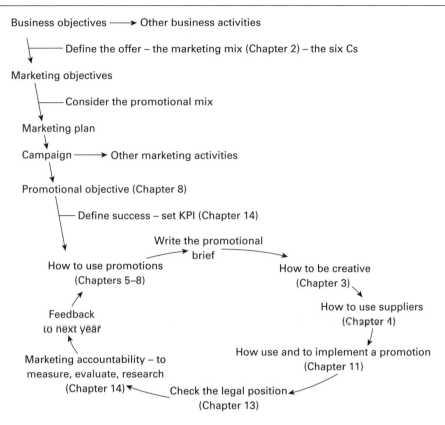

At any given time, it will be possible to specify which of the 12 objectives in Chapter 8 most coincides with both your overall marketing objectives and the campaign of which the promotion forms part. It is vital to get this right. Promotion agencies are sadly familiar with briefs that specify the objectives (often for a small-budget promotion) as 'to increase trial and repeat purchase, increase loyalty and increase trade distribution'. Desirable as it may be to do all these things, it is difficult to shoot at four goals at once. If your promotional objective does not overlap with any of the 12 in Chapter 8, it may be that you do not have a promotional brief, but a brief for some other kind of marketing activity – or, indeed, for a rethink of your business as a whole.

Taking the promotional objectives seriously (remember, just like business and marketing objectives, they should be SMART) means quantifying what the promotion is expected to achieve. For example, if the objective is increasing trial, it is important to specify how many triallists are sought, where they are to be found and the quantity of products or services they are expected to consume. Quantifying the objectives at the beginning enables you to measure and monitor the success of the promotion (a subject explored in Chapter 14).

FIGURE 11.2 Flowchart of the journey of a confectionery item from factory to end users

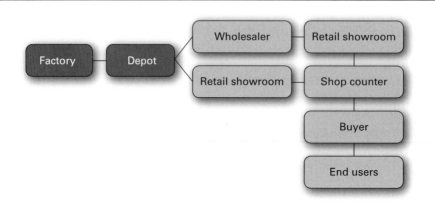

It is now possible to ask the central promotional question: 'Who do I want to do what?' This is when you move from the marketing objective to the promotional objective. The transition comes when you start thinking about the people who will help you achieve your marketing objective and the things you want them to do so that you can achieve it.

Figure 11.2 shows the movement of a confectionery item from factory to end users. Similar flowcharts could be drawn up for the movement of any other product or service; some would be simpler, some more complicated.

At each point on the chart, there are a number of people, who form the target for promotional activity. It is important to ask yourself four questions:

1 Who holds the key to the business problem of delivering the promotion? Is it the end user or the retailer? The buyer or the depot? Is it the customer?

2 What are these customers like? What other things do they do with their time? What are their motivations, interests and desires? What is holding them back from behaving as I would like them to behave? Is it children or friends? Who are they with when they are making the decision that I am interested in?

3 What exactly do I want them to do? Buy one product or more? Use it more frequently or for the first time? Tell their friends about it?

4 Who else on the chain has leverage? Some intermediary? Is it a boss or other staff member? What will persuade the retailer to put it on display?

Achieving behavioural change requires a high level of focus on these questions. It is the point at which marketing thinking moves from the general to the particular. It is no longer a matter of market share, penetration, segmentation and the other abstract categories. It is now about Julie Smith and her son Wayne trying to get the shopping done on a busy Thursday afternoon in Tesco in Birmingham, and spending less than a minute passing the gondola on which your product is located. What will make her choose one brand of vinegar rather than another? Will it be a coupon sent door-to-door, a Tesco multi-buy or an on-pack offer (if you can persuade Tesco to take it)?

Sarson's vinegar found a particular solution to these questions with its 'Shake on the Sarson's' promotion (Case study 9.19).

In the office stationery market, it is about the same Julie putting in an order for that week's needs for the small computer consultancy where she works part time. Julie is now a different kind of customer, taking on the role of a business buyer. What will make her choose one brand of sticky tape over another? Will it be an 'extra free' offer, a handy container, a straight discount or a personal benefit for her (if her employers will allow it)? Sellotape's 10,000 Lottery chances (Case study 9.7) provides one promotional solution.

In the drinks market, it is about the same Julie and her friends having a night out in a large, modern, suburban theme pub. What will encourage her to try out one brand of drink in preference to another? What will encourage her to try another within the limits of safe drinking?

In none of these cases is Julie alone. In the supermarket she is accompanied by Wayne. At work she is answerable to her boss. In the pub she is part of a group of friends. The social relationships of mother, employee and friend are very different and have different impacts on the way Julie will make her decision to choose one brand over another. Understanding the relationships and the contexts is crucial to finding the right means of encouraging Julie to do the thing you want her to do.

Thinking through Julie's needs and interests in relation to your business objectives is the key to promotional creativity. How will you evaluate the promotion and know whether or not it is a success? Chapter 14 gives you the answer: set the KPI and measure it; it's easy.

Promotional mechanics

Thinking about the variety of intermediaries and consumers you may want to influence, and their relationships and lifestyles, creates a bewildering number of options. After all, people are varied. The other side of the coin is the distinctly limited number of mechanics that are available in promotion.

A 'mechanic' in promotion refers to the particular things that consumers can be asked to do – a competition is a mechanic and so is a free mail-in. There are surprisingly few mechanics available, and all promotions use one or more of them. In many parts of the EU, law further limits the number of mechanics available to you. Objecting to one of them on the grounds that it has been used before is like objecting to a newspaper ad because newspaper ads have been used before.

The creativity and interest of a promotion do not lie in the mechanic itself, but in its relevance to your promotional objectives and to your target market, in the way you tweak it and vary it, in the content of an offer and in the way you put it across. Promotions have already been divided into price and value promotions. Mechanics can also be divided into those that impact immediately at the point of purchase and those that give a delayed benefit. Mechanics can then be classified as shown in Table 11.1; matching the nine key mechanics to the 12 objectives is shown in Table 11.2.

The matching ranges from 0 (not well matched) to 10 (very well matched). The ratings can be used as a rough guide to suitability. Very often it is the creative execution of

TABLE 11.1   Classification of promotional mechanics

Promotional type	Immediate	Delayed
Value	Free in-pack	Free mail-in
	Reusable container	Competition
	Instant win	Free draw
	Home sampling	Self-liquidator
	Free on-pack	Charity promotion
Price	Pence-off flash	Next purchase coupon
	Buy one, get one free	Cash refund
	Extra-fill packs	Cash share-out
	In-store coupon	Buy-back offer
	Finance offer	

a mechanic rather than the mechanic itself that is most effective at generating interest. Clearly, high-cost promotions like immediate free offers are more effective on almost every criterion than low-cost promotions such as self-liquidators.

If you have followed this process you will have a clear promotional objective in mind and you will have had an initial look at the mechanics that could meet it. Now it is time to look at matching the two together in an imaginative and effective way: it is time to see how to be creative.

Implementing the promotion

Now that you understand the crucial ingredients in devising a promotion, you'll be clear that, for your product or service:

- there's a marketing objective to be fulfilled for which you can specify a promotional objective, such as increasing volume or gaining trial;
- you know the strategic nature of the brand, its values and the offer in all its elements (the six Cs) and you have researched your customers' needs and established their communication canvas;
- a promotion, as the part of marketing that focuses on behaviour, is the right answer to a part of the marketing campaign that includes a need to draw attention at a specific time and at a specific place to a marketing activity; a sales promotion is when that time and place is in the retail space;
- you know how to convert the marketing objective into a promotional objective by answering the question, 'Who do I want to do what?' and then write a promotional brief;

TABLE 11.2 Linking the objectives to the mechanics: how they match up

Objectives	Mechanics								
	Immediate free offers	Delayed free offers	Immediate price offers	Delayed price offers	Finance offers	Competitions	Games and draws	Charitable offers	Self-liquidators
Increasing volume	9	7	9	7	5	1	3	5	2
Increasing trial	9	7	9	2	9	2	7	7	2
Increasing repeat purchase	2	9	2	9	5	3	2	7	3
Increasing loyalty	1	9	0	7	3	3	1	7	3
Widening usage	9	5	5	2	3	1	5	5	1
Creating interest	3	3	3	2	2	5	9	8	8
Deflecting attention from price	9	7	0	7	7	3	5	5	2
Gaining intermediary support	9	5	9	5	9	3	7	5	1
Discriminating among users	1	9	1	9	9	3	3	5	1
Restoring brand perceptions	9	5	7	3	9	1	1	1	1
Retaining brand perceptions	7	7	9	7	9	1	1	1	1

- you know of the need to define success, pick a KPI and then measure it to confirm that success (more of this in Chapter 14);
- the processes of brainstorming, list making and mind maps have been used to enable you to think imaginatively and creatively about promotional solutions (from Chapter 3);
- you have in mind the suppliers you can use and the ways in which they can help you devise and implement an effective promotion (from Chapter 4).

It is time to look at the nuts and bolts of implementing a promotion: budget, timing, communication, logistics and legalities. A simple three-stage cycle takes you from initial idea to completed promotion.

Budget

In many cases, the budget is given and you simply have to work within it. Will you be able to achieve all you want within the available budget? Are you sure? If not, go back to the beginning and start again. It is best not to try to cut corners, as it is usually more expensive in the long run.

What, though, if you have the freedom to set the budget? Money for promotions comes from the same pot as money for every other part of the promotional mix, though money for price promotions may be accounted for differently. There are five ways in which companies set their promotional budgets:

1 the amount spent last year, plus a little bit more for inflation and any expected market growth;

2 a fixed percentage of turnover, established over time for the company and industry;

3 the same as, or in ratio to, what major competitors spend;

4 the amount needed to achieve the defined marketing objectives – that is, what is needed, no more, no less;

5 in cost-cutting times, if you have not shown value for money from all your marketing, expect to be given the same as or less than last year.

The WKS survey showed that few firms changed their budget year in, year out, so it reduced in real terms and they did not change what they spent it on either. They ignored anything new – the new media, direct marketing, accountability and advertising other than press, TV or posters.

Starting with a blank piece of paper each year is a difficult task and, in practice, companies use one of the first three methods, a combination of them, or the last. Promotions can be costed as a separate and specific intervention in the market. The cost of the promotion and the margin it generates can be compared to the margin you would expect to make if you did not use the promotion. In fact it is wise to declare a marketing budget in two parts: the maintenance element, ie what you need to do to just stay in the market, and the extra needed to achieve growth, etc.

There is a simple piece of arithmetic that is basic to a promotion and deals with the relationship between promotional packs, proofs of purchase, opportunities to apply (OTA), redemption rate and cost. In this example, assume you are offering consumers the opportunity to mail in for a free model car on a packaged grocery product; the figures here are only illustrative to show the calculation and for comparison purposes. The sequence is as follows:

1 Your first decision is how many labels to print the offer on. Assume you want the promotion to last for a month. Take a month's volume, add 10 per cent for extra uptake and you can calculate the number of promotional packs required as being, say, 250,000.

2 Next, you decide how many proofs of purchase you will ask consumers to send in. Set it too low and your regular consumers have no incentive to buy more. Set it too high and your less regular consumers have no chance of participating. A good rule of thumb is to set it at the average level of purchase of the category (not your brand) in the promotional period – in this case, a month. Assume, on this basis, you decide on five proofs of purchase.

3 Now you can calculate the opportunities to apply (OTA). This is the number of promotional packs divided by the proofs of purchase. It is impossible for there to be more redemptions than this. In this case the OTA is $250,000 \div 5 = 50,000$.

4 Estimate the likely redemption level. This depends on the attractiveness of the premium, the ratio between proofs of purchase and purchase frequency, the amount of support you give to the offer, the strength of your brand and a host of other factors. Assume in this case a 6 per cent redemption rate. The calculation is then the OTA multiplied by the redemption rate: $50,000 \times 6$ per cent $= 3,000$.

5 Bring in the cost of providing the model car and receiving and handling applications. Here the estimate for handling a model car (cost, £1.00) is 80p. The total cost per redemption is thus £1.80.

6 Now you know the cost of this part of the promotion. It is redemptions multiplied by the cost per redemption, in this case $3,000 \times £1.80 = £5,400$. You can add to this the cost of artwork, special printing and other support for the promotion such as postage, packing the car. Assume this is £5,850, giving a total of £11,250.

7 Finally, you can express this figure as a cost per promoted pack by dividing it by the number of promoted packs. In this case it is $£11,250 \div 250,000 = 4.5p$.

This last figure is very useful. You can use it to compare the costs of different promotions on a like-for-like basis. You can use it to calculate how many extra packs you need to sell for the promotion to break even. If the cost is too high, you can also use it to go back to your calculations and try to find savings, for example, by asking consumers to contribute to the cost of postage, finding a cheaper model car, or increasing the number of proofs of purchase.

If you are running a coupon (see Chapter 9), the same calculation applies. Remember that the OTA are not calculated on the readership of a newspaper but on its circulation. Those with a higher number of readers per copy may have a higher redemption rate, but a coupon can be cut out only once.

You will also need to keep a careful watch on VAT. HM Revenue & Customs produces a series of booklets dealing specifically with promotions, business gifts and retail promotional schemes. They are, of course, subject to change, so you should make sure you have up-to-date copies to hand.

Valassis offers a handy calculator set out on Excel spreadsheets for direct mail, internet self-print and door-drop coupons. You just enter the figures in the spreadsheet and it does the calculation (see Chapter 15 for contact details).

Timing

Sales promotions (a promotion offered in the retail space) are often run to meet short-term market needs. They must also work with the lead times of intermediaries and suppliers. This makes timing a critical issue and one about which there is often conflict. It is important to be clear from the beginning about the following time constraints:

- when the promotion is needed to impact on the consumer;
- how long it will last;
- how that relates to the purchase frequency of your product or service;
- what lead times intermediaries require;
- how long you have for print and merchandise delivery;
- when you need your promotional concepts ready.

The time available at each stage strongly affects what can and cannot be achieved. Managing this can be significantly helped by using simple project management tools.

Communication

Every promotion is communicated in or on material of some kind. The options include:

- the wrapping of the product;
- leaflets in or with the product or service;
- leaflets separate from the product or service;
- advertisements in the press or on radio, TV, internet or posters;
- sponsored shows or events;
- posters, stickers and other support material;
- sales aids;
- mailshots;
- mobile marketing (including apps).

At an early stage you need to identify ballpark costs for what you want to do. You can firm them up later, but you need to know that the promotion is, in principle, affordable. To do this you need to select the appropriate communication media and estimate:

- the quantities needed;
- the specifications (colour, weight, frequency and so on);
- artwork, photography and other design requirements.

This can involve a great deal of getting in touch with print, media and other suppliers. A useful short cut is to obtain one of the published guides to print and media prices and base your estimates on that. Another is to keep a file of all promotions that you have costed and cannibalize the prices. Promotion agencies tend to be particularly good and quick at this, as they have a wealth of experience to draw on.

While the nuts and bolts are being worked on, time can be spent drafting the words that will be used to communicate the promotion. There are always two parts to the verbal presentation of any promotion: the upfront claim and the technical details, rules, instructions and other essential but secondary information.

It is common for agencies to present concepts showing what the printed material and advertisements will look like. This has one major danger: until the copy or scripts are written it is impossible to know how big the printed material will need to be. Often the concepts are presented and the budgets agreed but later someone has to ask for an increase in budget because the leaflet needs an extra page.

Write the copy or script first, even if only roughly. This will guide the designers and enable them to create a far better visual concept. Experience shows that the tighter the brief given to designers and copywriters, the better the results and the greater control you have over costs.

Use the websites of the IPM and DMA to obtain examples of the wording needed for coupons, etc. The Royal Mail on its website gives updated examples of direct-mail costs for different sizes of mailings.

Keep the creative approach simple. You have very little time to communicate your concept to the consumer. It is better to have a 'Win a holiday' headline than 'Bloggins summer spectacular'. The first communicates the benefits, the second nothing to those not directly associated with Bloggins. Remember too that research shows 'free' and 'new' are key words that trigger the shopper's subconscious mind to take a second look, as does a '£1' flash.

You'll also need to consider how the offer will be presented graphically. Whether it is communicated by leaflets, advertisements or in a small space on a pack, some form of graphics is needed. Even if you are doing the promotion yourself, some help will be needed here. It is important to reflect the style and feel of the offer in your graphic design and (if possible) enhance the underlying values of your product or service.

Logistics

Every promotion requires something to be given away, whether it is a prize, a coupon, a free mail-in premium or a charity donation. Having isolated what the offer consists of (win a holiday, send in for a kitchen knife, redeem a 25p coupon), it is possible to do the following:

- draw up a specification for the items involved;
- estimate the quantity needed;
- obtain ballpark costs.

Again, it is helpful to go to sourcing websites or have reference books to hand to short-cut the process of phoning or writing for samples and prices. Do use the internet to find samples and suppliers; you can quickly get quotes too. You can then turn to the operational characteristics of the promotion – how the promotion will actually work:

- Who will do what?
- Where will items be stored?
- How will they be distributed?
- What resources are needed at each stage?

The answers depend very much on the scale of the promotion and on your own resources. For a simple retail promotion, it may be no more complicated than arranging the printing and distribution of POP material. Other promotions can be very much more complicated and can involve marshalling half a dozen different organizations, a dozen types of printed material and offer materials of many kinds.

You'll need to ask yourself how feasible your promotion is. Be aware that much POP material is never displayed or properly displayed by retailers (*The Handbook of Field Marketing* by Alison Williams and Roddy Mullin explains how to overcome this). A brand manager once bought some excellent deckchairs at an extraordinarily good price for use as a dealer loader (these are gifts given to retailers; see Chapter 9). It meant that his offer would be far better than usual and far superior to those of his competitors. Unfortunately he forgot that most of the sales representatives were on the road for three days at a time, making 15 calls a day, and would have trouble fitting 45 deckchairs into a Ford Escort.

However, before you decide something is not feasible, ask yourself how it can be done rather than accept that it cannot. Be positive. Only when every option has proved impossible should you give up. After all, your great idea deserves to see the light of day.

Legalities

The legal and self-regulatory controls on promotions are discussed in Chapter 13, but it is worth discussing the subject briefly here.

It's best to start with the positive values that exist in your brand and in your relationship with your customers. Creative promotions have their origins in the values of a brand, in a shaft of lateral thinking that captures the imagination and fits the brief like a glove. However, sometimes you can get carried away with enthusiasm.

Ask yourself, does the activity conform to the various codes of practice and the law? If it does not, then the worst thing you can do is to try to bend the promotion to fit. This usually ends up by emasculating the promotion and making it too complicated.

Remember also to check how the activity will reflect on the promoter. Short-term gains that are achieved by an unfulfilled expectation on the part of the consumer will damage the company's reputation in the longer term. If something looks too good to be true, it probably is: remember how the Hoover flights promotion (Case study 9.4) almost killed the company.

A very simple rule to follow is to put yourself in the position of the consumer and think how you would feel if you were made this offer. In writing about direct marketing and door-to-door or mailshots I have always advocated trying it out with a letterbox, especially with other post. Does it look sufficiently different and exciting when it falls to the ground in a pile? If you would be unhappy, then so will your targets. 'Do unto others as you would be done to' is as applicable to promotions as to the rest of life. Think highly of consumers – they are neither stupid nor gullible.

A structured process

Managing the implementation of a promotion is no easy task. It helps if you divide the work into three stages, from brief to implementation, each separated by evaluation and decision phases, and resist the temptation to go straight to the detailed development of the first concept that comes to mind; see Figure 11.3. The three stages are:

1 Think through the possible solutions to the promotional brief. Define success. What KPI will you use to measure it? Reserve some budget to measure the KPI.

2 Develop your leading concepts in outline form.

3 Develop the top concept into an operational plan. Recheck the KPI.

We look at each of these, focusing on the work to be done at each stage – possible solutions, outline development and detailed development. Keep the stages separate, but remember it is all one process. Think of the stages as a series of loops.

Stage 1: possible solutions

Bear in mind the promotional objective and the promotional brief. Define success and set the KPI you propose to use to measure it. List possible concepts. Each concept will be described in a dozen or so words, often with further possibilities in brackets. A concept could be described as 'Competition: spot the ball (try a variant?) holiday prize (Tenerife? Florida?) plus vouchers for everyone who enters (if they cost less than £500).' Another may be even less specific about mechanics, but focus more on a theme: 'Win a holiday – competition or free draw – total prize pot £10,000.'

Now you have to apply a rough filter to the ideas you have developed. Figure 11.3 shows how it looks in flowchart form. This stage is the top part of the figure.

In the short-listing phase, you will need to go back to the marketing objective and promotional objective and see whether or not your brilliant idea is likely to achieve them. Keep the promotional brief to hand and remember how you defined success. To pick up the lager example from Chapter 3: will promoting it in tennis clubs really achieve a sufficient increase in sales? If it won't, you'll have to start again. Be particularly careful of the promotion that grips the customer, but not the objective. A promotion is there to meet a marketing objective, not simply to engage the customer.

Depending on the brief, you will end up with one or two possible solutions or maybe half a dozen. You can take these forward to outline development. Typically,

FIGURE 11.3   From the brief to the result

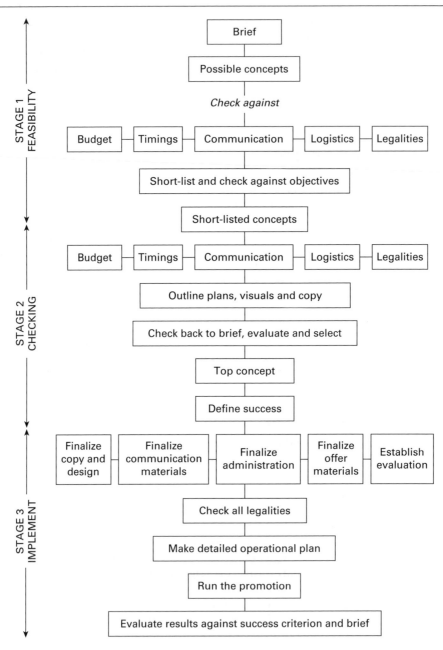

a promotion agency brings these items together on a 'concept board'. This is a rough illustration with the key message on it that instantly communicates the offer, backed up by one or two sheets of A4 on which are set out how the promotion will work and what it will cost. If you are doing it yourself, you will still need to see what the offer will look like and note down its key costs and operational characteristics.

Stage 2: outline development

The task now is to flesh out the details of your short-listed concepts and to establish whether or not they will actually work in practice. This process is shown in the middle part of Figure 11.3.

Working up the short-listed concepts is not a matter of doing different things to the first stage – it is doing the same things in more detail. So, for example, you will work out the detailed print specification and start writing the body copy. This process will narrow down the candidate concepts. You know that the concepts you are left with will work and how they will work. Now is the time to go back to the promotional brief and critically examine each candidate concept against it. Which really fits best? Which has strengths in one area but loses out in another? Which really meets the promotional objective? Which gives the most added value? And which will turn on your target audience the most?

For a big promotion, formal research is often advisable at this point, but research of some kind can be done for every promotion, simply by asking people you know. Friends, colleagues at work, customers can all be subjected to what is often (unfairly) called 'the idiot test'. Simply line up the concept boards, ask them to think themselves into the position of the target audience and rate your concepts on three criteria: clarity, attractiveness and accessibility.

It is surprising (and mortifying) how often your favourite concept will leave other people cold. You are too close to it to be objective. And even if the concept is clear enough, there will be points where it can be improved and ideas for these tweaks will come from the most unlikely sources.

At the end of this process, you are in a position to select the top concept. If it fits the brief like a glove and excites the people you show it to, you know you have a winner on your hands. At the very least you will have a sound, workable promotion that meets the brief you set. Now it must be turned into physical items, such as leaflets, posters and the like.

Stage 3: operational plan

This stage takes your top concept through to implementation. The elements of this stage are shown in the lower part of Figure 11.3.

This is the stage at which to check the criterion for success, set the KPI to measure and the budget to carry out the measurement, and to finalize and check all the secondary copy for the promotion – entry instructions, rules, descriptions of the prizes and so forth. It is imperative to follow the Code of Sales Promotion Practice in doing so. Use trade body websites to check (see Chapter 15). The rough visual also needs to be turned into artwork for all the various printed items for the promotion. Outside help will almost always be needed here.

The materials necessary to the promotion can now be obtained. It is normally possible at this stage to beat the ballpark prices obtained earlier because you now have a firm intention to proceed, so it is worth shopping around for better prices.

It is particularly important to pay attention to the operational plan. Many promotions fail despite excellent concepts, superb designs and exciting offers because a simple error has been made in the administration system. It is vital to go through this in the finest detail and to ensure that every aspect of delivery, handling and distribution is fully organized. Handling houses, and other suppliers described in Chapter 4, are crucial at this stage. A detailed operational plan sets out exactly what will happen when, by whom and how. A really tight plan leaves no room for error or misunderstanding and saves a great deal of time in the long run. After a while, the framework of a good promotional operational plan for your company will become established, so the process of drawing it up will become quicker as time goes on.

The operational plan must include contracts with third parties. They are of particular importance where the operation of a promotion depends critically on another company performing functions delegated to it. Contracts should always be drawn up for the following:

- *Joint promotions.* These are a disaster if the relationship turns sour, and one of the most effective ways of promoting if the relationship flourishes. A contract not only establishes the ground rules, but also obliges each party to think through all the eventualities before committing to a promotion.

- *Agency relationships.* A relationship with a promotion agency should always be governed by a contract setting out mutual responsibilities.

- *Premium supply.* Contracts beyond normal purchasing conditions are not generally necessary if you are making a one-off purchase of premium items. They are necessary if, for example, you are seeking to call off items for a promotion in the future or if a special item is being made.

- *Other specialists.* Contracts are advisable with handling houses, auxiliary sales forces, telesales operators, etc.

The formats of contracts vary enormously. Some companies write special contracts; others use long and complicated standard contracts. Many find that an exchange of letters backed by a set of standard conditions of trade provides the best balance. As promotional redemption rates are not always predictable, it is important to allow for changes in requirements in your contracts and to know on what basis the cost of any extra work is calculated.

Finally, you should establish responsibility for the marketing accountability and evaluation systems. You decided what success would be, you set a KPI and you need to make sure someone is responsible for measuring it. When you have the KPI results you will be able to evaluate the outcome against your definition of success. It is too late to think about how to evaluate a promotion after it has been run, when you have missed the opportunity to record much of the information. The time to do this is beforehand. There are various key measures that will flow from your objectives (discussed further in Chapter 8).

Now run it!

Now it is time to run the promotion. A promotion set up along the lines of the processes described here should run without a hitch, but it is always important to monitor its progress and be prepared to react to unforeseen developments. Redemption rates, in particular, should always be monitored closely against the expected rate. Remember, too, that a promotion ends when you have analysed all the available information to establish whether or not it achieved the objective set and your definition of success, and to draw out whatever lessons can be learnt.

The case studies in this chapter have been chosen because they illustrate the selection of promotional objectives and because of the way they make the link between business objectives and promotional mechanics. Every promotion in this book has something to say about the link between marketing objectives, promotional objectives and mechanics.

CASE STUDY 11.1   Kleenex facial tissues

This case study covers seven years of the 'Hay Fever Survival' promotion, run from 1991 by Kimberly-Clark, manufacturers of the leading brand of tissues, Kleenex facial tissues. Created by the Blue-Chip Marketing Consultancy, it is a rare story of consistent promotional development.

The original brief was simple and focused: to build a strategic platform to sell Kleenex tissues in the summer. Why hay fever? About 10 per cent of the population suffer from it, concentrated in particular geographical areas and on particular days when the pollen count is high. They are heavy users of tissues, but responsible for a small percentage of volume. Focusing on hay fever gave Kleenex tissues a promotional theme in the summer that used the demands of extreme product usage as a metaphor for best quality, softness and strength. While focusing on the hay fever sufferer, the offer had to appeal to all buyers of tissues.

The original promotional offer was for a free hay fever 'survival kit' in return for three proofs of purchase. It consisted of a toiletries bag containing an Optrex eye-mask, Merethol Lozenge pack, a travel pack of Kleenex tissues, money-off coupons for sunglasses and a room ionizer, and a 20-page hay fever guide from the National Pollen and Hay Fever Bureau. It was a partnership promotion, in which Optrex and Merethol provided their samples free. Why should they do so? Because Kleenex tissues could sample the hay fever sufferer in a way that no other brand could. Run on 900,000 packs, the promotion produced a 7.7 per cent response.

The next promotion bore a strong similarity to the original promotion, though now running on nearly 5 million packs and developed to include 'natural remedies'. In return for five proofs of purchase and 50p towards postage, the consumer received a toiletries bag containing an Optrex eye-mask, tube of Halls Mentho-Lyptus, a travel pack of Kleenex tissues and a hay fever guide from the renamed National Pollen Centre.

What happened in the next five years? It's a fascinating story of how promotions adapt to new needs and new opportunities – and how they can also lose their way.

In the first year, the recession forced a drop in the promotional budget. The toiletries bag was now unaffordable, and consumers were asked for 40p as a contribution towards postage. The contents remained the same but, to pick up on interest in that year in Europe, the guide became a European hay fever guide, with handy tips for travellers. There was also a new opportunity. Vauxhall had just launched the first family-priced car with a pollen filter, the Corsa. One was made available as the prize in a free draw. Despite this addition, the offer was objectively less valuable to the consumer than the original promotion, and redemptions dropped to 3.9 per cent.

Kleenex tissues then tried a new tack – a two-level offer. A new hay fever guide was available for one proof of purchase, and a set of samples for three proofs of purchase and 40p. A strong profile was given to a premium rate 'pollen line'. The creative treatment also changed. From focusing on 'hay fever survival', it now focused on 'those critical days' when the pollen count is at its highest. Extended to 4 million packs, the two-level offer was not a success. Redemption dropped to 0.3 per cent for the guide only, and 1.3 per cent for the sample kit.

This caused a rethink for the next year's promotion. Providing a clear and uncomplicated incentive to trial and repeat purchase became the priority. The premium rate phone number was dropped in favour of a link with the *Daily Mail* and Classic FM. The sample pack was slimmed to a new hay fever guide and three samples: Kleenex tissues, Optrex and Strepsils. The central offer was a high-quality AM/FM radio consumers could use to find out the pollen count. It could all be obtained for £3.50 plus five proofs of purchase. The 'hay fever survival' theme was prominently back. Response increased to 1.7 per cent, despite the higher requirement made on the consumer for both proofs of purchase and cash contribution.

This was not to last. The focus of the offer changed significantly. The central offer was a 'pollen-filter' Vauxhall Corsa to be won in a free draw each week for the 10 weeks of the 'pollen season'. The runners-up – 10,000 of them – received hay fever survival kits that included a new hay fever guide. Redemptions were 9.5 per cent.

Ten 'hay fever-free' family holidays then replaced the Vauxhalls as the prizes in the free draw with 6.4 per cent redemption. Unlike previous years, the option of 'plain paper' entries was included and did not require even one proof of purchase.

The wheel turned full circle. The promotion was a virtual remake of 1991, with the addition of strongly featured pollen count information in partnership with the *Daily Express* and Talk Radio.

In this seven-year period Kleenex's share of the branded tissue sector increased from 50 per cent in 1990 to over 70 per cent in 1996, recording increases every year. Its share of the total market increased to over 40 per cent, attracting extra volume from the 50 per cent of consumers who buy both Kleenex tissues and own-label tissues. Promotion was one of the key marketing weapons throughout this period and must take a major share of the credit.

Operating on-pack, at point of sale, in the media and with third-party endorsers, it was a thoroughly integrated promotion. Three factors that stand out in this case study undoubtedly helped: the ability to seize new opportunities such as the launch of the Corsa; the proactive relationship with third parties; and the close partnership that Kimberly-Clark has formed with the Blue-Chip Marketing Consultancy. It is the United Kingdom's most acclaimed promotion, winning 11 awards including an ISP Grand Prix and two on a European level.

What changed and what remained constant in the business objectives behind the 'Hay Fever Survival' promotions?

CASE STUDY 11.2   Zantac 75

Zantac 75 is a remedy for indigestion and heartburn that was launched in 1994 as an over-the-counter (OTC) version of Zantac, the leading prescription medicine. OTC products are medicines that the consumer buys without a prescription, but which are not placed on open shelves: the consumer must ask the pharmacist or pharmacy assistant for them, and will often seek his or her advice.

The difficulty Zantac 75 faced was that the product story was complicated. There were seven training manuals for sales reps to read. Unless reps could talk knowledgeably about the product to pharmacists, there was little chance that they would stock it, let alone recommend it to consumers. The promotional objective was simple: to ensure that reps were fully educated about Zantac 75 and able to present it effectively to pharmacists.

The Promotional Campaigns Group's solution was an e-mail game that took the theme of Zantac 75's world leadership in the prescription market. Each rep chose a world leader from a list that included Margaret Thatcher, Boris Yeltsin and Nelson Mandela. This identity was flashed on the rep's laptop computer every day. Every three days, a new episode of an amusing story about world leaders was sent by e-mail. The script was tailored to each rep's personality to increase involvement. Product learning was reinforced by questions from an imaginary Home Office, Treasury and Foreign Office.

All the reps participated, scoring an average of 90 per cent correct answers. Within four months, Zantac 75 had achieved 100 per cent distribution in independent pharmacists, and within six months it was the second most recommended brand of indigestion remedy in the United Kingdom.

Driving people to learn is hard work for learner and teacher alike. This promotion used a novel technique to make learning fun. It focused on product knowledge as the critical issue for the brand at that point in its life, and delivered the goods.

How had the manufacturers of Zantac 75 answered the 'Who do I want to do what?' question, and with what result?

How many categories of intermediary were involved in selling Zantac 75 to the consumer, and how did the promotion relate to their different needs?

CASE STUDY 11.3   Diabetes UK: 'Measure Up' message

Most of us equate waist measurement with the size of clothes we buy. Diabetes UK highlighted it as one of the risk factors associated with diabetes, together with the warning that 1 in 10 of us will be diabetic. A highly visible bright pink roadshow vehicle visited eight UK city centres. Visitors could drop in for information from medical experts and nutritionists as well as undergoing a blood-glucose-level test. The exterior of the vehicle carried heavy 'Measure Up' branding and hard-hitting messages. Each visitor received a 'goodie bag' with Diabetes UK literature and a sample pack of Shredded Wheat from the roadshow sponsor. The campaign was supported with mailings to healthcare professionals, posters and national press ads.

Awareness of diabetes and Diabetes UK was raised by 50 per cent amongst the target market during the campaign. After the campaign, 150,000 adults visited their GP for a diabetes test, and the combination of media and face-to-face activity achieved a reach of 33 million. This was a cause-related ISP 2007 Gold Award winner.

CASE STUDY 11.4   Music for schools

Schools were offered two entirely unconnected opportunities to build their collection of musical instruments. Both picked up on research evidence that schools were short of musical instruments and valued them highly. The promotions from Jacob's Club and the Co-op offer a contrast in objectives and execution round an identical theme.

Jacob's Club is the third biggest chocolate biscuit brand, with a 6 per cent market share. It is constantly faced with the challenge of larger brands and new entrants into a highly competitive market. Half its volume is purchased for use in lunchboxes.

Its promotional objectives included achieving a sales uplift of 25 per cent, increasing consumption in lunchboxes and reinforcing its family and caring image. The promotion, devised by Clarke Hooper and printed on 150 million packs, invited consumers to take the wrappers to school. The school could in turn redeem them for musical instruments. Direct mail to 25,500 schools resulted in 30 per cent of them registering. Telephone follow-up increased that to 90 per cent.

Nearly 14,000 schools claimed a total of 36,000 instruments worth over £800,000 at retail price. The entry point was low – a descant recorder worth £6.99 could be obtained for 295 wrappers, a spend of £29. Brand volume rose by 52 per cent during the promotional period, and household penetration rose by two-thirds.

The Continuity Company's promotion for Co-op was targeted at 16,000 schools near to the 1,300 participating Co-op stores. Recruitment was by direct mail, followed up by postal reminders. A total of 9,000 schools registered. The mail-out to schools included posters, wall charts and A5 leaflets to send home with each child. Co-op shoppers obtained one voucher with every £10 spent, which schools could redeem for instruments. There was a low starting point – just 35 vouchers entitled a school to a £5.99 descant recorder, representing an expenditure of £350. The Co-op promotion stabilized sales in the period up to Christmas. It also resulted in 190,000 instruments being claimed by schools.

Schools welcomed both promotions – 91 per cent told Jacob's that they would participate again, and 98 per cent said the same to the Co-op. Both have a number of factors in common: not being market leaders; appealing to families; having a broadly sharing, community image; and facing intense market competition. It is not surprising that their promotional analysis led them to very similar promotions. Both succeeded against their objectives, and both attracted considerable PR coverage. There are a number of details that are different, however:

- Jacob's backed the promotion with TV, the Co-op with press.

- Jacob's used telephone follow-up, which the Co-op did not.

- Jacob's enlisted the support of the Music Industries Association, while the Co-op used the endorsement of celebrities like Richard Baker and Phil Collins.

- Basically similar descant recorders required £29 to be spent on Jacob's Club or £350 in Co-op stores.

Does it matter that these very similar promotions ran at the same time? It would have done if KitKat and Club or the Co-op and Asda had run them, but Club and the Co-op are in different sectors. Analysis of similar promotional objectives can lead to similar solutions. The executional differences give a good example of how the way in which a promotion is carried out gives the promoter a range of options once the main approach has been decided.

To what extent were the objectives and business context of Jacob's and Co-op different in the 'Music for Schools' promotions?

Summary

Setting out the brief clearly and concisely is an essential first stage in devising a promotion. If the brief is not clear, your promotion will be built on sand. It is easy to miss out this stage if you are devising a promotion yourself, but it is a mistake. A good brief saves time, and well-defined objectives make the selection of mechanics straightforward.

The objectives and mechanics identified in this chapter do not constitute a rigid grid, but they are a good checklist for you to develop and apply. The rest of the brief will help you to organize the promotion in detail.

Implementing a promotion is a logical three-stage looping process. It is a mistake to try to take short cuts. The process can take a short time – just a week if necessary. The benefit of a system is that it takes you logically through all the stages and avoids costly mistakes. Following the system will not guarantee world-beating promotions, but it will ensure practical, workable promotions that achieve your objectives. It is vitally important to attend to issues defining success and setting the means of measurement (the KPI), budget, timing, communication, logistics and legalities in turning a promotional idea into a fully-fledged promotion and then to evaluate it so that lessons can be learnt before repeating the cycle. Look again at Figure 11.3 as a reminder.

Self-study questions

Use the following questions to identify what it is in particular that the four case studies illuminate. From the evidence presented, how successful were the promotions in achieving their objectives? What other mechanics could the agencies have considered to achieve those objectives?

11.1 How can a promotion be planned strategically?

11.2 What are the main points to include in a promotional brief?

11.3 What sorts of promotion are best for encouraging trial?

11.4 What sorts of promotion are best for encouraging repeat purchase?

11.5 What are the pros and cons of delayed and immediate promotions?

11.6 What are the different ways in which you can set a budget for a promotion?

11.7 If you offer a premium with three proofs of purchase on 150,000 packs, how many opportunities to apply will there be?

11.8 What are some of the main issues to watch for in contracts for promotional supply?

International promotions

12

When we speak of international promotions, we usually think of major, worldwide activity promoting a branded product in many countries, at the same time, under the same theme. A great deal more international promotion consists of activity that is designed in one country and implemented in another. It is multi-local rather than global.

A truly international promotion should appear in a number of countries, though not necessarily at the same time, nor in exactly the same form. This is the direction in which promotional activity has developed in multinational companies. There is no substitute for real-time understanding of markets: international campaigns must be built on up-to-date local understanding. This chapter concentrates on online opportunities because the opportunity is greater as the web is universal. Inserts and direct mail do work but press advertising is not always common. All online tools are available, from e-mail campaigns to search-engine marketing, banners and buttons. Across the 27 EU countries the language of business is increasingly English. Some facts about online trading activity in the EU are shown in Table 12.1.

TABLE 12.1 EU trading online (409 million citizens)

Country	Shopped online %	Average spend/yr (Euro)	Turnover (Euro billions)	Debit/ credit card (%)	Against invoice (%)	PayPal or similar (%)	Direct from bank (%)	COD (%)
UK	81	953	49.6	58		38	2	
Benelux	74	357	8.3	27	14	29		
Nordic	85	603	12.6	44	23	6		
France	72	423	22.7	55		36		
Germany	81	646	46.4	14	36	38	9	
Poland	59	194	6.3	10		21	43	24
Spain	60	308	12.2	34		49		13
Italy	45	215	11.3	25		55	5	13

SOURCE: postnord

The table shows the following:

- The United Kingdom leads on online purchases.
- Payments: It is interesting to see that whereas credit/debit cards are most popular in UK, France and the Nordic countries, they are less popular elsewhere.
- Paypal or similar is popular in Spain and Italy.

Some facts not shown in the table: four out of 10 consumers have bought from foreign sites. Germany leads here (34 million citizens/46 per cent of population) followed by the United Kingdom (28 million/54 per cent) then France (23 million/43 per cent); 56 per cent of the Nordic population have bought from a foreign site; 45 million Europeans have bought from the United States and 30 million from China, with UK citizens leading in each case.

According to international research from RetailMeNot and the Centre for Retail Research:

- Online sales in the US will grow by 15 per cent in 2014 to £189.3 billion, while in Europe, sales are expected to rise by 18 per cent to £131.2 billion.
- The UK, France and Germany are projected to be responsible for the bulk of this growth in Europe, accounting for 81 per cent of the online sales in the eight European markets expected in 2014. The UK is the largest market in Europe, with sales of £38.8 billion in 2013, and is expected to account for more than a third (34 per cent) of all online retail sales in the eight European markets surveyed in 2014. The report forecasts that £45 billion will be spent online in the UK in 2014 – an increase of 16 per cent on online consumer spend compared to the previous year.

Giulio Montemagno, SVP of international at digital coupon marketplace RetailMeNot, which owns Vouchercodes.co.uk in the UK, stated:

- In 2014, we are expecting to see online sales across Europe grow at a rate that is 11.9 times faster than in-store sales. In the UK, online retail is expected to increase by 15.8 per cent this year while the offline segment will grow by only 2.4 per cent. With such a competitive retail environment it's more important than ever that retailers look to mobile devices and the web to incentivize shoppers to make purchases online and in-store. Successful retailers will consider the internet not as a threat but as a powerful complement which can help them increase their sales.
- 46 per cent of Europeans and 55 per cent of Americans now shop online. Online shopping is particularly popular in Sweden and the UK where more than two-thirds of the population make purchases on the web; 71 per cent of Swedes and 67 per cent of Brits use the internet to shop. Online shopping is less popular in southern Europe, although it is growing: one in five people shop online in Italy (20 per cent), while one in three (32 per cent) use the internet to shop in Spain. Around half of people in France (52 per cent), Poland (51 per cent), Netherlands (49 per cent) and Germany (45 per cent) shop online.

- Phone interviews of 100 major retailers and 9,000 consumers, reveals that most consumers expect to shop online at least once a month in 2014. On average, European shoppers will make 15.2 online purchases this year with a typical basket size of £49, while American shoppers will make 15.6 online purchases, with an average spend of £71. In the UK, shoppers are expected to make 18.0 purchases online this year, spending an average of £59 each time.

- Throughout 2014, European shoppers are expected to spend £749 online, an increase of 18 per cent compared to 2013, while American shoppers are expected to spend £1,106 online, on average – 14.4 per cent more than in 2013. In the UK, shoppers are expected to spend £1,071 on the web this year – 15.8 per cent more than last year.

- Online retailers accounted for 6.3 per cent of all retail sales in Europe in 2013 and 10.6 per cent in the United States, and in 2014, this share is set to grow to 7.2 per cent and 11.6 per cent, respectively.
(Source: Internet Retailing, **http://internetretailing.net/2014/03/uk-retailers-expected-to-make-online-sales-of-45bn-this-year-study/**)

Internet Retailing reports:

The UK has the highest percentage of people who make a purchase every month on their smartphone (32 per cent) out of 18 European countries, including France (8 per cent), Germany (15 per cent), Italy (8 per cent) and Sweden (19 per cent). This is the key finding from Google-commissioned TNS research, which explores the growing importance of online platforms in the consumer journey, from research to purchase. The finding comes as Google launches a new website to help brands improve their website design and accessibility across mobile platforms. (**http://internetretailing.net/2014/03/uk-consumers-do-more-online-shopping-than-rest-of-europe-finds-google-as-it-launches-site-to-help-brands-exploit-mobile/**)

What are the dominant media?

It is not possible here to examine all the countries of the world. Here are examples from *The Marketer* of five to give a flavour of their dominant media (see **www.themarketer.co.uk/analysis/features/emerging-markets-5-channels-you-might-have-overlooked/**). A number of general points as to what to consider before implementing a promotion are then described.

Brazil: online video

Of all the Latin American countries, it's Brazil that digital marketers should watch out for. Brazil has the biggest online video audience in South America, with Brazilians watching over 4.7 billion videos in 2011. According to comScore, YouTube is the most popular platform for Brazilian online video viewers. YouTube reported that Brazil is its sixth biggest market in the world, reaching 79 per cent of the country's internet users and that its views from Brazilians grew 67 per cent from 2010. A survey by Forrester in 2011 showed that 86 per cent of Brazilians reported to watch online videos, more than people in the United States (80 per cent) and the United Kingdom (75 per cent). This is surprisingly high for a country where only 40 per cent of its citizens have internet access. SDL vice-president strategy and acquisitions Otto de Graaf says:

> Brazil has a very strong TV-watching culture and there's a lot of social media usage. This determines to some extent why video is very important. With the World Cup and Olympics coming up over the next couple of years, there are big opportunities for brands to get their message out.

Indonesia: e-commerce

The Boston Consulting Group named Indonesia 'Asia's next big opportunity' in a report released in March 2013. Its reasons are clear: Indonesia's middle class is projected to double to 141 million consumers by 2020, with economists forecasting growth of 30 per cent over the next five years. The combination of a stable political climate, a strong economy and a young population – the average age is 28 – explains why Indonesia can no longer be ignored. More specifically, it has the fastest growing e-commerce market in the world.

eMarketer reported in January 2013 that B2C e-commerce sales grew 21.1 per cent to $1 trillion in 2012 for the first time. This year sales are expected to grow 18 per cent, surpassing North America to become the world's biggest market for e-commerce sales. And with a growing middle-class, personal spending levels are rising by 10 per cent per year. The amount of internet users is also expected to hit 149 million by 2015 – all the more reason for marketers to explore this lucrative market.

India: smartphone apps

The statistics on India's mobile market look promising for potential investors. The country has mobile phone penetration of 72 per cent, with 69 per cent of phones being multimedia-capable. But what's proving to be particularly popular is India's domestic app market. According to professional services company Deloitte, the value of the Indian value added services industry, which includes mobile apps, was estimated at $3.4 billion in 2011. Figures from the Asia Pacific Research Group suggest the mobile application industry in India is predicted to exceed $4 billion by 2015. There is even a store in Mumbai that sells downloadable apps off its shelves: at Mobiworld, customers with smartphones can get mobile applications downloaded onto their phone using Bluetooth and a secure SMS code. The growing Indian app market is sure to provide many opportunities for mobile marketers.

China: social media

China, which boasts more than 1.35 billion inhabitants, has gone internet crazy. The country has over 591 million internet users, representing almost half the population. The China Internet Network Information Centre disclosed in June 2013 that 464 million citizens accessed the net via smartphones or other wireless devices. But perhaps the most revealing aspect of their web use is the enormous popularity of social media platforms, especially SinaWeibo, similar to a hybrid of Twitter and Facebook. It has over 600 million registered users in its database and over 60.2 million daily active users. So far, the social network seems to be doing well commercially. Weibo's advertising revenue skyrocketed 125 per cent in 2012 to £27 million in 2013. De Graaf says that unlike Westerners, China's population is particularly accepting of brands on social media sites:

> Westerners like social sharing, while on Weibo people tend to follow brands a lot more and use it as a source of information. The acceptance of brands on Weibo is much higher. Particularly with emerging economies this poses opportunities for luxury brands.

Ghana: mobile broadband

Business in Ghana is booming. Besides being in the world's top 10 fastest growing economies of 2013, Ghana also boasts Africa's highest penetration of mobile broadband. Twenty-three per cent of the population in 2011 were using mobile broadband, while fixed-broadband penetration stood at 0.3 per cent. Mobile operators invested heavily in 2009 and 2010, while internet service providers seemed unable to raise funds for new investments. For the telecom industry, this resulted in investment-to-revenue ratios of 65 per cent in Ghana, the highest in the world. Mobile phone penetration hit 100 per cent (of adults) in November 2013, and there is no sign of slowing down. An estimated 16 million mobile phones are used in this country with 25 million citizens (all ages), with many owning more than one SIM card.

Besides Ghana, there are opportunities in other countries in the developing world. According to a report by the International Telecommunication Union, mobile broadband continued to grow at a rate of 23 per cent between 2010 and 2011. Fixed broadband isn't doing as well, it's only growing at a global average of 10 per cent.

Havas Worldwide found: 'that half of Chinese online consumers have used a mobile device to shop, while 48 per cent of online consumers in Singapore and 42 per cent in India have shopped online with their mobile devices' (**http://contentz.mkt3416.com/lp/38068/308100/media/BC_Q4_mCommerce.pd**).

Types of international promotion

International promotions start with a highly successful, transferable promotion run in one country. This is how the famous Shell 'Make Money' promotion first travelled the world in the 1950s, long before internationally integrated marketing was common. It is not a long step for marketing people within the company to recognize that they should meet or at least communicate with their opposite numbers in other countries to pass on details of their successful promotions. These promotions may then be replicated in other countries by the originating company before their competitors can do so. The usual stimulus is money: the desire to split the origination costs with another group of people. Three things can be a particular focus of cost-saving promotion activity: the development of unique premiums; the use of character licences, such as Disney; and the exploitation of celebrity links, such as the international actors and models used for hair and beauty products. Corporate pressure for the standardization of promotions remains powerful. This has been driven by concern about the impact of varied promotional strategies on international brand identity, doubts about whether subsidiaries have an equal capability to design, implement and evaluate promotions, and the integration of retail customers on a regional basis.

The structure for managing the local/global balance in promotion has taken one of two forms. In one model, a worldwide promotions planning group is created that is responsible for all promotions throughout the world – a pattern followed by Coca-Cola and Pepsi. In the other, an essentially country- or region-based network becomes more proactive and, as a group, tries to find promotional solutions that will fit the needs of several countries. This is the pattern followed by Nestlé and a number of other leading companies. In both cases, the promotions will be planned in concept and outline in one country, allowing other countries to manage the local details within a global theme. The primary difference is not one of promotional effectiveness but of corporate culture: a strong belief in the efficacy of central control that dictates global strategy, or a far more consultative belief in the value of harnessing diversity. In both circumstances the economies of scale can be very attractive.

The three quite different forms of international promotion activity can be described in shorthand as 'single-country' (one country takes the lead), 'multiple-country' (several jointly plan for the rest) and 'borderless' (all participate). The difference is very important. The approach you will have to take initially will be different in each case. After that the details of creation and implementation will be the same.

Single-country

The process for promoting in another country is little different to that for promoting in your home country, but you do have to imagine a totally different 'village' to answer the question 'Who do I want to do what?' Crucially, you must make sure that you really know what that village is like. You need to know the people, the way they do business, their expectations and what is allowed by law and by custom, just as you do automatically at home.

Not all that long ago, an English company decided to promote its products in an Irish chain of supermarkets by offering a free draw for a tea set to be won in each store, every day for one week. By 11 o'clock on the first day, all the free-draw entry forms had been used up. All the stores were so jammed with people that no business could be done until new entry forms had been delivered and the crowds dispersed. It is hard to believe, but it is true. Not a good promotion! If only the promoter had realized that consumers in Eire were far less used to such promotions than shoppers in the United Kingdom.

Another example can be found in the clothing sector. An important sales opportunity is presented each year by the need to buy new clothes for growing children at the beginning of the school year in September. Thus, a form of 'Back to school' promotion has proved successful in every market. The promotion itself may be simple and similar in every market. What is different is the timing. In Japan and Europe it is possible to promote in August, when parents are beginning to think of the peace and quiet that lies ahead when the children return to school. In the Middle East, families tend to stay abroad on holiday until much later and therefore the timing of the promotion needs to be as much as two months later, in late September to early October.

Multiple-country

If a promotion is to run across several countries, it is likely that the greater the number of countries that you include the simpler will be your promotion. Often it will become a basic theme that may then be implemented locally using a variety of techniques. Coca-Cola and Pepsi are well known for their global promotional themes.

In 1996, Shell became the world's largest distributor of die-cast model cars, selling over 26 million via its worldwide 'Collezione' promotion. The international objective was to reinforce Shell's sponsorship of the Ferrari Formula One team. The model Ferrari cars were offered by the local Shell companies in any appropriate way they saw fit. Some gave them away with oil purchases and some redeemed them free on petrol sales, while others offered only a discount on the car in return for a smaller purchase of petrol. The promotional objectives were selected locally as the local situation dictated. In this type of international promotion, the global theme provides a stronger tool than any of the individual companies could afford to provide for themselves, as advantage can be taken of tremendous economies of scale. In 1997, this promotional activity was researched in South America, the Far East and Europe, and a new range of variations on a theme was developed for 1998. You could expect to collect your Lego Ferrari toy, only at your local Shell station, wherever you were in the world.

Multiple-country promotions on a regional basis are becoming increasingly possible as trading groups harmonize their laws and companies set up a single structure to market their products across a group of countries. This has long been the pattern in Northern Europe. It is also more and more the case in South-East Asia. If, as some argue, the fundamental building block of the future is regions rather than individual countries, promotion will increasingly take place on a multiple-country basis rather than either globally or nationally.

Borderless

The world is shrinking rapidly. There are now well-defined markets that cross geographical borders. While the customers may be from many different countries, they are often more similar to each other than they are to their fellow citizens. These markets will increase rapidly as the internet becomes a true marketplace. The brands to be found in international airports are already identical across the world, and hotel chains are similarly interchangeable from country to country. Loyalty is what the hotels and airlines want to promote, and they do this by a variety of frequent-flyer and frequent-visitor promotions. The key point is that the structure for truly global promotion is in place. The communication appears mainly at the point of use. Customers are more similar than different. 'Who do I want to do what?' can be asked and answered of frequent business travellers as a single 'village' across the world, and campaigns can be implemented on a truly global basis. All that needs changing is the language – and, in some cases, not even that. The Ramada duck (Case study 3.3) has been used worldwide.

Other well-defined cross-frontier markets are achieved by the spread of identical retail formats. Benetton and McDonald's are two very different retail formats that are identical across frontiers and appeal in each location to fundamentally similar people. However, it remains the case that there are fewer markets that are truly global than was expected 15 years ago and that the cultural factors governing behaviour remain persistently different. Even within B2B markets, there are radically different approaches to the relationship between groups and individuals, the taking of personal benefits from business transactions and the use of time. The disparities are even greater in consumer markets. For these reasons, a promotion more than any other part of the marketing mix needs to be planned globally but implemented locally.

Tips for international trading

1 *Law* – be aware of local laws governing distance selling (there is a limit when registering for VAT is required, and VAT varies), marketing and handling personal data. Local and national sales taxes may also apply.

2 *Websites* – engage professional translators for languages.

3 *Payments* – different preferences exist. In Islamic countries, the charging of interest is not permitted; Sharia-compliant finance must be offered. India sees cash on delivery as the favoured payment method for many online shopping experiences. This can obviously lead to difficulties and potential losses for the retailer. In Germany, 51 per cent of consumers wouldn't go back to a retailer that didn't offer their preferred payment method.

4 *Deliveries and returns* – find a firm with experience of distribution in countries.

5 *Cultural differences that impact* – especially for markets in the Middle East and Asia; it pays to know how a country's culture will impact interaction with your content.

Some specific cultural issues to be aware of include the following (Joe Doveton, Director of Conversion Services at Globalmaxer, reported by **https://econsultancy.com/ blog/63880-eight-cultural-differences-that-impact-conversion**):

- Colours:
  - Red is lucky in China, synonymous with beauty in Russia, and used for prices in France, but if you make your prices red in the UK, consumers will tend to assume a discount is being offered.
  - Green means go in Britain but death in Brazil (something to do with the mysterious green expanse of the jungle).

- In Japan, the word for blue is often used for colours that in English we would describe as green, such as a go traffic light. Many Bantu languages don't distinguish between green and blue; this can be anglicized as 'grue', for instance 'leaf grue' and 'ocean grue'.
- Use orange in Holland, the Dutch love it; avoid red, black and gold in Germany, as the Germans are sometimes uncomfortable with these colours.

- Website layout:
  - Many Arabic scripts read right to left and are right-aligned. Will this affect your site?
  - Many East Asian scripts can be written horizontally or vertically. Traditionally, Chinese, Japanese and Korean are written vertically, although some have started to be used horizontally, which makes sense for reading a screen rather than a paper scroll.
  - Asian readers are more comfortable scrolling down a long page.

- Calls to action
  - Skeuomorphism may have been rejected by Apple, and is slowly phasing out online in the West, but Eastern web users may be more reluctant to let go.
  - In Globalmaxer's tests, although colour can have an effect, the style and text of a button is most important to conversion rate.

- Faces
  - IKEA Saudi Arabia received criticism for airbrushing a woman from one of its catalogues. Although there are less women featuring in advertising in Saudi, the market isn't unhappy with locally attired women but having familiar faces in your marketing is important.
  - Ensure that context is considered if the subject or market is sensitive.

- Copy
  - Italians searching for low-cost flights: the most popular search term is not *voli economici*, the literal translation, but '*voli* low cost'.
  - There are examples in German, too, with work shirts being searched for with the phrase 'business *hemden*', only one word of the phrase being German.

- Technology
  - IE6 has over 24 per cent of browser share in China, so you can't afford to ignore it.
  - Flash sometimes has problems with Arabic script.
  - In the Russian market, use big online marketplaces to introduce yourself, before launching a standalone e-commerce operation.

- Context
  - Japan has a predilection for the cute *(kawaii)*, and for the busy web page. Germany on the other hand prefers simple web pages and messaging.

Localizing the global

Once you have identified which of the three types of international promotion you are to implement, you will be able to set realistic and achievable objectives. As with all promotions, it is better to keep it simple, especially when it is to happen halfway around the world. When you start getting down to the details, you should follow exactly the same process as outlined elsewhere in this book. However, you must take account of the particular characteristics of culture and law that continue to differ between countries in most consumer markets. A useful trade body is Trusted Shops, which offers membership, a 'kite mark' and advice on online trading in other countries including running promotions (see Chapter 15).

Laws

Every country has laws that may affect your promotion. For example, in Germany it is possible to run a competition or a sweepstake, but not a cashback offer. The rules are more subtle. If you run a competition, the answers must be easy to find on the competition form. You may then award the prize to the sender of the first correct entry received – a free draw in all but name. What's more, you are not supposed to have the entry forms near to the promoted product. That's the law, but it is normally flouted. Thus, to operate promotions effectively, you need not only a knowledge of the law but also that of local practice and culture.

Again in Germany, if you wish to band a premium to your product, you must ensure that it is very product-related and worth not more than a small percentage of the price of the main product. As a consequence, banded offers are hardly used and the consumer's expectation is that such offers may well be useful but are of limited value. Should you introduce a banded offer that is more exciting than is allowed, then not only will you have broken the law but you will run the risk of generating an unusually high demand that could create an 'out of stock' situation. Check the latest information with an expert or through a website; Trusted Shops provides some 25 pages of advice on legislation. New EU Law on Consumer Rights came into force in June 2014 which produces a minimum harmonization rule. Under Rome 1 Article 6, the law of the consumer's country of residence applies. For example before the EU Law takes force, a contract cooling-off period in the UK is seven days, in Germany it is 14 days but from June 2014 it is 14 days for both.

Logistics and trade

There are also differences in trade expectations and in the logistics required to support promotions. If a market is experienced in promotions, the trade will be equipped to handle and implement them. If not, your best ideas may never see the light of day, owing to confusion and lack of discipline. It is surprising how many support services we take for granted when we run promotions – post offices that are reliable, retailers who will redeem coupons fairly, and literate consumers. The absence of these could sink your promotion.

If you decide to supply the promoting companies with promotional items, find out about the customs regulations and the way the customs people really work. It is not unknown for items that are urgent to fall into some suddenly created and highly expensive import category if they are to be released within a year. If you use local suppliers, and it is often a good idea, make sure you have a local contact capable of managing them if things go wrong.

Often cultural differences require different techniques. In some countries, people want, and expect, an immediate reward: they live for today, not tomorrow. Thus, a collector scheme is less likely to succeed than a banded or free-product offer. A free mail-in might seem attractive, but will be totally useless in many developing countries.

Differences in practices of payment for drinks affect the way in which on-trade promotions can be run. A Smirnoff promotion assumed UK practice – that people go to the bar to order their drinks and then pay for them immediately. In France, the traditional practice is to sit at a table and be waited on or, if at the bar, to remain there. It is also the practice to collect a number of receipts and pay for them all when you leave.

However, different practices also create different opportunities. There are greater numbers of small, counter-service retailers in some countries than in others, the United Kingdom included. This means that promotions no longer possible in countries where the grocery trade is dominated by superstores can still be run in countries where the former situation persists. Great promotions of the past in one country can be a new opportunity in another. How can you make the most of them and avoid the other pitfalls we have discussed? The answer is to know the behaviour of your 'village' – both intermediaries and final consumers.

If you are promoting in a foreign country, you need allies who will act as your eyes and ears. Provided you ask the right questions, they will be able to come up with the answers. The difficult part is knowing which questions to ask. Also, whether you are promoting in a single country, promoting across a range of borders or dealing with a truly global market, the additional challenges make promoting even more fun than on your home ground.

Data protection law

The European Commission has made assessments of the enforcement and interpretation of data protection laws throughout the Community. The Commission is keen to increase the level of protection and enforcement and a new directive is in hand. The European Parliament has endorsed the proposed regulation and directive; see **http://ec.europa.eu/justice/data-protection/index_en.htm**. It is advisable to adopt positive consent for collection of personal data in all EU countries.

The first two of the following case studies illustrate the two primary forms of international promotion – one that is borderless because the market makes it possible to be so and one that operates across multiple, but different, markets. The next cases are sales promotions that ran in Singapore, Australia and Canada, but it could have been anywhere.

CASE STUDY 12.1   Tony Stone Images

Tony Stone Images, used by generations of art directors, sought brand differentiation to demonstrate that the company understands creative needs and is not just another stock photography supplier. The strategy devised by agency IMP was to associate Tony Stone Images with 'creative visual solutions' and to position the company as a partner rather than a supplier.

The core idea was the 'scamp', or scribbled drawing that 'creatives' use to indicate the picture they have in mind. A series of trade press ads featuring single-colour scamps, in place of the traditional full-colour photography used by competitors, extended to a range of merchandise incentives such as Post-It notes and a sweatshirt with a rough outline of a jogger helpfully arrowed 'jogger', and a calendar for the following year showing both scamps and the photographs that matched them, one for each month. A two-night break in New York competition featured a scribbled drawing of a skyline marked 'sunrise/sunset, wide angle skyscrapers'. Entrants were asked to identify the matching photograph in the catalogue, mark on a map where it had been taken and fax back their entries. A follow-up mailing offered a night out for two for identifying a 'lovey-dovey shot' in the catalogue and, as a tie-breaker, completing a half-drawn scamp. These competitions meant that the catalogue was browsed and that the product therefore stood out.

The mailing was translated into French, German, Danish and Flemish. It worked internationally because creatives are creatives the world over, photography is similarly international and the concept had universal appeal to the target audience. This is more than an illustration of international sales promotion: it is an example of using carefully thought-out and relevant incentives to make a wacky but deeply serious point about the positioning of a company and its relationship to its customers.

How did IMP answer the question 'Who do I want to do what?' in this promotion?

CASE STUDY 12.2   Umbro

The objectives were to extend the Umbro brand personality through promotion and to increase sales through retail chain Footlocker on a pan-European basis to the benefit of both companies. The promotion devised by IMP was to use the humorous, mickey-taking tone of voices familiar on terraces and in dressing rooms.

The core idea was to give purchasers of Umbro products an electronic swipe card that they took through a freestanding 'tunnel' in the shop. It would play one of two messages: 'You came. You won. You're walking out a winner. Claim your Euro '96 T-shirt from the cash desk', or 'What grief, what pain, you haven't won, but you can still win Euro '96 T-shirts with your game card'. Messages were recorded by recognizable football commentators from each country.

In Germany, cards had to be made available to shoppers who did not make a purchase. In Italy, the promotion had to be registered with the finance ministry for tax purposes. In the Netherlands, winners would hear a cheer in the 'tunnel' and then had to go to the cash desk and answer a simple question before they could obtain their T-shirt. The variances are important, but so is the transferability of the core concept of tunnel, swipe card and football razzmatazz. The promotion worked for Footlocker and Umbro because the hard work had been undertaken to devise an offer that simultaneously worked across countries, adapted to their specific rules.

What dangers, if any, do you see in trying to devise retail promotions that will work in several different EU countries?

CASE STUDY 12.3   Visible Vault

When radio station CFCW in Edmonton, Canada, was looking to boost its ratings, it approached PIMS-SCA for its traffic-building Visible Vault.

CFCW Radio had a vault filled with a moneybag worth $1 million. Contestants had to punch in a six-digit combination in an attempt to crack the code and win the prize. Day 20 of the promotion saw a $1 million winner, as a woman punched in the correct six digits that opened the vault. Marty Stevens, Promotions Director at CFCW, notified PIMS-SCA of the winner and relaxed, safe in the knowledge that it would pay the prize in full. The Vault is very portable, which enabled CFCW to take it to different locations, increasing awareness and visibility of the company. The bonus of having a winner provided plenty of exposure and was covered by all three major TV stations and two major newspapers in the area, as well as achieving greater ratings.

CASE STUDY 12.4 Boost Mobile Aus$1 million prize promotion

The Apollo Marketing Group created an Aus$1 million prize promotion for Australian mobile phone network Boost Mobile, to increase connection to the network. The promotion was open to three categories – consumers, sales reps, and traders and retailers. Four contestants were selected from each category of entries via a draw process and all 12 won a trip to Perisher Blue Ski Resort, Australia. Contestants then played a qualifying game which saw three of the 12 contestants go through to play for the $1 million. The final was televised live on 'The Today Show'. Each contestant chose a prize envelope from the $1 million Wall of Money and opened it to reveal if they were a winner. Mickaylah Lewis, who turned 21 the following day, chose her envelope from the Wall of Money and opened it to find the winning message 'Congratulations you've just Boosted yourself $1 million!' PIMS-SCA supplied the moneybag mechanic and the 300 secure moneybag envelopes to make up the Wall of Money, and paid out the $1 million live on Australian TV.

CASE STUDY 12.5 Great Singapore Duck Race

PIMS-SCA was approached by TOUCH Community Services, a Singapore charity, to cover the prize on offer in its Great Singapore $1 million Duck Race. The two objectives were to raise funds while increasing awareness of the charity, and to create a high-profile promotion with a limited budget. Participants were invited to 'adopt' a red duck by making a $10 donation to the TOUCH Services Charity. Each adopter was given an adoption certificate with a serial number. The red ducks were then randomly tagged with a number and assigned to each adoption certificate. If the first duck to cross the winning line was red, the 'owner' claimed the $1 million. On 12 November 2000, 100,000 plastic ducks, including 250 red ones, were released into the Singapore River for the 1.5 km race.

Due to the promotion's enormous success and public popularity, the event was repeated the following year. PIMS-SCA's role effectively increased funds and awareness for TOUCH by providing $1 million prize coverage and enabling TOUCH to run a high-profile promotion.

Summary

International sales promotion came about to achieve cost savings and ensure consistency. It differs depending on whether companies are centralized or decentralized in their structures, but the nature of sales promotion means that there are always cultural and legal factors to take into account.

Borderless promotions work where there is a single international target audience. In most cases, international promotions are multiple-country ones and vary in terms of timing and detail from country to country. Succeeding requires close attention being paid to the behaviour and culture of each market in which you are promoting.

Self-study questions

12.1 What are the main types of international promotion?

12.2 What must you take into account in planning a promotion that is going to run in several countries?

Promotion and the law

Promotional activity in the UK has long operated under the dual constraints of self-regulation and compliance with formal laws from Parliament.

In 1890, the leading poster companies set up a Joint Censorship Committee to exclude objectionable posters; this was soon followed by the first major piece of legislation for the industry, the Advertising Regulations Act, which gave local authorities power to control poster hoardings. Both these developments concerned posters (then the most publicly intrusive form of advertising) but now self-regulation and the law cover all forms of marketing from online to direct mail, radio to video-on-demand (VOD).

The balance between self-regulation and law has, however, varied over time, and even with the advent of harmonization in the EU, it still varies considerably between countries. For example, Germany has tended towards a focus on formal legislation while the United Kingdom favours self-regulation based on the guiding principles of all communications being legal, decent, truthful and honest with sufficient variation to allow for creativity but not deception. However, the picture is not black and white – all countries have a mixture of both. Despite some progress, there is still no single common legal framework for the operation of promotions across all Member States of the EU, so campaigns need to comply with the laws of each country and as a result this makes it challenging, if not impossible, to run pan-European campaigns.

In the Introduction we discussed the importance of building long-term customer relationships and the increasing public concern about the ethical status of the company behind the brand. Promoters who understand this will realize the importance of ensuring compliance with both the letter and the spirit of the relevant laws and codes of practice.

Self-regulation in the United Kingdom

The Advertising Standards Authority (ASA) was formed in 1962 with an independent chair and a remit to maintain the integrity of the industry. It is funded by a levy on most forms of advertising (currently 0.1 per cent) and is regarded as probably the best example of self-regulation in the world. The ASA oversees all forms of both broadcast and non-broadcast advertising as well as promotions and direct marketing, and enforces compliance with the BCAP or CAP Codes. Since February 2013, the ASA has had additional responsibility for marketing communications via e-mail, VOD, mobile and the web.

The Codes are the responsibility of the Committee of Advertising Practice (CAP), an independent body made up of those selling advertising (on TV, radio, posters, press, cinema, the internet), and those running the campaigns (advertising agencies and clients) and other trade bodies (for example, the Institute of Promotional Marketing). For non-broadcast campaigns, the ASA reviews complaints on the basis of the British Code of Advertising, Sales Promotion and Direct Marketing (CAP Code) whose fundamental principles are that all promotions should be:

- legal, decent, honest and truthful;
- conducted equitably, promptly and efficiently;
- seen to deal fairly and honourably with consumers;
- in line with accepted principles of fair competition; and
- in line with the spirit, as well as the letter, of the rules, and not bring the industry into disrepute.

The CAP Code is complementary to the law and in many respects is an enhancement of it, covering a broader range of topics in greater detail than Parliament could ever hope to legislate for. All marketers are strongly recommended to download a free copy of the CAP Code from **http://www.cap.org.uk/Advertising-Codes.aspx**.

Changes in the law inevitably lead to changes in the Codes, because it is not acceptable for the self-regulation system to operate at a level below the law. In fact most of the time, when the laws change, it is the drafting of the new elements of the Codes that provides more meaningful insight into how the laws are to be observed, and just as with the law, ignorance of the Code is no defence for not following it.

Enforcement of the Code is the responsibility of the ASA and while it does conduct audits and surveys, typically most compliance issues arise from a complaint made by a member of the public, a competitor or a trade body. The ASA receives over 30,000 complaints a year and about a sixth are non-broadcast complaints that are considered by the ASA in terms of whether they have breached the Code. Decisions are released weekly and frequently involve some big brand names and some consistent failings are often reported by the media as brands are 'named and shamed', potentially suffering reputation damage as a result. Some examples of complaints against brands and ASA decisions in these matters is given at the end of this chapter.

Unlike PhonePayPlus that regulates the premium rate phone industry, the ASA does not have the power to fine those in breach of the Codes. However, it does have a range of sanctions at its disposal that usually ensure compliance from responsible marketing companies that form the bulk of those on the complaints list:

1 The basic sanction is that 'the communication should not appear in that form again'.

2 The second-level sanction is a request that all future campaigns are pre-cleared for compliance by the ASA.

3 If the above fails, the ASA Council can write to members and request that they do not accept campaigns from the offending brand or company until

the matter is cleared up. This might work for big advertisers, but will have no impact where the offending communication was carried on the brand's own packaging or website, or via direct mail.

4 Where this is the situation, or the offender continues in defiance of ASA rulings, there is a final option: referral to the Competition and Markets Authority (formerly the OFT) that can impose an injunction and fines under statutory law for serious breaches and misleading communications.

This power has only been used in a handful of cases in the last decade, which could be seen as a weakness in the self-regulatory system, especially when the same names (notably tabloid newspapers, budget airlines and phone companies) appear year after year for the same or similar infringements of the Codes. However, the vast majority of companies both support and live in fear of the current self-regulatory system – no system is perfect, but it has enabled the UK to be the creative hub of the world and promotes consumer confidence in advertising and promotional claims in a way that a stricter, legislation-led regime overseen by industry outsiders would never achieve.

Chapter 8 of the CAP Code deals specifically with promotions. Some of the key areas of breaches relate to the availability, participation and administration of promotions:

- Promoters are expected to have sufficient quantities of their promotional products to meet likely demand. Phrases such as 'subject to availability' do not relieve you of your responsibilities.

- All prizes, gifts or rewards should be dispatched within 30 days. Demand should be estimated in advance, and sufficient stock bought to meet this likely demand; you should also have plans to meet unexpected demand. If all else fails, an item of equivalent value must be offered or a communication sent to consumers explaining the delay and providing an alternative option or delivery date.

- If there are limitations on participation, such as age or area of residence, or any costs that consumers must incur to take part, these must be clearly stated in advance, ahead of the moment of participation, and not buried in the small terms and conditions.

The word 'free' is one of the most powerful tools available to promoters, and its use is rightly carefully protected. If the consumer has to pay for anything other than the actual cost of postage, it may be a fine promotional offer but it is not 'free', so a claim such as 'Free watch, just send £1.99 postage & packaging' is not allowed because 'packaging' relates to something other than the cost of the 60p stamp required to send out the item. The same applies to the use of premium rate phone lines to claim a 'free' gift. In addition, the quality of the promoted item cannot be reduced to allow for the free offer, nor its price inflated to recover any of the cost of the free item.

On the implementation side, Chapter 8.24 of the Code requires winners of prize draws to be selected according to the laws of chance and by an independent person or under the supervision of an independent person. This would tend to exclude handling houses and agencies from being involved in this important area. The same is true of competitions, where the Code requirement is that there is a judging panel with at least one judge who is 'independent of the promoter and their intermediaries', as well as 'being competent in the subject matter'.

Instant wins, scratch cards and token promotions also have the same need for independent scrutiny, with an 'independent audit statement' required to ensure that all the stated prizes have been made available securely and distributed in accordance with the laws of chance, and not solely in a manner to fit in with the media or sales plan of the promoter.

For each of these mechanics, there is a requirement for an independent body to be involved in either winner selection or ticket allocation. But just who is independent? The ASA Sales Promotion Panel has stated that:

> the definition of an independent observer should exclude anyone who either had a contractual relationship with the promoter or worked for a company that had a contractual relationship with the promoter. This definition would not exclude people or companies paid a fee to act as independent observers provided they could demonstrate their independence.

So agencies, clients, handling houses and all those intrinsically involved in the client's business are not deemed eligible as the independent overseers of promotions. These measures are simple to implement in reality – a number of independent verification services exist – and are designed to not only ensure fairness but also protect promoters from claims of fixing promotions and other issues that could damage reputations and reduce consumer participation in campaigns.

A common and generally avoidable area of complaint relates to the rules of promotions – avoidable because it is not difficult to get the rules right with a little bit of time and some expert help. The Code provides clear guidance as to the key elements that need to be included in terms and conditions for competitions, free draws and instant-win offers but despite this many of these key elements are frequently ignored, missed out or not made available at the time of participation or purchase – a Code requirement. Of course space on-pack or in an advert is at a premium, but summary conditions should always have the basics on entry conditions: the closing date, a description of the prizes, the criteria for selecting or judging winners and the availability of a winners list, as well information on where the full terms can be obtained from. Participants should be able to access *and* retain the terms and conditions throughout the promotion. It is prudent not to print the terms on (for example) the proof of purchase section that has to be sent off for winner verification.

Promotions directed at young children are an area of particular sensitivity – not least because the Code definition of a child is anyone under the age of 18 and various rules relate to marketing to those under 16 and 12. For example, no promotions for food brands (except fresh fruit or vegetables) are allowed to be aimed at primary school children and there is a ban on campaigns aimed at under-12s for any product if it seeks to get the children to pester their parents to buy it, nor should you seek to obtain personal information on those under 16 without parental consent. Additionally the Code requires that promoters do not take unfair advantage of children's lack of experience, encourage them to make excessive purchases, or cause conflict between them and their parents.

The CAP Code also has specific rules for the advertising and promotion of alcoholic drinks, financial services, vitamins, health products, slimming products, cosmetics and medicines because these areas have greater legal oversight, have presented significant difficulties for consumers in the past or been open to abuse by promoters. There are also specific rules about environmental claims, distance selling, employment and business opportunities.

Although all this may appear complex and complicated, the Codes are written in plain English and should not present any difficulties for an honest promoter seeking to run reasonable campaigns. The ASA and CAP websites contain useful guidance notes on the Codes and any updates or new views on implementation and recent adjudication, plus there is confidential Copy Advice Service that can provide simple feedback on proposed campaigns (see Chapter 15 for contact information). However, there is a downside to seeking their advice: it may not always go your way, and if you fail to follow their advice, you will not have a leg to stand on if there is a subsequent complaint. There are also various law firms that offer advice on promotional marketing compliance as well independent verification companies and the IPM's own Legal Advice Service (£300 a go for non-members for advice).

If the CAP Code were the only set of rules promoters needed to know and follow, life would be simple, but there is a plethora of codes of practice, many of which are turgid, repetitive and entirely without teeth. Just as clubs think they need ties, so trade associations think they need codes. You should make your own judgement about which codes matter in your business. For example, there are references to sales promotion in codes produced by the Consumers' Association for business sponsorship of educational materials, for financial services promotion produced by the various financial regulators, for the pharmaceutical industry and for many other industry associations. The following codes can be particularly relevant to sales promotion:

- British Promotional Merchandise Association Code of Practice;
- Direct Marketing Association Code of Practice;
- Mail Order Traders' Association Code of Practice;
- Promotional Sourcing Association Code of Practice;
- Promotional Handling Association Code of Practice;
- PhonePayPlus Code of Practice.
- The Internet Advertising Bureau's 'Good Practice Principles'.

The codes change frequently, so it is worth seeking out the latest editions from the relevant associations; see Chapter 15.

UK law

Although there are many laws that affect the conduct of sales promotions, very few of them were actually designed for the specific purpose of controlling promotional campaigns. There are laws on packaging, product safety and statements at the point of sale or those that relate to consumer credit, gambling, the health sector and so on. However, there are in effect just two main laws that provide the main bulk of the legal framework that affects the sort of campaigns that you are most likely to be involved in.

The Gambling Act 2005

This Act led to a complete change in the regulation of prize promotions. The biggest change is that it allows lotteries in a promotion – or to be exact it redefines 'lottery'. Schedule 2 of the Act tells us that a lottery will only exist if people pay for goods or services at a price or rate that reflects the opportunity to participate. So, if the price is not loaded to take account of the promotion, then promotions based on chance, such as instant wins requiring product purchase, will be acceptable and there will no longer be any need for a free entry route.

As far as competitions are concerned, that is games of skill, the existing restrictions involving forecasting the result of future events are now under 'betting'. If a promotion does not satisfy the new requirements as they relate to games of skill, the worst that can happen is the scheme is regarded as a game of chance, and a game of chance is perfectly legal so long as there is no loading of the price of the product or service to take account of the promotion. When this is based on chance, the whole promotion will be regarded as being based on chance; so long as people do not inflate the price of their product or service, they can run any prize promotion they like with any combination of skill and chance. So in practice, promotions with prizes are virtually free of any legal control.

The Gambling Act 2005 relates to Great Britain, ie England, Scotland and Wales. In theory, Northern Ireland still operates under the old Betting, Gaming, Lotteries and Amusements (Northern Ireland) Order 1985, which banned games of chance where a purchase (product or otherwise) was required. So promoters and agencies will need to consider whether to exclude Northern Ireland from UK prize purchase-linked games of chance, include a 'No purchase necessary' option just for residents of Northern Ireland, or offer a 'no purchase necessary' route for the whole country. The NI Assembly declared in 2013 its intention to bring its laws in line with those of the mainland and they are not seeking to enforce this law which they acknowledge is out of step with both Great Britain and EU law.

The European dimension

When it comes to self-regulation, the European Advertising Standards Alliance (EASA) provides a measure of coordination across Europe and acts as a central postbox ensuring that cross-border complaints are sent to the relevant national self-regulatory body. However, laws can vary widely and although they are becoming more aligned, there are still a few oddities. For example in France there is the need to reimburse entrant's cost of internet usage upon request. In Sweden, games of chance are banned, whether or not they are linked to a purchase, and in Italy, Spain and Portugal prize draws need to be registered with the authorities, fees paid, insurance bonds bought and public officials engaged to oversee winner selection.

It is a complicated area and you should seek specialist advice before launching a promotion in a foreign country, however simple it may appear. Despite these variations, harmonization across the EU has taken a big leap forward in recent years with the introduction of the European Directive on Unfair Consumer Practices (UCPD) and a number of rulings in the European Court of Justice that have overturned some limiting national country laws.

The UCPD was enacted in EU Member States in 2008 (in the UK it is called the Consumer Protection Regulations 2008 – CPR 2008) and is consistent across all countries in banning outright 31 marketing practices that it was felt were against the public interest. It requires 'maximum harmonization' meaning that not only do Member States have to comply with all the requirements of the Directive, they are not allowed to impose any additional laws that are any tougher than those in the Directive.

The CPR 2008 seeks to provide a modern, simplified consumer framework replacing lots of older laws. Where there is a breach, it is most likely that the promoter will be deemed responsible, but agencies will normally also be liable under their contracts of service with clients. It is important to note that the CPR covers not only what you say, for example, in terms of marketing claims, but also 'misleading omissions'. The CPR also has a ban on:

- 'Practices which are contrary to the requirements of professional diligence';
- 'Practices which are misleading or aggressive'; and
- '31 specified practices in any circumstances'. The key ones for marketers are provided in Table 13.1.

TABLE 13.1   Key consumer protection regulations affecting marketers (2008)

CPR Schedule 1 Paragraph number:	Grade	The implications for marketers
2. Displaying a trust mark, quality mark or equivalent without having obtained the necessary authorization.	Low	Make sure all endorsements are approved.
6. Making an invitation to purchase products at a specified price and then: a) refusing to show the advertised item to consumers; or b) refusing to take orders for it or deliver it within a reasonable time; or c) demonstrating a defective sample of it, with the intention of promoting a different product (bait and switch).	High	Ensure that you have sufficient stock of an item before advertising it.

TABLE 13.1 *continued*

CPR Schedule 1 Paragraph number:	Grade	The implications for marketers
7. Falsely stating that a product will only be available for a very limited time, or that it will only be available on particular terms for a very limited time, in order to elicit an immediate decision and deprive consumers of sufficient opportunity or time to make an informed choice.	Low	Ryanair and Easyjet have both suffered issues with this requirement.
10. Presenting rights given to consumers in law as a distinctive feature of the trader's offer.	Low	Avoid highlighting what is common or taken as the norm.
11. Using editorial content in the media to promote a product where a trader has paid for the promotion without making that clear in the content or by images or sounds clearly identifiable by the consumer (advertorial).	High	Ensure that sponsorship or advertorials are clearly separated from editorial.
16. Claiming that products are able to facilitate winning in games of chance.	Low	Avoid excessive claims, frequently used in direct mail.
18. Passing on materially inaccurate information on market conditions or on the possibility of finding the product with the intention of inducing the consumer to acquire the product at conditions less favourable than normal market conditions.	Low	Examples would be 'buy now, before the price rises' or 'only available in this shop'.
19. Claiming in a commercial practice to offer a competition or prize promotion without awarding the prizes described or a reasonable equivalent.	High	Ensure that your fulfilment procedures are 100% reliable. Have the prizes in stock before you start.

TABLE 13.1 *continued*

CPR Schedule 1 Paragraph number:	Grade	The implications for marketers
20. Describing a product as 'gratis', 'free', 'without charge' or similar if the consumer has to pay anything other than the unavoidable cost of responding to the commercial practice and collecting or paying for delivery of the item.	High	'Free' is a crucial word for marketers. Genuinely free gifts offered with the purchase of another product at its normal price will not be prevented. It is primarily aimed at obvious abuses of the word.
22. Falsely claiming or creating the impression that the trader is not acting for purposes relating to his trade, business, craft or profession, or falsely representing oneself as a consumer.	High	This effectively outlaws buzz marketing and all forms of marketing for a brand that purport to come from someone other than the brand, eg 'consumer' blogs.
28. Including in an advertisement a direct exhortation to children to buy advertised products or persuade their parents or other adults to buy advertised products for them.	High	ASA rules already limit advertising to children; this takes it a stage further. 'Children' are under the age of 12.
31. Creating the false impression that the consumer has already won, will win, or will on doing a particular act win, a prize or other equivalent benefit, when in fact either: – there is no prize or other equivalent benefit, or – taking any action in relation to claiming the prize or other equivalent benefit is subject to the consumer paying money or incurring a cost. Note: this only applies to winners claiming a prize: The Gambling Act already disregards the payment of a phone call or a standard rate text or stamp as being a payment to enter.	Low	Avoid excessive claims. Do not use the term 'instant win' unless one will know that one has won and what one has won at the time of entering. Unique codes would not meet this requirement.

In addition to the UK legislation outlined above, there are other rules and regulations to be considered; for example:

- Ofcom: all broadcasters running 'pay to enter' votes or competitions need to have independent audits.
- PhonePayPlus, the regulator of the premium phone industry, has rules on how pricing and rules are communicated on air or in press etc.
- Portman Code: for responsible marketing of alcoholic beverages.

Finally, with so many promotions now being run on social media, you should be aware that the main platforms have their own rules that are in addition to national laws and codes. For example, rules on Facebook (as at April 2014, but regularly changing) include:

- Caution is required because Facebook accounts are available to those aged 13 years old or over, but most promotions are aimed at those over 18 years old.
- Entry into a promotion can now be made simply by someone 'Liking' a business page or posting a message or comment on it (but abuse of fake accounts/likes is common).
- You can insist that only fans of your page can access the promotion.
- You can link entry to the promotion to a user providing content (for example, a photo, video or other content) but do ensure you moderate entries: you cannot insist that they post a photo with them in it, due to inaccurate tagging.
- You should not post a 'You have won' message on someone's wall, it is too public. Ideally contact them directly using data gathered as part of the entry process.
- You should distance yourself from Facebook in your terms and conditions, ie: 'This promotion is in no way sponsored by Facebook...'.
- You should have solid terms and conditions that are easily accessible before entry and do not change.
- You should have the usual data protection opt in/opt out options available if you are gathering personal data.

The rules for Twitter are:

- You cannot allow entry into a prize draw by getting people to retweet more than once – it is a form of spam.
- Make sure that you use a unique hashtag to gather entries, otherwise it can be embarrassing.
- If you use celebrities or other paid-for spokespeople to communicate your messages you must make this clear, usually via use of #ad or #spon in each of the messages.
- Your terms and conditions should be summarized in a tweet, for example, UK res, 18+. Closes 31/12/XX and a web link to the full terms and conditions, or use a second tweet.
- You should have the usual data protection opt in/opt out options available.

The following case studies are taken from ASA adjudications and deal with typical infringements of the Code. Some infringements are obvious, others less so. When answering the questions that follow each example, bear in mind that the ASA Council is not infallible – it may make judgements that you or others want to dispute.

CASE STUDY 13.1   *The Sun* and Twilight: the movie

The Sun newspaper ran a promotion offering a 'Free Twilight, the Movie wristband. Just send £1.99 post & packing'. When the wristband was sent out, the envelope had a 46p stamp on it. A complaint was made that the item was not free because the newspaper was charging more than the actual cost of the direct postage. The complaint was successful and *The Sun* was told not to repeat the offence and to only charge for postage and no other costs such as packing, administration or packaging.

> *What could* The Sun *have done to keep this promotion within the Code if it still wanted to use the word 'free'?*
>
> *If it didn't use the word 'free', how else could it have described the promotion?*

CASE STUDY 13.2   Sandisk and Argos

Argos ran national press adverts proclaiming 'Half Price 4Gb Sandisk Memory Sticks. Limited availability...'. The offer proved popular and the stores soon ran out. The ASA received a number of complaints and investigated. It was not pleased with the findings: 'we considered the small print was not sufficient to warn consumer of the very limited nature of the offer... and because Argos had not made a reasonable estimate of demand and the ad did not make clear the limited stock, the ad was misleading and must not be repeated'.

This situation is not only against the CAP Code but also clause 6 of the CPR, and is often called 'bait advertising', which involves communicating an amazing deal to get people into your store and, when that product is no longer available, switch them and upsell them to a more expensive product.

> *How could Argos have ensured that the consumer offer on the memory sticks was clear within the meaning of the Code?*
>
> *Assuming all the ads were pre-booked, what steps could Argos have taken to ensure that it stayed within the Code when stocks ran out?*

CASE STUDY 13.3   The VIP trip

Red Bull ran a promotion in 2012 to support its sponsorship of a team in Formula 1. The prize was headlined, 'VIP Trip to the Belgian Grand Prix' but the eventual winners were far from happy with their experience. It turned out the VIP experience consisted of Ryanair flights to Cologne (in Germany) and a long taxi ride at their own expense to their hotel in Maastrich (in Holland). The hotel was a basic three-star and the two male winners had to share a bed. Then it was another long taxi ride (over 45 miles) to the race track, where they had regular grandstand seats, but they had to leave before the end (when Jenson Button from the UK won) to make their own way to Brussels (at least still in Belgium) for a flight back home.

Quite naturally the ASA did not like it: 'information relating to the different locations of the event, airport and hotel, and that travel to and from them was not included... was significant information likely to influence consumers' understanding of the promotion and should therefore have been stated clearly in the promotional material'. It also objected to the use of the term 'VIP Trip' when none of the elements were exclusive or of a high enough quality to warrant the description.

What words could Red Bull have used in its marketing headline to keep within the Code?

How do you think that this situation arose?

Summary

Promotion is a practical, nuts-and-bolts affair and there are a lot of detailed rules to follow, both in the codes and in legislation. There are also some broad principles that reflect good business practice. The collective need of promoters to avoid intrusive legislation makes it important to follow both the spirit and the letter of the ASA Code. Following the Code is not difficult if you use one of the copy-checking services available to help you. If in any doubt, contact the IPM (if you are a member) or a specialist legal practice. Each country has different laws governing sales promotion, and you need to take them into account.

I gratefully acknowledge the help of Philip Circus, Jeremy Stern and Ardi Kolah in preparing this chapter. Philip's book *Sales Promotion and Direct Market Law: A practical guide* (2007) is available from Tottel Publishing; see Chapter 15. Philip Circus is a partner in Lawmark (**www.lawmark.co.uk/philipcircus/**). Ardi's book *Essential Law for Marketers*, second edition is available; see Chapter 15.

Self-study questions

13.1 How do you make sure your promotional copy accords with the codes of practice?

13.2 What are the most frequent causes of promotions being criticized by the ASA?

13.3 What are the main principles of the codes of advertising and sales promotion practice?

Marketing accountability and promotional insight

Marketing accountability is best carried out by a marketer defining the promotion success and setting the KPIs, with someone else carrying out the measuring and recording of the KPIs (use finance – then it will be believed!). The marketer then compares the figures with the success definition, and an evaluation is produced.

An IPA research report shows that ROI is not well understood, especially by marketers, so use a KPI. Only 12 per cent of marketers have a very clear idea of the impact different activities have (*B2B Marketing's Leaders Report*, 2013) and only 6 per cent of B2B leaders can calculate ROI all of the time. Measuring marketing ROI used to be easy: the ROI of a direct mail piece could be calculated by simply subtracting the total production costs from the revenue directly generated by the response. When e-mails arrived on the scene, ROI was equally easy to calculate. To make ROI more difficult to measure, some of today's marketing techniques may not actually include a marketing message or a call to action (such as social updates on sites like LinkedIn). So what can be done?

Success, KPIs and evaluation

Promotions are undertaken to achieve specific promotional objectives, which are normally part of a campaign to achieve a marketing objective. They cost money. So it is absolutely critical that you ensure your promotions prove to be value for money. Define the success criteria of your promotion, setting KPIs by which to measure, then measure and finally evaluate to see if you have achieved success. The lessons learnt can be borne in mind for the next cycle of promotion (see Figure 11.1).

An IPA report shows that only 20 per cent of marketers evaluate the effect of communications on profit, yet marketers are now required to become more accountable to retain their budgets and jobs. The reasons for not measuring are various:

- Individual promotions seldom have the budgets that justify an additional amount for marketing accountability.
- Promotions can, in many respects, be measured by sales results.

- There is often not the time to define success, set a KPI, or measure and evaluate market accountability before the next promotion is due.

The point is made in the book *Value for Money Marketing* (by Roddy Mullin) that marketing accountability has to become part of company culture before it is routinely applied. However, those who do evaluate their promotions know the benefits it brings, short and long term. It justifies budgets to accounting persons. It is suggested that the marketing budget is split into two – the first part for 'maintenance', ie retaining the existing market share level (sustaining and building the engram, relationship and social media support, local promotion) – and the second part for revenue expenditure (to achieve growth, the launch of new products etc, to add excitement, fun and contingency promotions). You will only know of the maintenance figure if you have records of marketing expenditure and market share over the years. You will only know what promotions really work for the future if you record it.

The purpose of marketing accountability

Like a lamp-post, marketing accountability should be used to shed light, not to lean on. Once marketing accountability is part of a company's culture then there will be records of what works and what does not. Marketing accountability is an iterative process that will very rapidly save you money. There are three main stages of promotional marketing accountability:

1 *Think accountability.* Define success. Set KPIs. Make someone responsible for measuring the KPIs. Thinking accountability and planning for marketing accountability are excellent inputs into strategic questions such as how to split your marketing promotion (communication) budget between advertising, promotional offers, direct marketing and publicity. It has the added benefit of providing evidence and facts to put in front of finance directors to demonstrate the effectiveness of marketing and show value-for-money marketing. It assumes that a culture of marketing accountability exists and that all other marketing activities are also accountable in order to make the budget allocations. Promotions will, of course, be on to a real winner if it is the only accountable activity.

2 *Measure.* You can do this in a test stage to identify the particular promotional concepts that will meet the objectives you have, or monitor throughout a promotion, or just collate the collected measurements at the end. Be aware if you are measuring a change in behaviour or attitude that you may have to measure the KPIs before your promotional activity as well, so you can record the resulting change.

3 *Evaluate.* Compare the effect and impact of promotions you have undertaken with your definition of success and feed this evaluation into the planning of future promotions.

A good evaluation system, one used by all those in the organization who run promotions, is consistently applied and makes the results available to everyone who needs to know now and in the future. It is a key to collective learning in any company or agency and, over time, becomes a valuable asset.

Keeping evaluation knowledge

The challenge in setting up an in-house evaluation knowledge system is knowing what you need to record and what you can reasonably discard. The challenge in operating it is finding the time to do the recording while the evidence is still available, and knowing what to circulate, what to put on your database and what to keep in manual files (samples of print, merchandise, etc). Make the system too complicated and you run the risk that it will not be used. Make it too simple and you will not have the information you need next time round.

In promotions, this challenge is tougher than it is in many other areas of business because promotions are so varied and so often conducted by staff who move on to other jobs. Many agencies have built a spreadsheet of response rates to different coupons, free mail-ins and other offers. These are invaluable, but are at the pinnacle of a good system. The place to start is recording the basic data for each promotion you run.

How an evaluation knowledge system works

The most practical approach is to produce a document wallet containing all the key information about a promotion. You can organize your data under the following four headings. Under the first three, you can either write an appropriate paragraph or include a piece of paper in your file. The last one requires you to stand back from the evidence and think.

1. Background and objectives

List here the products on which the promotion ran, the quantities involved and the name of the promotion. Also record the three key points that led you to undertake the promotion: the marketing objective, the promotional objectives and the answer you gave to the question 'Who do I want to do what?' Including the reason why the objective was set ('We faced a major challenge from a new competitor') locates the promotion in a context that may be forgotten in a year's time.

2. Description

This is a detailed description of what the promotion involved. You may be able to include your operational marketing plan but, before you file it, make sure you update it to show what actually happened, not what you planned to happen. Make sure you include:

- the offer made to the consumer;
- the mechanic (including detailed rules and entry requirements);
- the operational structure (who did what, agencies and suppliers used);

- communication materials (type and quantity);
- media support;
- timings;
- trade/intermediary support;
- sales-force activity (if relevant);
- the KPI used for measurement;
- copies of all relevant printed or video material;
- suppliers and contacts.

3. What happened

There are three primary measures of the results of a promotion and they relate, respectively, to promotional response, sales and finance. In many cases, it is simplest to include the evidence in your document wallet rather than to spend time entering it into another document. For example, if your handling house gives you an analysis of applications for a free mail-in, simply include that piece of paper. Make sure you cover:

- *Marketing accountability:* how success of the promotion was defined, whether the KPI set was reasonable, and a record of the KPI measurement, evaluation and analysis of the result against the success criterion. You should note whether the result met, nearly met or did not meet the success criterion you set.
- *Promotional response:* consumer uptake of the promotion, trade participation, the results of any market research or surveys undertaken, any feedback from insight (social media, etc) and a note of any consumer, trade or sales-force comments. Did the press comment or journalists report?
- *Sales:* sales figures for the periods before, during and after the promotion, the results of any continuous surveys of market share, distribution and penetration, and relevant figures for competitors' products.
- *Finance:* the cost of all material produced for the promotion, any trade discounts, fees and other costs, and any calculations that you make about the profit contribution the promotion made.

Sales and finance data will, in most cases, be information generated by other parts of the company. Make sure you include information that helps in promotional evaluation; do not include information just because it is available.

4. Analysis

Did the promotion work? How you answer this question depends on the culture of the company. To listen to some brand managers and agency personnel, there's never been a promotion that didn't transform the fortunes of the promoted product. For the analysis to be useful, however, you must be as honest as possible. You should refer back to the promotional objective, the brief, and the success criteria and KPI you set.

You should include statistics – how the promotion performed against quantitative objectives set for participation, sales, penetration and market share and how it performed against the operational marketing plan you set, the budget and the timings. You should also include comments: an assessment of the lessons learnt from it, particularly what you would do differently next time, and the experience it has given you of suppliers, trade partners and internal departments. Sometimes stock during a promotion is not replaced on the shelf or a delay is caused in restocking. Such occurrences affect the result.

The analysis section is not just a matter of reporting that sales increased by 11 per cent against a target of 10 per cent. If a major competitor suffered a production blip at the same time, you need to record it. Analysis is about why a promotion performed as it did. The answers are not always easy to find, but repeated and honest analysis makes the process easier.

What to look out for

Putting a promotion finally to bed with a document wallet containing the information and analysis listed above is the basic building block of a marketing accountability system. Before you put it away, though, you need to make sure that:

- the wallet is indexed and accessible so others can find it;
- any basic data that can be held on a central database, for example response levels, are transferred;
- there is a debrief meeting so that experience is shared.

The enemy of good evaluation is the next job, but resist the temptation to switch to it.

Taking these steps would, in most companies, transform the quality of promotional evaluation. It would even give you the information you need to enter your promotions for, and maybe win, an IPM award.

For a promotion, marketing accountability can be used to address the following type of questions; the answers enable better planning next time:

- Did the promotion achieve the objective?
- What was the cost to achieve the objective of that promotion?
- Was the promotion value for money?
- How did the promotion compare in value-for-money terms with other marketing activities or promotions we have used to achieve the same objective?
- Was the KPI used the most appropriate and was it effective?

Promotional insight

Research is useful to support decisions on the use of promotions in general and choosing one in particular. It is important to draw out something useful rather than have a load of statistics – insight is actionable. This is in-depth analysis and over-comes the marketer who thinks they know it all. It is dangerous to rely on a hunch or 'gut feel'. Do the research.

Questions: general attitudes to promotions

- How do particular groups of intermediaries and potential customers respond to promotional offers?
- What kind of promotional offer do they find most compelling?
- What other products and services would they link your own product or service to for the purposes of joint promotions?
- How do they react to different kinds of charity offer?
- What frequency of purchase is it sensible to aim at in constructing proof-of-purchase requirements?
- What was the impact of a promotion on brand values and on the reaction to the promotion by those who did and those who did not take up your offer?

There are various ways in which you can go about doing promotional research:

- *Doing it yourself.* This is the only way to undertake factual desk research and evaluation of sales patterns, as only you will have access to the data. Because resources are normally limited, the more you can do the other types of research yourself the more likely they are to be done.

- *Using specialist researchers.* Most market research companies will undertake promotional research, and a number have developed specialist methodologies in the field.

- *Including it in an agency brief.* Promotion agencies now have longer-term relationships with clients and often have in-house resources in market research. It can make sense to build both a marketing accountability and a research element into every brief if you use an agency.

The greatest advances in this area have been made in promotions to children and young people, where changing fashions have made it critical to understand the issues that motivate them. On a larger scale, it is too much for one brand. There is immense scope for it in alliances such as that between Cadbury Schweppes, Bass, Kimberly-Clark and Unilever to pool research and database information.

These questions are answered by a mix of field research (where you ask people or pay market researchers to ask the questions) and desk research (where you find out and use the field research of others). A useful book is *Why We Buy* by Paco Underhill; see Chapter 15.

Questions: which promotions to use

The following have a bearing on the selection of a particular promotional concept over others:

- the level of response you can expect from a particular offer with particular entry requirements;
- the effect on response rates of changing a particular element in the promotion, for example the number of proofs of purchase required or the nature of the premium item;
- the clarity of communication in the particular way the offer is themed and expressed;
- the effect on the image and value of your product or service made by a particular promotional offer;
- the level of spontaneous interest in, and therefore the attractiveness of, different promotional concepts.

The most sensitive issue is always the response rate. For a free mail-in this can vary from 3 to 15 per cent or more. On-pack coupons can be redeemed at rates of anything between 5 and 25 per cent. This variance has enormous implications for your budget, so reducing the area of uncertainty is crucial. It is important to be clear about which of these questions actually have a bearing on your choice between a number of competing promotional concepts. In many cases, all the concepts will have a similar effect on the image and value of your product or service and it will be pointless to explore the matter further.

The questions are best answered by desk research for data held by you from previous sales promotions or from studying the data of others. The straightforward in-house part of evaluative research is collecting together all the factual data on response rates, sales patterns, consumer complaints and other readily measurable variables. This type of evaluation should be standard operating practice and is covered in the 'Market testing' section below.

All mail-in promotions produce a list of people who took up the offer. This forms an excellent basis for running a simple postal questionnaire. Getting to those who did not take up your offer requires rather more effort in list building, but it is important to obtain proper comparisons. More in-depth research into consumer reaction to promotions can be obtained via group discussions.

Desk research has the major advantage that you can do it, at your desk, and at nil or low cost. If you can answer the questions – or at least narrow the amount of uncertainty – by means of desk research, it is always best to do so.

There are three main data sources for desk research, and they can be built up over time to provide you with the material you need to evaluate competing promotional concepts:

1 *Your own promotions.* Details of your own past promotions are the best and the first form of research data. The evaluation system recommended in the section 'Keeping evaluation knowledge' above should be used after every promotion. Using this data for research purposes means identifying similarities and differences between past promotions and your promotional concepts, and intelligently estimating from there. The data can also be used to identify the promotions that will work with particular target groups and to achieve particular objectives.

2 *Competitors' promotions.* It is possible to build up a fair amount of market intelligence about the promotions run by your competitors, their likely cost and their likely effectiveness. It should be standard practice to get hold of every promotional pack and collect every promotional leaflet issued by your main competitors. From these you can list the nature of the offer, the entry requirements and the theme used. Rather more detective work is required to gain an estimate of costs, response rates and effectiveness:

   – For a prize promotion, simply cost the prizes on offer. For a premium promotion, obtain and cost the premium on offer. Make an estimate of the quantity of leaflets and other support material, and cost these too. This should give a rough indication of budget.

   – Use your own sales data, and continuous market research data if you subscribe to them, to establish whether or not any discernible sales effect has been achieved by your competitors' promotions. Other tracking studies can measure their impact on awareness, distribution and other variables.

   – Make your own subjective assessment of the clarity of communication of the offer, and its impact on brand values, awareness and other less quantifiable measures.

3 *Wider promotional activity.* There are various sources of information about promotions in a wider sense. These include:

   – trade magazines (mainly online), see Chapter 15;

   – regular features on promotions carried in the weekly advertising and marketing press, in particular *Marketing*, *Marketing Week* and *Campaign*;

   – publications (online) from the IPM and, in particular, the annual brochure describing winning promotions entered for the IPM awards;

   – occasional research reports published by a variety of business information and research organizations, including Internet Retailing, Mobile Marketer and Mintel;

   – conferences on promotional issues, normally in London, at which leading practitioners describe and discuss promotions they have undertaken and trends in the industry.

Those few companies that employ an in-house promotion manager benefit from the build-up of expertise in this area, and it is also a particular strength of promotion agencies. However, anyone spending any significant sum on promotions should make it their business to monitor and evaluate wider promotional activity and learn from it.

Field research

Field research involves collecting information directly from the market by way of a sample designed to be representative of your target market. There are five main methods that can be used for promotional research:

1 Street interviews, which provide quantitative responses to a relatively simple set of questions. As a means of testing the response to promotions

immediately after purchase, interviews outside superstores can be particularly effective.

2 Hall tests (where consumers are invited into a nearby church hall or similar venue), which also provide quantitative responses, but allow more opportunity for detail. This can extend to creating a simulated buying situation and comparing consumer behaviour.

3 Group discussions or focus groups, which provide considerable qualitative information on consumer attitudes and are often used before quantitative testing.

4 Analysis of social media. Of all the methods, this is most likely to provide individual and social feedback on promotional ideas.

5 Postal, internet (e-mail) and telephone questionnaires, which have major cost savings over face-to-face interviews. Because of the need to see promotional offers, their use in promotional research is largely restricted to planning and evaluative research.

The use of all these types of field research is a science in itself and, as such, is outside the scope of this book. Many are now advocating greater use of the analysis of social media. The reason for this relates to the gap between what people say they do and what they actually do. It is well known that consumers understate their expenditure on socially disapproved activities such as smoking and drinking. In the same way, they understate their enthusiasm for promotional offers. Field research can be misleading if it takes at face value what people say rather than what they do. Paco Underhill's book *Why We Buy* is invaluable here, as it is all based on what people do. See also *Shoppernomics* by Roddy Mullin and Colin Harper; details in Chapter 15.

Market testing

Market testing overcomes the gap between what people say they do and what they actually do: it measures actual behaviours in the marketplace. This technique is prohibitively expensive for most applications of market research because it involves placing a product or service out in the market and producing it in low, uneconomic numbers. However, for promotional research, it is much more feasible. It is often quite possible to sticker a small quantity of a production run with a particular offer and use it as a door-drop sample. For service companies the exercise is even simpler – just produce a short run of the leaflets or other material communicating the offer and try it out in one part of your market.

Clearly, there are logistical and planning aspects to take into account, of which the most important is the time required to organize and evaluate the test. Some promoters believe that the danger of good ideas being seen and adopted by competitors makes field testing impossible. Others believe that lack of field testing means that really innovative ideas are held back, as promoters do not have the faith to take a risk. One of the major advantages of a strategic approach to promotions is that the time for proper market testing can be built in.

Other measurements

Big data analytics

EPOS data can determine what is bought and when and which items were on promotion. Store cards will place that with customers. Analysis by time of day and day of the week may also show when it is best to offer promotions.

With marketing software it's also possible to determine what the most popular/successful communication channels/tools were. For B2B, was a particular white paper downloaded many times? How many comments did a recent blog post receive?

By taking an overview of the latest customers' journeys through the sales funnel, patterns and trends can be identified such as conversion points, media consumption, frequency of interactions and sales tipping points. By understanding this data, it's possible to continuously update the marketing channels and messages to send out to shopper/buyers.

Web audits

Another aspect of market accountability is how your website is performing. You need your website to work for you, to make the most of the new and existing content you produce. On-page content remains a major factor for achieving top search rankings. As such you should undertake a website audit. Put your technical hat on. Now replace your hat for another marked 'Content'. Audit/benchmark your existing content. See which content templates and formats have been performing well. Take a look at your goals to see how you're doing, and target areas for improvement (via the production of new content, and the optimization of existing content, etc).

Finally, you should definitely spend some time benchmarking the competition. This is mainly about the content they produce (and how it is distributed), but should extend to social. What's working for them? How frequently are they updating their content, their distribution channels, and their social networks? Can you correlate a competitor's content marketing campaign with its performance (eg website metrics, social metrics, and trading performance, where available)?

The key findings from investigating your website will include:

- *Engagement rate:* the number of prospects that engaged with your business/marketing channels.
- *Lead rate:* the number of prospects that converted to a lead.
- *Conversion rate:* the number of leads that converted to a sale.
- *Closed business:* the total revenue generated.
- *Pipeline:* the number of leads that end up on the forecast.

Delivery costs and e-commerce

A major factor in e-commerce is delivery, set to cost retailers £6 billion in abandoned baskets in 2014 (Internet Retailing). The latest eCustomerServiceIndex from eDigitalResearch and IMRG questioned 2,000 online shoppers and found 77 per cent of them had abandoned an e-commerce shopping basket in the last year. When asked why, some 53 per cent of them said delivery costs were too high, while 26 per cent put something in an online basket 'just to check' delivery costs, and 18 per cent decided not to buy because the estimated delivery date was too long. Other reasons came from the 44 per cent who said they'd changed their mind about making the purchase while 39 per cent wanted longer to think about it. Some 65 per cent of those who abandoned the checkout because they felt delivery costs were unreasonable then went on to search online to find similar goods elsewhere. One in five made no purchase at all, while 8 per cent went to a store to buy.

Investment in better parcel tracking, timed delivery slots and other innovations has gone some way to improving customer satisfaction with overall customer experience, but these results clearly show that issues related to delivery are still a massive barrier to purchase for a large number of online shoppers. Linked findings showed most shoppers would prefer not to pay more than £5 for small or medium-sized goods to be sent to them, with most expecting not to pay at all. Reasons cited for checkout abandonment also included out of stock (21 per cent), limited information on which to make a purchase decision (12 per cent), security concerns, limited payment options, and unclear returns policies (both 8 per cent).

A similar assessment can be extended to promotions to discover if abandonment of a purchase of a product was with or without a promotion.

Summary

Proper marketing accountability, defining success, setting KPIs, and measuring and evaluation make sure that you are getting your money's worth from your promotional expenditure and that you are spending it on the right things. There is no excuse for failing to evaluate every promotion, or for failing to do the basic desk research beforehand. This should be planned into every piece of promotional activity.

Use of field research and market testing depends on your budgets, but will help to reduce uncertainty. In the end, research cannot make the decisions for you, particularly in such a fluid and fast-moving field as sales promotion. However, to help you plan in the future and compete for budget with your finance director, marketing accountability is essential. Marketing does not have the luxury of not giving value for money.

Self-study questions

14.1 What is the process of obtaining marketing accountability?

14.2 What must you record for effective evaluation?

14.3 What are the main types of research you can use in sales promotion?

14.4 Why do you think so little research goes on into sales promotion?

Further information

Trade associations

Advertising Standards Authority (ASA) and
Committee for Advertising Practice (CAP)
Mid-City Place
71 High Holborn
London WC1V 7QT
Tel: 020 7492 2222
Website: **www.asa.org.uk**
Offers copy advice by e-mail.

British Promotional Merchandise Association (BPMA)
52–53 Russell Square
London WC1B 4HP
Tel: 020 7631 6960
Fax: 020 7631 6944
E-mail: **enquiries@bpma.co.uk**
Website: **www.bpma.co.uk**
Has a list of members' products and services. Charter members are the tops.

CAP's Copy Advice Service
Tel: 020 7492 2780
Fax: 020 7580 4072
Website: **www.cap.org.uk**
Offers advice online, plus related cases.

CAM Foundation
Moor Hall
Cookham, Maidenhead
Berkshire SL6 9QH
Tel: 01628 427190
Fax: 01628 427399
E-mail: **camfoundation@cim.co.uk**
Website: **www.camfoundation.com**
Contact: Alaina Roberts

Covers specific areas of marketing communication and promotional aspects of marketing for those pursuing a career in advertising, PR, media, market research, direct marketing or sales promotion through examinations.

Chartered Institute of Marketing
Moor Hall
Cookham, Maidenhead
Berkshire SL6 9QH
Tel: 01628 427500
Website: **www.cim.co.uk**
The home of the professional practitioner in marketing. Offers training courses on most marketing subjects.

Chartered Institute of Purchasing and Supply
Easton House
Easton on the Hill, Stamford
Lincolnshire PE9 3NZ
Tel: 01780 756777
Fax: 01780 751610
E-mail: **info@cips.org**
Website: **www.cips.org**

Direct Marketing Association (DMA)
70 Margaret Street
London W1W 8SS
Tel: 020 7291 3300
Fax: 020 7291 3301
Contact: **james.milligan@dma.org.uk**
E-mail: **info@dma.org.uk**
Website: **www.dma.org.uk**
Europe's largest trade association in the marketing and communications sector, with over 900 corporate members. On behalf of its membership, the DMA promotes best practice and self-regulation, through its codes, to maintain and enhance consumers' trust and confidence in the direct marketing industry. The DMA has set up the Direct Marketing Authority as an independent body to monitor industry compliance. Offers an extensive range of assistance on its website, including codes of practice.

Incorporated Society of British Advertisers (ISBA)
Langham House, 1b Portland Place
London W1B 1PN
Tel: (020) 7291 9020
Fax: (020) 7629 5355
E-mail: **davide@isba.org.uk**
Website: **www.isba.org.uk**
Trade association for advertisers.

Institute of Practitioners in Advertising
44 Belgrave Square
London SW1X 8QS
Tel: 020 7235 7020
Fax: 020 7245 9904
E-mail: **mark@ipa.co.uk**
Website: **www.ipa.co.uk**
The IPA is the trade body and professional institute for leading agencies in the United Kingdom's advertising, media and marketing communications industry. It can provide guidance on what it is like to work in advertising, the variety of jobs that exist, what sort of skills are needed, how to go about getting into the industry and which agencies are actively looking for graduates.

Institute of Promotional Marketing (IPM)
70 Margaret Street
London W1W 8SS
Tel: 020 7291 7730
Fax: 020 7291 7731
E-mail: **enquiries@theipm.org.uk**
Website: **www.theipm.org.uk**
The website has a 'Display' site containing nearly 200 examples of award-winning promotions showing the market background, mechanics used and results. Coupon guidelines and checklists for promotional mechanics are also available. The ISP's purpose is to protect and promote professional and effective sales promotion. It provides professional qualifications at all levels. The IPM sponsors the Marketing Intern Hub (Tel: 020 7291 7730, e-mail: **info@themarketinginternhub.co.uk**, website: **www.themarketinginternhub.co.uk**)

Marketing Agencies Association
4 Quebec Street
London W1H 7RP
Tel: 020 7535 3550
Fax: 020 7535 3551
E-mail: **scott.knox@marketingagencies.org.uk**
Website: **http://www.marketingagencies.org.uk**
Offers communication agencies supplying a range of services legal advice, training, management and best practice tools. Will help find an agency through its Search and Selection service.

Point of Purchase Advertising Institute (POPAI)
Highfields Farm, Huncote Road
Stoney Stanton
Leicestershire LE9 4DJ
Tel: 01455 271856
Fax: 01455 273918
E-mail: **info@popai.co.uk**
Website: **www.popai.co.uk**
Trade association for point of purchase, point of sale.

Trusted Shops GmbH
Strubbelrather Str 15c
50823 Cologne
Germany
Tel: 02033645906
E-mail: **naveen.aricatt@trustedshops.com**
Website: **www.trustedshops.com**
Trusted Shops has three products for online shops: customer reviews, which provide proof of quality and a good sense of customer service; certification and 'trustmark', which show the reliability and professionalism of a shop; buyer protection, which contributes to reducing the number of shopping baskets abandoned during the ordering process. Trusted shops produces a handbook for online retailers which has 25 pages of information on EU legislation.

Voucher Association (VA)
Contact: Andrew Johnson
Tel: 0870 241 6445
E-mail: **andrew@ukgcva.co.uk**
Website: **www.ukgcva.co.uk**
The VA has 56 issuer and service members and five social members, representing many of the key players in the industry.

Agencies that have supplied information

Global Loyalty Pty Ltd
Sarah Richardson, General Manager
Level 2, 710 Collins Street
Docklands
VIC 3008
Australia
Mobile: +61 438 923 300
Tel: +61 3 9097 1764
E-mail: **sarahrichardson@globalloyalty.com.au**
Website: **www.globalloyalty.com.au**

Mediator Communications Ltd
166/168a Camden Street
London NW19PT
Tel: +44 (0)20 7436 3380
E-mail: **letstalk@mediator.co.uk**
Website: **www.mediator.co.uk/**
Mediator is a young, independent marketing communications agency with a background in creating partnership campaigns. Clients include: Arla (Castello), Alton Towers, UKTV, LEGOLAND, Zipcar, Haven, Superdrug, Just Eat and Thorpe Park.

Valassis Ltd
Weldon House, Corby Gate Business Park
Priors Hand Road
Corby
Northants NN17 5JG
Tel: 01536 400123
Fax: 01536 400678
Retailer helpline: 0845 6005133
E-mail: **rayres@valassis.co.uk**
Website: **www.valassis.co.uk**
NCH Business Solutions, part of Valassis UK, is a leader in redemptions, settlement and analysis and has been operating in the United Kingdom for over 30 years. It handles 80 per cent of all coupons in the United Kingdom.

Promotional suppliers

PIMS-SCA
First Floor, Dudley House
169 Piccadilly
80–82 Regent Street
London W1J 9EH
Tel: 020 7255 7900
Fax: 020 7493 8161
E-mail: **fiona@pims-sca.com**
Website: **www.pims-sca.com**
Interesting case studies. New media capable; text-and-win promotions. As a registered Lloyd's Broker and working with some of the largest insurance companies in the world, it guarantees complete financial security for every promotion.

General

Ardi Kolah, Guru in a bottle
Author of *Essential Law for Marketers*, an indispensable book that's written in non-legal jargon and language that's easy to understand and follow.
Tel: 0208 542 8786
E-mail: **ardi.kolah@guruinabottle.com**
Website: **www.guruinabottle.com**

Charities Aid Foundation
Website: **https://www.cafonline.org**

Consumer Focus (formerly National Consumers Council)
Victoria House
Southampton Row
London WC1B 4AD
Tel: 020 7799 7900
Fax: 020 7799 7901
E-mail: **contact@consumerfocus.org.uk**
Website: **www.consumerfocus.org.uk**

Lawmark
The Marketing Law Advisory Service
Philip Circus MA, MPhil, DCA, FISP
Tel: 01798 813750
Mobile: 077680 78576
E-mail: **philip.circus@virgin.net**
Website: **www.lawmark.co.uk/philipcircus/**

Office for National Statistics
Customer Contact Centre
Office for National Statistics
Room 1.101, Government Buildings
Cardiff Road
Newport
South Wales NP10 8XG
Tel: 0845 6013034
Fax: 0 1633 652747
E-mail: **info@ons.gsi.gov.uk**
Website: **www.ons.gov.uk**

Which?
2 Marylebone Road
London NW1 4DF
Tel: 020 7770 7000
Fax: 020 7770 7600
E-mail: **which@which.co.uk**
Website: **www.which.co.uk**

Sourcing promotional merchandise

The Sourcing Team
Gill Thorpe, FCIPS, Managing Director
www.sourcing.co.uk
Global sourcing and procurement, specializing in promotional products, providing both standard and made to order products for public and private-sector clients; branded items used for product launches, exhibitions, events and general corporate merchandise requirements.

Magazines

B2B Marketing, http://www.b2bmarketing.net/

CIM (online magazine, Australia and New Zealand), http://www.cimmagazine.com/

Digital Marketing (online magazine), http://digitalmarketingmagazine.co.uk/

Field Marketing and Brand Experience, http://www.fieldmarketing.com/fmbx-magazine/

Internet Retailing: http://internetretailing.net/

The Marketer, magazine of the CIM, http://www.themarketer.co.uk/

Marketing, 174 Hammersmith Road, London W6 7JP (Tel: 020 7413 4150; Fax: 020 7413 4504; website: www.marketingmagazine.co.uk/)

Marketing News, www.ama.org/publications/MarketingNews

Marketing Week, 12–26 Lexington Street, London W1R 4HQ (Tel: 020 7970 4000; Fax: 020 7970 6721; website: www.marketing-week.co.uk)

Mobile Marketer, www.mobilemarketer.com/

Mobile Marketing Magazine, mobilemarketingmagazine.com/

Pragmatic Marketing, www.pragmaticmarketing.com

Promotional Marketing (online magazine), published by the Institute of Promotional Marketing: www.promomarketing.info An up-to-date monthly magazine covering promotional marketing and incentive strategy.

Sales and Marketing Management, www.salesandmarketing.com/

References and further reading

Circus, P (2007) *Sales Promotion and Direct Market Law: A practical guide*, Tottel Publishing, Haywards Heath

Harper, C (2014) *Beyond Shopper Marketing*, Storecheck Marketing, Farnham Common

Kolah, A (2004) *Essential Law for Marketers*, Kogan Page, London

Mullin, R (2001) *Value for Money Marketing*, Kogan Page, London

Mullin, R and Harper, C (2014) *Shoppernomics*, Gower, Farnham

Sharp, B (2010) *How Brands Grow: What marketers don't know*, OUP, Oxford

Underhill, P (2003) *Why We Buy: The science of shopping*, Thomson Texere, London

Williams, A and Mullin, R (2008) *The Handbook of Field Marketing*, Kogan Page, London

INDEX